The Broadcast Television Industry

James R. Walker
Saint Xavier University, Chicago

Douglas A. Ferguson
Bowling Green State University

with contributions by
John Long
California State University, Chico

Kevin Sauter
University of Saint Thomas, St. Paul, Minnesota

Allyn and Bacon
Boston • London • Toronto • Sydney • Tokyo • Singapore

I would like to dedicate my portion of this book to my father, the late Wynn C. Walker, a wonderful man, who supported and encouraged me in every way.   JRW

I would like to thank Jim Walker for trusting me to contribute my half of this book. I am indebted to previous broadcast employers in Ohio for my training and education. My efforts are dedicated to the emotional support of my wife, Cindy, and the gentle guidance of my mother, Lorraine, who departed during the writing, and my father, Ralph.   DAF

Vice President, Editor in Chief: Paul Smith
Series Editor: Karon Bowers
Senior Editor: Joseph Terry
Editorial Assistant: Leila Scott
Marketing Manager: Kris Farnsworth
Editorial Production Service: Chestnut Hill Enterprises, Inc.
Manufacturing Buyer: Megan Cochran
Cover Administrator: Jennifer Hart

Library of Congress Cataloging-in-Publication Data
Walker, James Robert.
    The broadcast television industry / James R. Walker and Douglas A.
Ferguson.
        p.   cm.
    Includes bibliographical references and index.
    ISBN 0-205-18950-4
    1. Television broadcasting--United States.   I. Ferguson, Douglas
A.   II. Title.
PN1992.3.U5W35   1997
384.55'0973--dc21   97-37598
                                                              CIP

Printed in the United States of Amerca

10   9   8   7   6   5   4   3   02   01

Contents

Preface

In a little more than fifty years, broadcast television has become a part of everyday life. In the United States, television sets are on for an average of more than seven hours a day. The majority of that viewing is of programs originating on broadcast stations and networks, delivered by the airwaves or through cable lines. The national television networks have grown from four to seven in a little more than a decade and are the single most important force in the development of new entertainment and information programming.

Broadcast television continues to prosper for several reasons. Although network competition has increased, the number of additional television signals that can be added in most geographic locations is limited because of the increased interference produced by new stations. Thus, while established cable networks face increased competition from new cable services and local cable systems face new competition from digital satellite services, most broadcast television stations have little current concern about new broadcast competitors. This scarcity of broadcast stations in many markets has driven up station prices. In addition, recent regulatory changes have allowed more stations to be owned by individual corporations, creating more demand for broadcast stations and further increasing the value of each station. In addition, network broadcast television is still the most effective vehicle for delivering the large national audience desired by many advertisers. Thus, after the advertising slump of the early 1990s, broadcast television revenues rebounded quickly and profits increased significantly. "Plain old television," as broadcast television is often called, is still a pretty good business.

But the future of broadcast television is far from secure. In the last two decades, cable has grown into a major competitor and it attracts a younger viewing audience that, as it grows older, may abandon broadcast television. New digital television compression technologies may greatly expand the number of local broadcast competitors. The rapidly growing World Wide Web may expand greatly the number of video distribution channels as many web homepages become personal television services. While broadcast television has successfully navigated changes in the media environment in the past, it may not be as successful in the future.

In this volume, we hope to provide perspective on the challenges facing broadcast television in the United States. We review its technology, its history, and the economic forces that drive its programming decisions. We analyze the programming contributions of both national networks and syndicators, and local stations. We devote a chapter to public television—the major alternative to the dominant commercial television system. We also dedicate a separate chapter to the extensive body of research on the impact of television on individuals and society. Finally, we speculate on the future of broadcast television in the United States. We hope you find the volume an informative and valuable overview of "plain old television."

ACKNOWLEDGMENTS

We want to thank several people who have helped us with this project. Al Greco, the Mass Communication Series editor, offered encouragement and steady guidance throughout the development of the manuscript. Rob Bellamy of Duquesne University provided the initial inspiration and outline for this book, reviewed several chapters, and was a most valuable resource for its creation. Judith Hiltner, our excellent "in-house" editor, made scores of suggestions to better the book, improving it immeasurably. The following reviewers provided detailed, accurate, and essential comments that greatly enhanced the final manuscript: Alan B. Albarran, Southern Methodist University; Benjamin J. Bates, University of Tennessee at Knoxville; and Marvin R. Bensmen, University of Memphis. Finally, we want to thank the many fine people at Allyn and Bacon who worked to make this book a reality.

1

Broadcast Television

Advantages, Technology, and an Overview

In our opening chapter, we will document the advantages of broadcast television over its main rival, cable. While cable television has expanded the variety of programming available, broadcast services are still the most watched channels on cable systems. In addition, some of the most popular programming on cable are episodes of programs that originally aired on broadcast *networks*. We will show how the efficient technology of broadcasting is applied to television, providing nearly universal service to U.S. homes. Finally, we will provide an overview of our investigation of the broadcast television industry in the United States.

THE VIRTUES OF PLAIN OLD TELEVISION

On one side is broadcast television and on the other is cable. On one side is a transmission system that is invisible, almost perfectly reliable, subsidized by scarce public resources (the airwaves), and accessible with all standard television receivers from any but the most remote locations. On the other side is a transmission system that often uses unsightly aboveground wires, has all-too-frequent interruptions, and often offers a lower quality picture and sound. On one side is a television signal that can be received by over 98 percent of U.S. households with no direct fee. On the other side is a signal that is currently received by only 65 percent of the nation's households because it charges over $20 a month for its most basic service.[1] On one side is a system that has maintained two-thirds of its audience, despite an enormous increase since 1975 in the number of competing signals received by the average home. On the other side is a system whose financial success has been aided by its status as a local monopoly, a status that is rapidly changing. Yet, despite these contrasts, it is broadcast and not cable television that often seems under siege.

Our purpose here is not to demean cable television; its dramatic rise in the 1980s and multimillion dollar profits are evidence enough of its success. In the 1990s, cable has started conversion to *fiber-optic transmission,* which will increase the quality of its transmission and greatly expand its channel capacity. But broadcast television, or "plain old television" as it is sometimes known, is an industry of remarkable, and often overlooked, strengths. It is a mature industry with a strong structure built during a fifty-year history. However, because it is universal and familiar, its presence is taken for granted. After a period of declining ratings, due to competition from cable, the broadcast television industry has rebounded and station sales are booming.[2] In 1996, one minute of advertising on broadcast television's highest rated weekly programs passed the $1 million dollar mark.[3] Although newer networks offer few hours of programming per week, since 1985 the number of national commercial networks has doubled from three to six.

Recent changes in FCC regulations have increased the number of stations that any group can own and opened previously closed production and *syndication* markets to broadcast networks, increasing the value of network programs when they are sold in syndication. These changes have led to "mega-mergers" between ABC and Disney, CBS and Westinghouse, and Time Warner and Turner Broadcasting System. In each case, the merger has increased the degree of broadcast television, cable, and nontelevision media integration. Broadcast television networks are diversifying into newer media, while maintaining their core broadcast businesses. In truth, it is no longer broadcast television on one side and cable on the other, but, increasingly, broadcast and cable television on the same side.

However, as the broadcast and cable television industries move closer together, it is worth examining the special characteristics of each. In this volume, we will focus primarily on the broadcast television industry in the United States, mentioning cable and other television distribution systems only as they affect the broadcast system.

Although it may well change in the future (see Chapter 10), broadcast television stations are, for the present, more valuable than ever. The Telecommunications Act of 1996 increased the licensing period for stations from five to eight years, and the percentage of homes that can be reached by any set of group-owned stations from 25 to 35 percent. This loosening of ownership limits has further strengthened the already strong demand for most broadcast television stations. The average television station sold for nearly $5 million in 1974 just before the start of the cable revolution. The average station sold for nearly $25 million in 1995.[4]

Part of reason for the increasing value of television stations is their relative scarcity. The national plan for slightly over 2,000 stations established in 1952 has not been significantly expanded. The most commercially attractive station allotments have been utilized. For those interested in expanding their television holdings, there is little alternative except the purchase of existing stations. The demand is high and the supply is fixed.

The situation is just the opposite for cable television, in which competition is more plentiful and likely to increase rapidly. Newer cable systems and those undergoing rewiring can carry many more competing signals, providing more competition among a rapidly growing number of cable networks. Cable's fast-growing competitor, the *digital satellite system (DSS),* has a 1,000-channel capacity. Because of regulatory changes, local cable systems are facing competition from powerful telephone companies as well as DSS. Although lacking the capacity to be a serious video competitor at the moment, the Internet's *World Wide Web* is increasing its ability to deliver video, audio, graphic, and print information with a degree of specialization that cannot be matched by cable. Equipment that allows web access using an ordinary television is already being marketed. The comfortable era for cable television, characterized by local monopolies with minimal regulation, is clearly drawing to a close. Like its broadcast counterpart, cable television will need to adapt to increased competition.

BROADCAST TELEVISION TECHNOLOGY

The most significant advantage that broadcast television has over its competitors is its use of electromagnetic radiation, in the form of radio waves, as its means of transmission. Radio waves are accessible with ordinary receivers (televisions or radios) from most locations within the broadcast range of a station's transmitter. By carefully connecting affiliated stations nationwide, the major television networks can reach over 98 percent of all households in the country. In contrast, cable transmission requires the installation and maintenance of expensive *coaxial* or fiber-optic cable to transmit signals from the headend (main operational facility) of the local cable system to each customer's home. Because of the high cost of wiring and the limited number of potential customers, very rural areas are particularly overlooked by this distribution system. However, broadcast television can offer nearly universal (98 percent of households) service to a community with only a transmitter, electric power, and, most importantly, a *channel* (band of frequencies) in the electromagnetic spectrum.

Nonetheless, cable television also has important technological advantages. The most significant of these is the most obvious: its capacity for many channels. In addition, in mountainous regions or areas far from broadcast transmitters, cable television may be the only source of high-quality television. Indeed, cable television started as *Community Antenna Television (CATV),* a means of bringing improved reception and more stations to communities that were poorly served by broadcast television.

Spectrum Allocation

The channel used by a television station in the United States requires 6,000 *kilohertz* (6 *megahertz*) of electromagnetic spectrum space. Compared to FM radio (200 kilohertz) or AM radio (10 kilohertz), television is spectrum-hungry, because it must include both video and audio information. The intense spectrum needs of television limit the number of possible channels that can be allocated to the medium if the many other needs for spectrum space (government, military, two-way radio, cellular telephone, marine, international shortwave radio, and so on) are to be accommodated.

In the United States, the *Federal Communications Commission (FCC)* has allocated twelve channels (2–13) in the *Very High Frequency (VHF)* part of the spectrum and 56 channels (14–69) in the *Ultra High Frequency (UHF)* part of the spectrum for use by television stations. Figure 1-1 shows the order of broadcast television and radio channels in the United States.

Because a broadcast television station signal is local, dozens of stations can share each of these channels without interfering with each other, as long as adequate geographic separation (a minimum of 200 miles) is maintained. By 1995, 1,544 television stations were assigned to these 68 channels in the United States,[5] with VHF channels averaging 60 stations per channel.[6] However, this long-standing system is undergoing rapid change. In 1997, the FCC gave final approval to a new allocation plan that will allow existing stations to operate their current broadcast signal and a second high definition signal until conversion to the new high definition television system is completed. Thus, the next several years will see a historic change in broad-

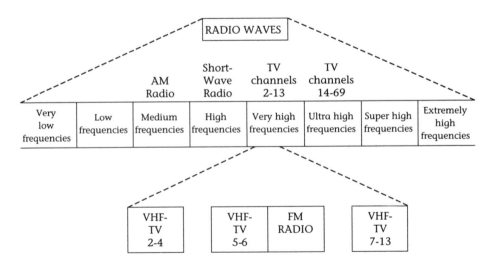

FIGURE 1-1   Order of Television Spectrum Assignment

cast television transmission—the most significant since the creation of UHF television in 1952 (see Chapters 2 and 10).

Television Signal Transmission

All broadcast television stations transmit two *carrier waves,* one for video and one for audio information. The carrier waves link the station transmitter and television, providing a continuous stream of picture and sound. The video information is *modulated* (embedded) onto the carrier wave using amplitude and phase modulation. Amplitude modulation is used in AM radio. The audio information, usually in stereo, is added using frequency modulation, the system used in FM radio. The television signal also carries closed captioning that provides written information for the hearing-impaired. The television receiver extracts the modulated audio and video from the carrier wave and converts it from electrical energy to pictures and sounds.

The television carrier wave is a *direct wave,* moving in a direct, or line-of-sight, pattern as it radiates from the station transmitter. Direct waves radiate in all directions at once, unless they are shaped by a directional antenna. As the line-of-sight waves move out from the transmitter, they appear gradually to move higher and higher into the sky, as one moves away from the transmitter, because the earth is gradually curving downward. This characteristic reduces the coverage distance of both broadcast television and FM radio, which also uses direct waves. Direct waves can also, depending on the frequency used, be stopped by solid objects such as mountains or buildings. Thus, one of the keys to increase the coverage area of a television station is to position the transmitting tower at the highest point, such as the tallest building or mountain, in a particular market. Several stations can share the same transmitting tower as long as the channels they use are adequately separated on

Direct waves move in a line of sight pattern. As the earth curves,
they move off into space.

FIGURE 1-2   Direct Wave Propagation

the electromagnetic spectrum (see Figure 1-1). Increasing the electrical power of the signal can also increase the distance that a clear signal can be received, although this effect is much greater for AM radio than for television, because of television's use of a line-of-sight (direct) wave.

Controlling Interference

Although it is in the economic interest of commercial stations to increase the populated, geographic area that can receive its signal by using greater tower height and signal power, signal strength must be controlled by the FCC to reduce interference among stations. Broadcast television stations sharing the same channel or adjacent channels must be positioned and engineered to minimize interference among their signals. Interference among stations on the same channel, *co-channel interference,* is controlled by geographically separating stations, typically by locating the stations several hundred miles apart, limiting the stations' power and antenna height, and using directional antennas that focus the broadcast signal away from the nearer sharing stations. Stations on adjacent channels (side by side on the electromagnetic spectrum) in the same location (market) can also interfere with each other. This is called *adjacent channel interference.* Thus, stations in the same market are not assigned adjacent channels. However, some markets have been assigned VHF channels 4 and 5, or VHF channels 6 and 7, because frequencies are located between these two channels that have been assigned to other radio services. This eliminates any adjacent television channel interference.

The amount of spectrum space allocated by the FCC limits the number of possible stations in a particular market, making access to the public's airwaves for broadcasting very valuable, especially in large metropolitan areas. When large market stations are sold, the asking price is generally many times the value of the station's buildings, equipment, and other facilities. The buyer is really paying for the transfer of the broadcast license and the right to use public property. The sale is always conditional; the FCC must approve the *license transfer.* Without FCC approval, the station's facilities are useless for broadcasting purposes.

Networking

As we note in Chapter 2, the local broadcast television station was the source of most programming for a brief period before and after World War II, but by the late 1940s programs emanating from networks were beginning to dominate most station lineups. By the 1960s, over 60 percent of the programming broadcast by local stations came from networks. The process of television networking, the linking of stations to a central location that is sending either a live or videotaped program, started with expensive systems of interconnecting *coaxial cables.* Thousands of miles of cable were required to link a single network's affiliates. Consequently, a national network using coaxial cables was not achieved until 1951 and it took even longer for networks to reach into many markets. Later, stretches of the coaxial cable were replaced by *microwave relay* stations. The only corporation with the technical capacity and capital resources to activate this complex and expensive system was the monolithic AT&T, which at the time had a monopoly on both long-distance and local telephone service in the United States. AT&T rented its television networking capacity to ABC, CBS, and NBC at a cost that represented a substantial part of the fixed expenses for each network.

The high cost of reaching a network's nearly 200 stations and, especially, the restricted number of broadcast stations, limited the network service to three players for much of the first four decades of television. However, the communications satellite, starting with Telstar in 1963, would recast the technology and economics of television networking. The communications satellite would reduce networking costs dramatically.

At the heart of modern television networking is the *geostationary satellite,* located 22,300 miles above the earth's equator. The satellite is called *geostationary* because it rotates at the same speed as the earth, and thus, from the perspective of an

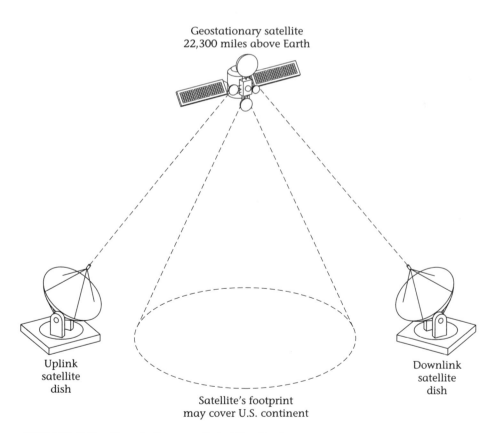

FIGURE 1-3   Geostationary Satellite System

earth-bound observer, it appears to stay in a fixed location. From a satellite dish called an *uplink,* a super-high-frequency electromagnetic signal is sent to the satellite, where it is received, amplified, and returned to earth. Older satellites used the 4–6 gigahertz (billion hertz) C band, while newer satellites use the 12–14 gigahertz Ku band. The returned signal can be received by any satellite dish *(downlink)* aimed at the geostationary satellite within an area as large as the continental United States.

This huge *"footprint,"* in which the satellite's signal can be received, is central to the efficiency of satellite distribution. One uplink and one geostationary satellite replace thousands of miles of coaxial cable or hundreds of microwave relay stations. This efficiency is only the start. Some satellites can carry two dozen transponders, each wide enough to carry six broadcast-quality television signals. Thus, one communication satellite can carry many times as many signals as AT&T's entire land-based system handled in the era of three-network television.

The efficiency of satellite networking helped to trigger the cable revolution of the 1970s and 1980s, as well as rapid growth in radio networking and syndication. The latest product of this technology is the digital satellite system, which uses high-power satellites and digital *compression* to deliver hundreds of television signals to viewers with eighteen-inch receiving dishes.[7] Broadcast networks moved from land lines to satellite networking in the early 1980s. Satellite technology is also employed by local stations to transmit remote news broadcasts from satellite dish-equipped news vans back to local stations.

At the heart of broadcast television's financial strength are the virtues of its technology coupled with the scarcity of its channels. Well-established, nearly universal, and very reliable, broadcast television uses technology that requires minimal cash outlay by consumers beyond the purchase of a television. Although it cannot provide the variety of channels available on cable, most of the country can receive six commercial networks and one noncommercial broadcast network.

OVERVIEW OF THE BOOK

In the remaining nine chapters, we will progress from the historical foundations of broadcast television, to current policy and industry practice, to the individual and societal impacts of television, and, finally, to its future. Specifically, we will review the development of both the commercial and public broadcast television systems (Chapters 2 and 8), examine the economic and regulatory systems that control television (Chapters 3 and 4), inspect the local and national businesses that create and deliver television programming (Chapters 5 and 6), outline the process of audience measurement that is essential for these commercial enterprises (Chapter 7), summarize what researchers have learned about the impact of television (Chapter 9), and speculate about the future of broadcast television in an era of rapid technological and structural change (Chapter 10).

We have chosen to examine the development of commercial and public television separately because they evolved from different economic structures and were promoted to achieve different goals. Commercial television was engendered in the business sector to reap profits, while public television was nurtured by educational institutions to foster social good. In Chapter 2, which traces the evolution of commercial broadcast television, we will examine the development of television technology from early experiments with a weak mechanical system to the setting of nationwide technical standards by the FCC in the 1930s, 1940s, and 1950s. An account of the evolution of national networks and station structures will follow. Then, we will look at the growth of television programming in a less competitive "first generation" of television, in which only two major networks and one smaller network dominated the medium. Next, the impact of cable television's rapid rise starting in the mid-1970s will be assessed, leading to an analysis of television's second generation. Finally, we will look at the recent consolidation of the television industry, setting the stage for our later discussion of television's future in Chapter 10.

The two forces that most directly control the television industry in the United States are the economic system in which it must operate, and the regulations imposed on it by the federal government. Chapter 3 documents broadcast television's economic system, one that is concerned with efficiency and restricted by the laws of supply and demand. The television industry in the United States is advertiser-supported; broadcasters are in the business of producing audiences, and programming is merely the means to an end. Because of its ability to reach a nationwide audience, there are few substitutes for large-scale network entertainment and news programs. Some of the most popular programming offered by competing television services was developed for broadcast stations and networks.

While Chapter 3 analyzes the dominant market forces controlling programming, Chapter 4 documents the power the federal government exercises over the use of the airwaves by the television industry. Since the airwaves are considered public property, the government arbitrates among competing interests, controlling interference among stations, standardizing the technology used for broadcasting, and promoting healthy competition among industry rivals. The Communications Act of 1934, as amended, is the most significant law affecting broadcasting. The Act created the Federal Communications Commission (FCC), which serves as the government's interface with the commercial television industry. The FCC is strongly influenced by all three branches of the federal government: executive, legislative, and judicial. The competing segments of the television industry routinely influence FCC decisions, often appealing its actions to federal courts. Citizen groups can also bring pressure to bear on the FCC and the television industry.

Chapter 5 is devoted to a detailed review of the workings of local television stations. Using a representative large market, Minneapolis/St. Paul, we explore the diversity among local stations. Local television is still the dominant delivery system for television programs; the most widely watched shows come to the viewer through the conduit of a local station. However, programming that is specifically local in content comes in the form of newscasts or other occasional local productions generated by most stations. We will discuss these in some detail. These station-produced programs are still the most prominent element of *localism* in U.S. broadcasting, and localism is crucial to the industry. Still, network fare and syndicated programming, programming bought by the station, fill most of a station's schedule. A station's network status is the single most important factor in describing a station. Local stations can be divided into a relatively small number owned and operated by the networks (O&Os), those contractually affiliated with the networks (affiliates), those affiliated with limited networks, and those with no regular network connection.

Chapter 6 analyzes the national television industry that uses the local station as its gateway to the mass audience. We review the development and current status of each of the major national broadcast networks (ABC, CBS, NBC, Fox) and the growing pains of two new players (The WB and UPN). The yearly cycle of network program development and the scheduling process are examined in some detail. The other source for new national programming, syndication, is discussed in detail. This direct selling of programs, both network *reruns* and, increasingly, original programs, has grown from an afterthought in the late 1950s to the most dynamic portion of the national television industry.

As we note in Chapter 7, commercial television is obsessed with the measurement of its audience for two reasons. First, because networks must attract huge audiences, they conduct research on sample programs *(pilots)* to help them estimate the popularity of new programming. Second, the broadcast industry must verify for advertisers that its programming is attracting an audience that is both large and valuable to advertisers. To accomplish this, the networks employ ratings companies, chiefly Nielsen Media Research, to prove that their programs are being watched by a sufficient number of viewers in the desired *demographic* categories to justify the network's fee for carrying an advertiser's commercials.

However, the commodity that a network sells, the audience's attention, is tentative. Viewers often pay little attention to programs and even less to commercials. The ubiquitous remote control device makes it very easy for viewers to "zap" commercials by pushing a button. Even without technological assistance, viewers zap commercials, by shifting their attention to reading or conversation, or by straying to their bathrooms or kitchens. In this active viewing environment, program ratings can only serve as rough estimates of actual program viewing.

Chapter 8 will be devoted to the public television system, a predominately noncommercial alternative broadcast service. The public system was triggered by the desire of institutions of higher education to create a "university of the air" that would bring the benefits of universities to distant listeners. However, increasing government support in the 1960s for a system that could overcome the limitations of a profit-centered commercial television led to a redefinition of noncommercial television from "educational" to "public." As Chapter 8 will document, the public system has long struggled to find a stable source of funding and to insulate itself from governmental intrusions into its programming.

The impact of television on individuals and the larger society is the subject of Chapter 9. Over four decades of research have examined the possible negative effects of the medium, including minority stereotyping, propagating a limited "television" world, modeling aggressive behavior, undermining academic achievement, and compromising the political campaign process. Although considerable evidence documents many of the negative effects ascribed to television, the medium has become the major source of entertainment and information for most citizens of the United States.

In Chapter 10, our final chapter, we see a future of continued dominance by the major media corporations of the broadcast media. However, it is not clear what the next generation of broadcast technology will look like. Satellites may distribute national programs directly to individual homes. If this happens, individual stations may well become specialized channels, featuring local and regional programs and repeating the transformation of networks in radio. In addition, alternative, menu-based systems of program selection could further erode the mass audience and its advertising base. However, if the audience becomes a more active participant in program choice, they probably will pay more for the privilege. One thing is certain as we look to broadcast television's future—programs and commercials will not disappear, but systems that deliver them will continue to evolve. However, before we venture too far into the medium's future, we need to examine television's rich past, the subject of our next chapter.

NOTES

[1]*Broadcasting & Cable Yearbook 1996,* Vol. 1, (New Providence, NJ: R. R. Bowker), p. xxi.

[2]Tim Jones, "Hot Media Properties? Plain Old TV," *Chicago Tribune,* July 28, 1996, Sec. w, pp. 1 & 6; Tim Jones, "The Visible Hand of Wall Street Rewrites Newspaper Giants' Script," *Chicago Tribune,* September 29, 1996, Sec. 5, p. 1; and Tim Jones, "An Old Glow, and Dynamic Prospects," *Chicago Tribune,* December 16, 1996, Sec. 4, p. 1.

[3]Joe Mandese, "How Much? Try a Million a Minute," *Electronic Media,* September 16, 1996, p. 3.

[4]*Broadcasting & Cable Yearbook,* op. cit., p. A-100.

[5]Ibid., p. xxi.

[6]Ibid., pp. C145–C146.

[7]A recent lowering of prices is giving a big push to DSS, but its major limitation, compared to cable, is its inability to carry local broadcast stations. See Lee Hall, "Price War Giving DBS a Big Push," *Electronic Media,* September 2, 1996, pp. 1 & 2.

2

A History of Broadcast Television

No history of commercial broadcast television confined to a single chapter can be more than a sketch, and a very selective one at that. In this chapter, we will concentrate on the development of broadcast television, referring to cable only as it has affected the broadcast industry. Our history will examine four major topics over three generations of television: (1) the technological development of the medium, (2) the growth of its regulation, (3) the creation of the major television networks, and (4) the evolution of television programming.

Although we examine these topics separately, we will show how they are interdependent. Simply put, technological development stimulated government involvement, resulting in regulation. This government action had profound effects on network ownership and development, and that in turn largely dictated programming changes. None of these factors worked in isolation from the others, although for organizational clarity we will often treat them separately here.

In varying detail, we will examine developments in technology, regulations, networks, and programming over three generations of television.[1] We will concentrate on the first generation of broadcast television, which lasted from the early twenties to the mid-seventies and included a long period of development followed by a twenty-year "golden age" for broadcast, network-dominated television. The second generation saw the rise of cable television, first as a competitor for network television and later as both a competitor and a collaborator. The second generation also saw a rapid increase in the number of stations that were not affiliated with a network *(independents)*. These stations later provided affiliates for new broadcast networks (Fox, The WB, UPN). The third generation of broadcast television lies in the near future: a future with many more competitors, improved picture quality, and an increased concentration of ownership. This third generation will be treated only briefly in this chapter, but in more detail in Chapter 10.

THE FIRST GENERATION OF TELEVISION: FIFTY YEARS TO OVERNIGHT SUCCESS

In the first half of the 1950s, television expanded rapidly in the United States. Set ownership grew nearly 700 percent between 1950 and 1955, from 4.6 million to 32 million receivers.[2] During the same period, the number of stations grew from 98 to 522.[3] The effects of television on its entertainment rivals, the motion picture and radio industries, were extreme. In 1946, its peak year, the U.S motion picture industry grossed $1.7 billion. By 1958, gross revenues for movies were under $1 billion ($680 million in 1946 dollars),[4] while network radio lost most of its major stars to the electronic upstart. Television was a feeble presence at the 1948 political conventions, but by 1956 both parties felt obligated to provide delegates with instructions on how to be TV savvy.[5] Talk about television was everywhere in the early 1950s, and the emergence of the medium was one of the defining elements of the decade.

However, the volcano that was television in the early fifties had been building for thirty years. Only after government and industry had joined forces did the medium explode.

Television's Technological Development

Both the concept and the technology of television are older than popularly imagined. An 1879 illustration in *Punch* magazine actually anticipated interactive television. It shows a family in their home watching a tennis match, while they talk to one of the players on a telephone. French artist Albert Robida offered illustrations three years later that seem all too contemporary. Television is envisioned as a tool of learning (a professor at a blackboard), a source of breaking news (a Mid-Eastern battle rages before the living room viewer), a purveyor of base entertainment (represented by a slightly clad dancing woman performing for a fat, bearded man smoking a cigar), and a hawker of dry goods (a woman inspecting fabric offered by a merchant).[6] Well before the end of the century, these visions began to trigger the energies of inventors. In 1884, the German inventor, Paul Nipkow, devised a practical system for separating a picture into a series of lines that could be transmitted.[7] Variations on the *Nipkow disc* would make a crude but viewable form of "mechanical" television available by the mid-1920s.

A False Start: Mechanical Television

Nipkow used a series of holes in a whirling disc to scan an image, each hole passing at a different position over the image. The disc had to complete one revolution in order to fully scan a single frame. To achieve the illusion of motion, the disc had to scan an object several times a second. Thus, central to all *mechanical television* systems are electric motors. One motor drives the disc in the television camera that scans an image, and the other, built into the television receiver in the earliest systems, drives the disc reproducing the image. Speeding up the disc produces more scans of an object. Faster speeds, combined with more holes in the disc, produced a clearer picture. But speeding up any motor also decreases its reliability. Thus, mechanical television was faced with a paradox: As it increased picture quality, it malfunctioned more frequently.

Despite this critical flaw, several corporations (General Electric, AT&T, RCA) and two fiercely independent developers, John L. Baird in Great Britain and Charles Francis Jenkins in the United States, worked intently in the 1920s and 1930s to improve mechanical television. By 1925, both Baird and Jenkins demonstrated working systems that could reproduce silhouettes,[8] and a color version was demonstrated in 1928.[9] The original mechanical systems used a selenium cell to convert into electrical impulses the light scanned by improved versions of the Nipkow disc. These impulses could be transmitted over wire or by radio waves, using conventional radio transmission of the sound. The basic mechanical television receiver was a relatively simple device; plans for building homemade receivers were featured in radio hobbyist magazines.[10] Indeed, these publications abounded with articles about television, although the popular press reaction was more guarded.[11]

In the latter half of the 1920s, mechanical television blossomed in the laboratory. More reliable *cathode ray tubes* replaced the spinning wheel in receivers. As the number of lines used to construct the television picture (lines of resolution) increased from 48 to 240, the images became clearer and entrepreneurial interest increased.[12] By 1929, there were fifteen experimental television stations in the United States[13] and Baird, Jenkins, and others marketed do-it-yourself kits and finished receivers. In a much publicized event, Secretary of Commerce, and soon to be President, Herbert Hoover, appeared on AT&T's version of mechanical television.[14] AT&T's system was designed to act as a telephone with pictures, prompting one writer openly to speculate on the many social problems that would result from adding sight to the home phone.[15] Ernst F. W. Alexanderson, legendary inventor at General Electric, and others worked on large-screen projection models for motion picture audiences.[16] Television seemed poised to overtake emerging radio as the major in-home entertainment medium. But timing is crucial for a new technology, and mechanical television's timing couldn't have been much worse.

The stock market crash of 1929 and subsequent Great Depression quickly dried up the capital necessary for future marketing of existing mechanical television systems. Radio manufacturers and networks were more concerned with exploiting an already popular medium than with developing a rival. RCA chairman David Sarnoff was a consistent critic of the new technology.[17] Because faster whirling discs were needed to improve picture quality, mechanical systems were becoming less reliable. Finally, a system with much more potential based on electronic, rather than mechanical, scanning of images was emerging in corporate and individual laboratories. Developers would continue working on mechanical television in the 1930s, and John Baird would succeed in convincing the British Broadcasting System to test an advanced version of his system in 1935.[18] But by the middle of the decade, the mechanical system lost its claim as a serious rival to electronic television.

An Electronic Competitor

Electronic television solved the reliability problem of mechanical television by replacing the electric motor and Nipkow disc scanning system with an electronic image system or electron gun. The first version of the electron gun was developed by independent inventor Philo T. Farnsworth and was central to his *image dissector,* one of two competing electronic television camera pickup tube designs.[19] In the camera, Farnsworth's image dissector used an electron beam to scan the photosensitive surface of the pickup tube one line at a time. In a modern U.S. television system, each of the 525 lines of resolution is scanned every 1/30 of a second, producing one image. Electronic image scanning is both much faster and much more reliable than any mechanical system.

A variation of Farnsworth's scanning system was incorporated by RCA in its rival pickup tube design, the *iconoscope.* Russian immigrant Vladimir Zworykin demonstrated a primitive version of the iconoscope to Westinghouse in 1923, but his pickup tube reached maturity with RCA's support in the 1930s. However, the image dissector and its electronic scanning system that Farnsworth developed in his modest radio shop was so essential that Zworykin had to use it in order to improve the iconoscope. After a successful court challenge by Farnsworth, RCA was forced to break with its tradition of owning its patents and began a cross-licensing agreement with Farnsworth.[20] Zworykin is widely touted as the "father of television," but Farnsworth's contribution was equally essential.

With RCA controlling critical patents in electronic television, the new system became a priority for chairman David Sarnoff, who committed one million Depression-era dollars to its development.[21] He became a champion of the medium and the major driving force for its development in the 1930s. From this point on, television would become an extension of, and later a substitute for, network radio. RCA held the dominant position in radio broadcasting with two major radio networks (NBC Red and NBC Blue) and several powerful stations. Catapulted by its commanding position in both radio manufacturing and broadcasting, RCA would become the most powerful force in the introduction of television.

A Start for Television

Sarnoff's enthusiasm for television made it the focal point of RCA's exhibit at the 1939 New York World's Fair. The "World of Tomorrow" fair highlighted an optimistic, technologically enhanced future that sharply contrasted with the economic depression of the past and European and Asian conflicts of the present. Franklin Roosevelt's opening speech at the World's Fair on April 30, 1939 became the first televised presidential address. Public areas were set aside at the fair for curious visitors to view television. During the next year, RCA's experimental station W2XBS (later WNBT, then WNBC) began daily broadcasts to the New York area, offering its own drama, music, sports, cooking, and variety programs. Quickly dismissing fifteen years of extensive mechanical experiments, RCA recounted its successes in a yearbook inaccurately titled "Television's First Year."[22]

At the Federal Communications Commission (FCC), RCA pushed for the adoption of its 441 lines of resolution electronic system. With a substantial head start on all of its competitors, RCA saw little reason to delay. However, the FCC's new chairman, James Lawrence Fly, responding to criticism from other radio interests (DuMont, Zenith, Philco, CBS), RCA's precipitous marketing of receivers, and fearful of monopoly, moved cautiously.[23] Establishing standards for broadcast television would freeze certain aspects of development, and in this respect broadcast television differs from most technologies. Once a system was established, once stations were developed and equipped, and once receivers were purchased in large numbers, it would be difficult to change broadcast standards because the spectrum space needed for television transmission would not accommodate competing systems. Although RCA protested, the FCC sought a wide range of expert judgments before establishing standards.

Setting Standards

In 1940, the FCC formed the *National Television System Committee (NTSC)*, composed of 168 engineers appointed by the Radio Manufacturers Association (RMA).[24] The committee worked until March, 1941, when it made its recommendations to the FCC. The FCC approved the NTSC system of electronic television on April 30.[25] The system required a 525-line picture that changed thirty times a second, and each television channel would require 6 MHz of spectrum space. Video transmission would employ the amplitude modulation (AM) used by radio at the time, while sound would use the clearly superior frequency modulation (FM), championed by its developer, the renowned radio inventor Edwin Howard Armstrong. A compatible color system that would work with black-and-white receivers was not approved because of its poor quality.

The standards represented a defeat for RCA on two fronts: RCA had wanted adoption of its own 441-line system and also had been locked in a tough fight with Armstrong over the development of FM radio. Next, the FCC granted licenses for commercial television stations. The first of these stations began operation on July 1, 1941. A rate card (price list) from that first year for NBC's WNBT in New York shows that sixty seconds of time could be purchased for $8 in prime time[26] (thirty seconds on a recent Super Bowl fetched $1.3 million).[27] Less than six months later, television's second beginning would come to an end as the United States entered World War II. During World War II, a few stations remained on the air with very limited schedules, including air-raid instructions, but commercial exploitation of the medium would wait until both personnel and materials became available at the end of the war.

Color Television Fails

RCA was more successful battling the other giant of radio, CBS, over standards for color television, although not initially. Both CBS and RCA worked extensively on developing color television after the war. The CBS system produced the best picture quality and, after an intense fight with RCA, succeeded in convincing the FCC to adopt its system in 1950.[28] However, unlike the NTSC standards, government adoption of the CBS color system did not mandate industry acceptance. CBS also had no major manufacturing arm and would need to rely on other companies to produce their new system. By 1952, U.S. consumers had purchased over 15 million black-and-white television receivers and CBS's color system was not compatible with any of them.[29] The infant television industry, just starting to turn a profit, would need to replace much of its current television production equipment with CBS's new system. Even more critically, because frequency space is scarce, the CBS system could not operate at the same time as the current NTSC black-and-white system. The television industry voted with its pocketbook, choosing immediate profit over a "colorful" but economically questionable future.

Color Television Succeeds, But Slowly

RCA continued to develop a fully compatible, if technically weaker, color system. In 1953, they succeeded and their compatible system was adopted as the industry standard by the FCC. However, color equipment both for stations and consumers was very costly. In 1955, an average color television cost $500 ($2,800 in current dollars), while a black-and-white one cost only $138.[30] In 1965, when the figures were $356 for color ($1,700 in current dollars) and $106 for black-and-white, only 5.3 percent of the nearly 53 million homes with television in the United States had color sets.[31] Conversion costs made color programming a luxury that only RCA and its NBC network, whose network logo began to include a peacock, could afford. CBS and ABC saw little reason to invest millions to subsidize RCA's color process. Conversion to color was an even larger burden for local stations with smaller revenues. In 1959, NBC broadcast 700 hours in color, while CBS and ABC offered almost none.[32] Only after all three networks made a substantial commitment to color programming with the first full-color season in 1966–1967 did the color receiver sales start to surge. By 1976, 75 percent of U.S. households had color receivers.[33]

Bigger, Cheaper, and Remote-Controlled

By 1980, 83 percent of all U.S. households had color televisions and the conversion to color was nearly complete. However, fewer than 16 percent of households had remote-controlled receivers, less than 40 percent had more than one receiver, and the standard living room set had either a 19- or 25-inch diagonal picture. The eighties saw an enormous increase in sales of remote-controlled receivers, reaching 77 percent of homes by the end of the decade,[34] and a 20 percent increase in the number of homes with multiple receivers.[35] By early 1992, 95 percent of all color televisions came with remote controls. Both trends were the result of sharp decreases, adjusted for inflation, in the cost of new television receivers that stimulated strong sales throughout the decade.[36] The principal family television also grew to a 27-inch picture, while over 2.2 million consumers invested in large-screen projection televisions between 1990 and 1994.[37] Handheld receivers (Watchman) also became widely available, although their use seemed restricted to spectators wanting instant replay at sporting events.

The 1980s brought improved sound quality in receivers with wide adoption of stereo broadcasting, but improvement in picture quality has been limited by the 525 lines of resolution standard set in 1941. A noncompatible *high-definition television (HDTV)* system was developed in the 1970s by NHK, the Japanese television network, but was never introduced in the United States because of the compatibility issue. A grand alliance of major manufacturers, including Zenith, AT&T, Philips Consumer Electronics, Thomson Consumer Electronics, and others has produced a standard for digital HDTV that uses the same amount of spectrum space as a conventional broadcast signal. In 1996, the FCC had established a long-range plan for the introduction of a new HDTV system. Stations would be given additional spectrum space to broadcast both a conventional and high-definition digital signal for up to fifteen years. We will discuss the prospects for HDTV in more detail in Chapter 10.

Regulating a New Medium

Because broadcast television in the United States grew out of broadcast radio, it inherited the regulatory structures that evolved in the 1920s and 1930s to control radio (see Chapter 4 for a fuller discussion). Briefly, because the electromagnetic spectrum space assigned to broadcasting is scarce, and because there are usually more groups that want to use this spectrum than available space, the federal government developed a system of renewable licensing for radio stations. Even if demand is limited, the federal government still maintains authority over the spectrum use because it is considered public property.

At first, scarcity was not an issue, and licenses were granted to any party willing to submit the appropriate form and pay a fee. But as competition for licenses increased, radio interference increased proportionally. In response, Congress passed the Radio Act of 1927, which established the Federal Radio Commission (FRC) to review license applications and renewals. Stations were required to operate in "the public interest, convenience, and necessity." This public interest standard was applied to local broadcast stations, not networks, except for network-owned and -operated stations. However, by the start of television's major advance after World War II, networks were the dominant forces in the radio and infant television industries.

Finding Frequency

Despite the influence of NBC and CBS, the FCC's main problem after establishing the NTSC standards in 1941 was finding enough spectrum space for television. A television channel requires 600 times the spectrum space of an AM radio channel. In addition, the progress in electronics produced by the war created greater demand for spectrum space for two-way radio and military applications. FM radio also had obtained a significant piece of the electromagnetic pie just before the U.S.

entry into the war. But, television's postwar potential was clear to many; the FCC received 144 applications for television station licenses by 1946.[38] The major regulatory battles in the first few years of postwar television would involve finding spectrum space.

The first victim of this spectrum crush was fledgling FM radio. FM service had been authorized by the FCC in 1940 using the 42 to 50 MHz section of the very high frequency band (VHF). By the time of U.S. entry into World War II, nearly 400,000 FM receivers had been sold and 58 stations had construction authorization.[39] Pressure from television forces, especially RCA, convinced the FCC to shift FM in 1946 to its current location (88–108 MHz). The move had devastating consequences for FM, contributing to a long delay in its development as an economically viable medium. However, 1948 television also lost one round of the spectrum fight. Pressure for more frequencies for two-way radio led the FCC to appropriate the spectrum space assigned to channel 1 for that purpose. The channel 1 was dropped from television receivers produced for the United States. But television's loss was only temporary. The FCC quickly concluded that a national system of television would need more than the twelve channels (2–13) assigned to television on the VHF band of frequencies.

The Television Freeze

In 1948, the FCC began a temporary freeze on station licensing to allow its engineers to revise their earlier plan for station development in the United States. Following the radio model, much television programming probably would come from networks, but television service would be provided by local stations. The FCC wanted to develop a plan that would provide for locally based television service, maximum nationwide coverage by television, while minimizing interference. This initiative involved the development of an allotment plan that would provide the channel assignments for local television markets throughout the country. Although FCC anticipated only a six-month freeze, the complexity of the engineering task, combined with the infighting among competing television interests, led to a four-year freeze. The long delay in station development meant that some significant markets (Little Rock, Arkansas; Austin, Texas) had no television stations, while only 24 markets had multiple stations.[40] A few markets, notably New York and Chicago, had an abundance. In addition, the pre-freeze stations' early start would give them a significant, long-term competitive advantage over their post-freeze rivals.

The freeze on new station licenses ended when the FCC issued *The Sixth Report and Order* on April 14, 1952. The order unveiled a master allotment plan that assigned frequencies for 2,053 current and future stations, providing at least one broadcast station to all but the most remote locations and multiple stations in most markets.[41] The plan required the utilization of 70 new channels in the Ultra-High Frequency (UHF) band. However, in deference to the 15 million VHF-only receivers already sold by 1952, channels 2–13 were maintained. Although the plan provided the necessary channels, it did not require manufacturers to equip television receivers with UHF tuners. Thus, in markets with both VHF and UHF stations, UHF stations were at a distinct competitive disadvantage. This problem would cripple the development of UHF television until after 1962 when Congress required VHF and UHF tuners on all sets sold in the United States.

UHF faced other technical limitations. Signals degraded faster than in VHF transmission, leading to poorer reception for some viewers and requiring UHF stations to spend more for electric power to improve signal quality. Quality UHF reception also required a separate antenna. However, UHF would be helped by the rise of cable starting in the mid-1970s. Cable transmission gave UHF stations picture quality equal to VHF stations and assigned many UHF stations channel numbers in or near the VHF range (2–13), making UHF stations easier for viewers to find.

In addition to providing for new channels, the FCC's master plan for television also included two other key decisions, one with long-range consequences. First, following a precedent set for FM radio in 1945, and at the urging of its first woman commissioner, Frieda Hennock, the FCC reserved about 11 percent of the allotments for educational television stations: a decision critical for the future development of public television. Although few educational stations were built initially, the protection afforded to educational television by the FCC guaranteed that the necessary frequency space would be available for the development of a nationwide public television service in the 1960s. Without protection, most of the prime allotments in the larger markets would have been commercialized. Second, the FCC reaffirmed its earlier acceptance of a standard for color television. But, as we noted earlier, CBS's noncompatible system would not be adopted by the industry.

The Sixth Report and Order provided a remarkably stable plan for broadcast television, but the reliance on the UHF band for additional stations created a dichotomy among stations in many markets. Pre-freeze stations located on the VHF band were usually affiliated with NBC or CBS, who also owned the strongest radio networks. Many post-freeze stations were forced to use the UHF band and affiliate with the weaker ABC or *DuMont* networks. This weakness in affiliates contributed to the early demise of the DuMont Network and limited ABC's success, until its affiliate lineup grew stronger in the mid-seventies. The structure put in place by *The Sixth Report and Order* created enough competitive stations for two-and-a-half, but not three major networks.

Building Three "Golden Webs"

Historian Erik Barnouw characterized the 1930s and 1940s, radio's acme, as the age of the "golden web."[42] Three dominant networks, CBS, NBC Red, and NBC Blue (later ABC), employing their interconnected stations, produced the most successful programming and made radio a national medium. The big three broadcast television networks were spun from those webs and were financed by their gold.

The first few years of postwar television were characterized by dominant stations. Like the prewar NBC station WNBT (later WNBC), the postwar stations produced much of their own programming. New stations had new studios and new personnel excited by the prospects of producing for the new medium. Networks did not offer a regular schedule until 1947, when stations along the East Coast were linked. The first major network season in 1948 included stations in the Midwest. Live national networking was not available until 1951. This early station activity produced some major talents, including Ernie Kovaks in Philadelphia, and a cluster of new personalities with a low-key style that became known as the *Chicago School of Television* (Dave Garroway; puppeteer Burr Tillstom's program, *Kukla, Fran and Ollie*). Local sports, especially baseball, boxing, wrestling, and *Roller Derby,* filled hundreds of hours with minimal rights fees. The brief period of local dominance in entertainment production continued, in a more limited way, throughout the next three decades in daytime talk/variety programs, sports, and children's programs.

But the economic lessons of network radio were not lost on the television industry. Like television, radio started as a local medium with each station producing all of its programming. But networks developed quickly because of the economy of scale they provided. Networks can absorb much higher production costs because the revenues produced by a national audience are so much larger than those produced by a local one, even in the largest markets. Larger production budgets can purchase the most expensive talent and the best facilities, frequently producing superior ratings. Thus, as AT&T's capacity to link stations together increased, first regionally and then nationally, networks began to dominate television as they had radio.

Although there were four early national television networks (ABC, CBS, DuMont Television, and NBC), they can be most accurately seen as two contrasting sets of two: the established networks (CBS and NBC) and their weak competitors (ABC and DuMont).

Established Networks

Both the CBS and NBC television networks had the enormous advantage of growing out of established radio giants. They were in a better financial position, because their radio profits could be used to finance television. They also had an established program pool to exploit. Hit radio programs were gradually shifted to television between 1948 and 1952. The transition often started with the simulcasting of the program on both media. Frequently, the program's sponsor shifted to television, along with the program. Usually, the program's popularity also transferred to television. In all, a staggering 216 prime-time television network series were also aired on network radio.[43] CBS's chairman William Paley was particularly adept at raiding talent from other radio networks.

Their strong financial position and superior programming made it relatively easy for CBS and NBC to sign up stations with the strongest VHF signals in a market as affiliates. Indeed, many of the new television station licensees were long-time radio network affiliates. The four-year television freeze on new station applications further strengthened the position of CBS and NBC by making stations very scarce. Before *The Sixth Report and Order,* many markets lacked even a second television station, making it difficult for ABC or DuMont to find any affiliates at all. By 1954, NBC and CBS had 78 percent of all affiliated stations.[44]

The dominant duo were also well-connected to major advertisers. They had been delivering the mass national radio audience for over twenty years and could be trusted to do the same in television. As advertising agencies turned to the new medium, they turned to their established contacts at CBS and NBC.

Weak Competitors

ABC and DuMont had different origins, but shared a common problem: a weak affiliate line-up. The ABC radio network was created when the FCC forced RCA to sell one of its two networks to comply with the Chain Broadcasting Rules of 1941 (upheld by the U.S. Supreme Court in 1943). NBC Blue, the more public affairs oriented and less commercial of RCA's two networks, was sold to Edward J. Noble, owner of the candy company that produced Life Savers. ABC's new ownership revamped its radio network line-up and attracted audiences with its new quiz shows *(Stop the Music),* and by signing crooner Bing Crosby, who was nearing his peak as a motion picture star. ABC was able to attract Crosby because it was willing to let him use tape-recording equipment rather than following the established practice of producing two different network feeds for eastern and western time zones.[45]

The DuMont Network shared NBC's roots in electronics manufacturing. Founder Allen B. DuMont's picture tubes were at the core of many first-generation televisions. Like Westinghouse and RCA during radio's golden years, DuMont used television programming to stimulate the sales of new receivers and increase production of receiver components. Network and station operation was also a way to diversify his interests.

Between 1947 and 1955, ABC and DuMont offered network television programming, but were never truly nationwide networks. The lack of affiliates in many markets meant that neither network could compete on equal footing with the dominant duo's national coverage. ABC strengthened its financial position substantially in 1951 when it merged with the cash-rich United Paramount Theaters, headed by Leonard Goldenson. Though less famous than the flamboyant William Paley of CBS or the legendary David Sarnoff of NBC, Goldenson would become the guiding force behind ABC until its sale to Capital Cities in 1985.

While the United Paramount merger improved ABC's lot, DuMont's position grew weaker as competition increased among television manufacturers. DuMont's withdrawal from network operation in 1955 was ABC's salvation, freeing stations in important markets to affiliate with ABC. Still, it would take two decades for ABC to reach affiliate parity with CBS and NBC.

Programming: Imitation, Innovation, and Stagnation

Network television programming characteristically exhibits imitation, innovation, and stagnation. Programmers attempt to minimize risk by imitating the successful formulas and established talent, those that have generated high program ratings. Only when such imitation fails, or their resources are limited, do programmers pursue more innovative forms and new personnel. Sometimes, innovation is the product of unique individuals with new ideas, rather than the consequence of ratings pressure.

After a period of experimentation, network television in its first generation became a closed system and, ultimately, a stagnant one. Because of the limited number of available VHF stations in most markets, new national networks could not develop. When competition is limited and all major competitors are sharing equally in the success of the business, they have little motivation to try the untested. Such was television by the late 1970s toward the end of its first generation: three relatively equal competitors (ABC, CBS, NBC) using the same formulas and strategies. But broadcast television actually moved through several periods of imitation, innovation, and stagnation during its first generation.

Imitation: Radio with Pictures

Because three of the four television networks sprang from radio parents and film studios initially boycotted television, much of the earliest network programming was radio with a video component. As we noted, many radio programs were transferred to television and some were *simulcast* on both radio and television. Many of these radio transfers endured well into the 1950s *(Burns and Allen, The Jack Benny Show, You Bet Your Life)*. The television version would employ the same set, talent, and even the large clumsy ribbon microphones used in the radio version. The long-running television version of Groucho Marx's quiz program, *You Bet Your Life,* is an excellent example of this type of primitive adaptation. Like radio ads, television commercials often were integrated into the program: performers seamlessly transformed into pitchmen. The television version of *Martin Kane, Private Eye* featured a tobacco shop where Kane received his phone messages. After the detective got the message and left the store, the shopkeeper would begin pushing the sponsor's cigarette brands.

For established programs, television required little innovation. Early network newscasts, for instance, featured a correspondent sitting at a desk reading a script with a picture of George Washington on the wall behind him. To add visual interest, the newsreader rose and moved to the front corner of the desk. Later, still photographs and newsreel footage were added to make the broadcast more visually interesting.

Television also borrowed all of the established radio formats. Soap operas, quiz programs, musical variety shows, situation comedies, Westerns, and mystery/detective shows all were produced in the first years of network television. Except for musical variety and westerns, all are common formats even today. There were few filmed programs, little coverage of location events, and network programming was limited at first; early television often was produced live in studios, usually with three cameras. Consequently, some formats fared better than others. Quiz shows, soap operas, and variety shows were easily adapted to the new medium. Action–adventure programs were the least workable, because such programs required elaborate sets or real backgrounds and because physical action is very difficult to stage in real time. Studio action shows taken from radio *(Captain Midnight)* were not as appealing on television. The child's imagination produced far more vivid images than the shabby sets, cheap costumes, and awkward struggles of the TV version. But, children's programs with appealing hosts and colorful characters *(Howdy Doody, Captain Kanagroo)* or with filmed action *(Hopalong Cassidy, The Lone Ranger, Superman)* prospered.

Television also revived the disappearing variety entertainment form of Vaudeville. Many of the great Vaudeville comics were absorbed by radio (George Burns and Gracie Allen, Jack Benny, Bob Hope, Jimmy Durante) and then passed on to television, all the while maintaining their popularity. Others (Fred Allen, Eddie Cantor, Ed Wynn) had long runs on radio and a short stay on television. Some, most notably Milton Berle, had repeatedly failed on radio, but became television sensations. Where radio rewarded verbal wit and sharp characterizations, television rewarded visual shtick: physical comedy, loud costumes, and outlandish makeup.

Early television's connection to Vaudeville was also the result of the medium's strong urban presence before 1952. The television freeze meant that a disproportionate number of network affiliates were located in large cities, and, prior to national network interconnection in 1951, they were confined to the Northeast and Midwest. Many of the early stars were familiar to these viewers from their Vaudeville days, and their humor resonated with urban ethnic populations. As television became a truly national medium during the 1950s, the popularity of some early successes (Milton Berle, Sid Caesar) faded.

Innovation: Theater of the Air

Although radio had presented critically acclaimed anthology dramatic series *(The Mercury Theater of the Air), live televised drama* became the format that critics have most tightly associated with television's "Golden Age." Live network television drama, initially produced in New York and later in Hollywood, schooled a generation of producers (Fred Coe, Worthington Miner), directors (George Roy Hill, John Frankenheimer, Delbert Mann, Sidney Lumet, Arthur Penn, Franklin Schaffner), actors (Charlton Heston, Paul Newman, Joanne Woodward, James Dean, Walter Matthau, Jack Lemmon), and especially writers (Paddy Chayefsky, Horton Foote, Reginald Rose, Rod Serling). Typically produced with only a few sets, with mostly close-up shots, and in real time, live television drama accented the bond between word and actor. The human face was its most compelling image.

This innovative form was born primarily out of necessity. Early television needed programming that could be produced cheaply and in quantity. New York provided an abundance of inexperienced, inexpensive but talented writers and actors, and the necessary production facilities. Because most programming was supervised by advertising agencies located in New York, the agency could stay in close contact with producers.

Live television drama was the pressure of live theater on a television timetable. As in theater, performers had to memorize lines and actions. Once the production began, there was no reprieve. Mistakes had to be covered on the spot. Added to the normal stage pressures was a weekly grind. Next week there would be a new play to produce, and another the week after. As CBS correspondent Charles Kuralt marveled in his loving look at 1950s TV, *When Television Was Young,* "there has never been anything like it."

In 1955 at television drama's peak, about fifteen new dramas were aired each week,[46] and some of them were not very golden. But as the form evolved, the best of live television drama was immortalized on the Broadway stage *(The Miracle Worker)* and in motion pictures (Paddy Chayefsky*'s Marty,* which won the Academy Award for best picture in 1955, Rod Serling's *Requiem for a Heavyweight,* Reginald Rose's *Twelve Angry Men,* Horton Foote's *The Trip to Bountiful).* Jose Ferrer won an Academy Award for his motion picture performance in *Cyrano de Bergerac,* a role he developed first on television. The form dominated prestige television in the 1950s, although it decreased sharply in the last half of the decade, disappearing entirely by the fall of 1959.[47]

Live television decline can be traced to technological and industry changes. The development of videotape recording by Ampex in 1955 ended the need for live performances. Productions could be taped and later edited to eliminate errors. The emphasis shifted from small, intimate stories to more elaborate productions, including an extraordinarily complex production of *A Night to Remember,* the story of the Titanic disaster. In addition, advertisers were moving from full or partial program sponsorship to the purchase of individual spots in many different programs. Because they were not as closely associated with any particular program, advertisers became more interested in a program's rating than its perceived quality. The weekly anthology drama with its higher prestige but lower rating suffered. At almost the same time, major Hollywood studios began to produce programs on film. Hollywood's production practices, honed during decades of the "studio system," proved more appealing to television audiences.

Imitation: B Movies for TV

Hollywood suffered a sharp downturn in the 1950s as a direct result of television's success and an earlier antitrust action that separated film production and distribution. For many viewers, television delivered entertainment on a par with or even superior to low-budget motion pictures, often called B movies. As movie theater attendance dropped, production was cut back. The pictures that were produced offered what television could not provide: color, wide-screen projection (CinemaScope, Panavision, VistaVision), large-scale spectacles, exotic locations, and established stars *(Ben Hur, King of Kings, Spartacus).* But the studio facilities, developed to support a much larger number of productions, were underutilized. The antitrust rulings of the previous decade had cut the cord that once bound the studios and the theater chains. It was clear that Hollywood needed a new distributor for its product, and television was it. As a result, by the mid-1950s, Hollywood reversed its earlier hostility to television and turned to the new medium as a source of steady work.

ABC, the weakest network, was particularly aggressive in courting Hollywood. Capitalizing on Chairman Leonard Goldenson's long-standing ties to the motion picture industry, ABC signed deals with Walt Disney Productions in 1954 and Warner Brothers in 1955. Production facilities that once churned out B movies now became entertainment television's new home. Television networks still selected programs, but major Hollywood studios and a few upstart independents became the principal makers of network television programming. It is a symbiotic arrangement that has lasted four decades.

The first generation of new Hollywood contributions exploited live television's major weakness: the presentation of action. By far the dominant action genre to emerge was the B movie staple: the Western. Stock footage of cavalry charges and wagon trains were spliced with back-lot western towns patrolled by Stetsoned marshals. Westerns had strong appeal to smalltown Americans, who by now were more fully integrated into the national television audience. The Western explosion was television's propensity for imitation at its extreme. In 1960, network television featured eighteen hours of Westerns. Later, as the advertisers began to demand more urban, upscale audiences, Westerns would lose their appeal to networks. By 1976, the genre had disappeared, returning very infrequently in the last two decades.[48]

Innovation: Pat Weaver's New Ideas

Although all television programming is derivative to some degree, the medium did begin to exploit its unique dimensions by developing new program forms. Perhaps the greatest innovator in early television was Sylvester "Pat" Weaver, who was president of NBC from 1949 to 1956. Weaver was the son of a successful roofing manufacturer in Los Angeles, and was educated at Dartmouth. He started his broadcasting career at the Don Lee CBS regional radio network in 1932 and was the major television developer at Young & Rubicam advertising agency before joining NBC.[49] His greatest contribution was extending quality network television into morning and late-night hours with *Today* in 1952 and *The Tonight Show* in 1954. *Today* became the trademark format for the early morning magazine program, now offered by other networks and many local stations. It was a mixture of hard news, weather, celebrity interviews, how-to demonstrations, and entertainment features, skillfully woven together by likable hosts. Weaver selected Dave Garraway, who had developed his own special style in Chicago as the program's first host, but several others (Hugh Downs, Barbara Walters, Tom Brokaw, Jane Pauley, Bryant Gumbel) have carried the torch during the program's long history. From its start, *The Tonight Show* had a much stronger entertainment mix. Under Steve Allen's direction it emphasized sketch humor; Jack Paar was the master of the celebrity interview; and during his thirty-year run, Johnny Carson simply became the show (the title changed to *The Tonight Show Starring Johnny Carson*). Ignoring the program's title, Americans simply asked "Did you see Carson last night?" Weaver's early morning and late-night successes turned marginal time periods into NBC profit centers.

Weaver's vision for television also acknowledged its potential for providing extraordinary experiences. As an advertising executive and network programmer, he understood that television needs to deliver the mass audience to advertisers, and the successful weekly series and daily programs did just this. But both commercially and culturally, television must offer a break from the routine. His concept was the *spectacular,* programming so special that it would draw critical attention and acclaim to the medium. The spectacular concept was reinforced by NBC's need to produce high-quality programming using its color system, in order to stimulate the sales of RCA's color receivers. Weaver frequently turned to Broadway for special material. The 1955 production of *Peter Pan,* starring Mary Martin and Cyril Ritchard, is perhaps the best remembered spectacular from the 1950s. The production was so remarkable that it has been repeatedly rebroadcast. As the concept was imitated by other networks, it became a standard programming strategy used to gain a momentary ratings boost. The spectacular became known simply as the *special.*

Specials have taken a variety of forms. Some are longer episodes of regular series (the final episode of *M*A*S*H* or a marriage in a family comedy). Others are yearly events, such as the Academy Awards and Grammy Awards and, of course, the Super Bowl. In the 1970s, two new forms of special programming were pioneered by ABC's future programming chief, Brandon Stoddard: the *made-for-television* movie and the *miniseries.* Made-for-television movies were developed to meet the need for new material to fill the successful motion picture blocks *(Saturday Night at the Movies)* that had increased in numbers during the preceding decade. Ironically, the success of television had reduced the number of theatrical motion picture releases at the very time the medium was demanding more. Made-for-television features became a more important component of the movie mix, as earlier exposure on pay cable networks (HBO, Showtime) and in-home video rentals decreased the television ratings appeal of theatrical motion pictures in the 1980s. Miniseries were a natural extension of made-for-television movies. Extended over eight nights in 1976, ABC's *Roots* became a national sensation, demonstrating television's capacity to deal with the country's racist heritage through the story of one African American family. The last episode of *Roots* is the third highest rated U.S. television program. *Roots* touched off a run of successful, multiple-night miniseries *(Holocaust; Shogun; Roots, Part 2; The Winds of War).* After production costs began to exceed the ratings and publicity benefits in the late 1980s, the miniseries typically were scaled back to two-night special events.

Television has been a consistent source of innovation in the coverage of special events and sports. The national nominating conventions of the Democratic and Republican parties, presidential elections, and historic events such as the space launches, the Kefauver Organized Crime Hearings (1951), the assassination of John F. Kennedy (1963), and the Watergate hearings (1974) highlighted the ability of national networks to cover real events happening in different locations or over many days. Sports has been a consistent showcase of new technology, including the long telephoto lens in the 1950s, instant replay in the 1960s, portable cameras in the 1970s, and sophisticated electronic *graphics* in the 1980s. Major sports events such as the Summer and Winter Olympic Games, the Super Bowl, college football bowl games, the baseball World Series and All-Star Game, and the NCAA and NBA play-offs are the zenith of network sports, producing prestige, publicity, and, with the Super Bowl, eight of the top fifteen highest-rated programs.[50]

Scandals Then Stagnation

Fifties television fell victim to two scandals: *blacklisting* and *quiz show rigging*. Blacklisting emerged from a red-baiting plague that infected television as well Hollywood; the quiz show rigging was a product of the television industry's own slavish devotion to ever higher ratings.

Blacklisting

The successful explosion of the atomic bomb in 1949 and the hydrogen bomb in 1953 by the Soviet Union produced a period of national paranoia in the United States. Anti-Communist groups used these successful tests as "proof" that traitors must be undermining the country's security. Unscrupulous politicians, including the junior senator from Wisconsin, Joseph McCarthy, exploited these national fears.

One manifestation of this national hysteria was the blacklisting of creative talent in television. Private, anti-Communist groups would compile lists of writers, directors, and actors who were believed to be Communists or to have Communist sympathies. The most famous list was published by a group of ex-FBI agents in a booklet entitled *Red Channels*. Blacklisted professionals had committed no crime. It was legal to be a member of the Communist Party. Many of those listed were not even associated with Communist activities, only with events that had been attended by Communists. Some, including actor Everett Sloan, were confused with others.

Blacklisting was particularly insidious because there was little possibility for appeal. Blacklisting groups were judge and jury, and their sentence, professional banishment, was final. Networks and stations cooperated because they feared a public relations nightmare or advertiser boycotts if they appeared to be "soft on Communism." Some of those unfairly listed were able to have their names removed, but the stigma could never be completely lifted. Blacklisted writers would employ "fronts" who would take credit for teleplays and pass most of the fee on to the writer. But blacklisted actors had little recourse. In a state of despair provoked by his blacklisting, Philip Loeb, who for several years had a leading role in the CBS series *The Goldbergs,* committed suicide. Although Loeb's reaction was extreme in the 1950s, blacklisting silenced some of television's most talented contributors.

One victim sought legal recourse and, with persistence, helped break the blacklisters' hold. Dismissed by CBS in 1957, popular New York radio comedian, John Henry Faulk, sued the blacklisting organization, Aware, Inc., for libel. His suit took five years, but in 1962 he was awarded $3.5 million in damages. But, due to the death of the principal defendant, he collected only a small portion of this award.[51]

However, the Faulk case made blacklisting as financially untenable as it had always been morally.

The Quiz Show Scandals

While blacklisting grew out of a misplaced sense of patriotism, television's second major scandal was a product of simple greed. One television format recycled from radio is the quiz show. Radio quiz shows had been low-budget affairs with programs generally emphasizing contestant competition over reward. But on television, the $64 question became the $64,000 question. Starting with the success of *The $64,000 Question* in 1955, the number and prizes of prime-time quiz shows inflated rapidly. By 1958–1959, there were twenty-four network quiz shows, representing a $100 million investment.[52] Although networks scheduled these programs, they were produced for sponsors by advertising agencies. As competition heated up among the glut of shows, a few producers found they could increase ratings by manipulating the contests. Programs featured the return of winning contestants each week until they won a grand prize or were beaten. The drama escalated with each passing week, and was intensified by casting some contestants as heroes and others as villains. Producers would supply answers to the contestants who could provide the best show and the highest ratings. The public, however, believed they were watching a real, not a fictional, drama.

On one of the most successful programs, *Twenty One,* the hero for several weeks was a Brooklyn everyman named Herbert Stempel. But as his popularity faded, producers told him to lose to a charming young Columbia University instructor from a family of academic patricians. With Charles Van Doren as a winning contestant, *Twenty One* had hit its own ratings jackpot. In an age of American intellectual self-doubt, triggered in part by the Soviet Union's successful launch of Sputnik, Van Doren became popular culture's idealization of learning. His face was everywhere. Once his bachelor status became known, he received marriage proposals. *Today* offered him a $50,000-a-year position as its Educational Editor. However, disgruntled contestants, including Herbert Stempel, began to leak word of the rigging. In 1958, a New York grand jury investigated quiz-show fraud, but the judge in the case prevented the release of the jury's lengthy report. During the following year, congress examined the quiz shows. The scandal reached its peak with Van Doren's admission of guilt on November 2, 1959.[53]

The networks were embarrassed and embattled. They responded with a major public relations campaign and made substantive changes. Big-money quiz shows were dead on prime-time television, and so was advertising agency control of programming. From this point on, networks would contract with independent producers and Hollywood studios for programming. Networks would have final authority on all scheduling. Advertising agencies would provide only the commercials, and commercials would be clearly separated from programs. As we noted earlier, advertisers were already moving to become much less identified with particular programs. Most moved from complete program sponsorship to program participation, and spots from many advertisers would appear during a commercial break. By the end of the 1960s, only 3 percent of network programming was produced by advertising agencies.[54]

Stagnation: Commerce Not Art

By the middle of the 1960s, television had reached a point of stagnation. The established two had become the comfortable three. ABC was still in a weaker position, but was profitable. Network television seemed to mirror the oligopoly in the automobile industry: three major players (GM/NBC, Ford/CBS, Chrysler/ABC), of which one (Chrysler/ABC) was a bit weaker.

Both NBC and CBS had several long-running shows *(Ed Sullivan, To Tell the Truth, What's My Line, Bonanza, The Wonderful World of Color)* that provided season to season stability for their line ups. Typically, they finished the yearly ratings in nearly a dead heat. With less to lose, ABC was more likely to innovate. Some original ideas *(The Flintstones,* a prime-time cartoon, and *Peyton Place,* a soap opera offered on multiple nights) were successful, but most new concepts failed. ABC also focused more on younger viewers *(The Mod Squad, Shindig, The Young Rebels),* those most willing to try new programs.

But, in general, there was little motivation to experiment. The television pie was large enough to make virtually all players profitable. Some critics suggested that a station in a major market was not a license to serve the public interest, but a license to print money. During the 1960s and 1970s, the number of program types decreased with live drama, Westerns, quiz programs, documentaries, and variety programs (in the 1980s) suffering the greatest losses.

After twenty years in the shadows of the "big two," the 1970s brought new status to ABC. The network's new clout came from an improved daytime and prime-time schedule, fueled by new youth-oriented daytime soaps, and strong prime-time situation comedies *(Happy Days, Laverne and Shirley, Mork and Mindy, Three's Company).* The 1971 Prime Time Access Rule had also helped ABC by forcing rivals CBS and NBC to abandon thirty minutes a night of their more successful programming, while allowing the weaker ABC to concentrate on filling fewer hours. In addition, changes in the ratings sample used by A. C. Nielsen tended to favor ABC's more urban audience. As a result, ABC won the yearly prime-time ratings race for the first time in the 1975–1976 season. The competition among the three networks became even more balanced between 1976 and 1979, when ABC raided CBS and NBC affiliates, convincing twenty nine of them to switch.[55] Parity among the comfortable three was complete.

In the 1960s and 1970s, limited competition meant that programmers could concentrate on offering the *least objectionable programming.* Viewers generally decide to watch television first and then select a program. As long as a particular program is deemed the best, or least objectionable, of the available offerings, it will keep its viewers. Programmers found that viewers who like a particular program type *(situation comedy)* often watch several programs of the same type scheduled consecutively (block programming). With remote controls in only a small minority of homes, *tuning inertia* during program breaks prevailed. If a network could capture a household at the start of prime time, it could often keep it for an evening. Even late-night television was stable. Everything that CBS or ABC tried failed and *The Tonight Show with Johnny Carson* remained king. For competitive gratification, networks focused on improving news, sports, and special events coverage, while the philosophy for entertainment programming was to "not mess with success."

THE SECOND GENERATION OF TELEVISION: COMPETITION FOR "THREE BLIND MICE"

In his review of network television's recent history, *New York Daily News* reporter Ken Auletta tagged NBC, CBS, and ABC the "three blind mice" for their delayed reactions to the changes that swept television in the 1980s.[56] The decade began with three major networks controlling nearly 90 percent of the prime-time audience. It ended with these networks struggling to hold on to 60 percent of that audience, facing two well-entrenched competitors, the Fox Network and the cable television industry.[57]

The plight of network television was shared by many mature industries in the 1970s and 1980s, when they faced new competition after a period of stagnation. The *deregulation* of the airline industry led to enormous change, and the big three automakers had to struggle to recapture a substantial portion of the U.S. market it lost to Japanese and Korean competitors. Television set and equipment manufacturing, once closely aligned with broadcasting, virtually disappeared in the United States. The situation for broadcast television was not nearly so desperate. Overlooked in the rapid rise of cable television and videocassette recorders in U.S. homes was a substantial increase in the number of television stations. In 1975, there were 706 commercial stations in the United States, but by 1989 the number had risen to 1,062, a 50 percent increase.[58] Once the advertising recession of the early 1990s ended, network television revenues, if not ratings, were as strong as ever.

The Cable Threat

In 1972, the FCC seemed to cast the privileged position of broadcast television in stone. The FCC's regulation of cable put severe limitations on the growing industry. Initially cable, or Community Antenna Television (CATV) as it was known in its early years, seemed to benefit broadcasters by extending their signals into rural and mountainous areas. However, the cable industry's importation of distant broadcast signals soon started bringing new competitors into local broadcast markets. Although the 1972 cable rules did legitimize a cable industry with aspirations that went beyond CATV, it put severe restrictions on that industry while protecting broadcast television by severely restricting the number of distant signals and imposing requirements of community, educational, and government access. The 1972 rules put the brakes on cable's expansion beyond its CATV base in areas poorly serviced by broadcast television.

The infant subscription television service, Home Box Office, challenged the FCC's cable rules in court. In 1977, a federal court overturned the most restrictive of the rules. Cable systems now would be free to develop and import an unlimited number of new channels. Developments in satellite transmission, deregulated in 1972, had greatly reduced the costs of national networking of video signals. HBO was soon distributing its signal to hundreds and then thousands of cable systems throughout the United States at a fraction of the cost incurred by the broadcast networks still using AT&T land-based networking. The opportunity was also seized by a young owner of a small station in Atlanta using UHF channel 17. In 1976, Ted Turner rented satellite space for WTBS, making it available nationwide as cable's first *superstation*. Thus, Turner began his move from small-time broadcaster to cable tycoon.

The new economics of networking, combined with reductions in production costs and a growing mass of syndicated programming, triggered a burst of new cable networks. Between 1976 and 1980, most of the major players in the cable revolution (ESPN, CNN, MTV, USA Network, CBN—later the Family Channel) came on dish. New broadcast/cable superstations (WGN, WOR) followed WTBS's successful lead, while HBO found subscription competition from Showtime. With an ever-increasing number of channels to offer, the demand for cable services grew. One by one major metropolitan areas awarded cable franchises. Between 1975 and 1988, the percentage of cable households jumped from 14 to 50 percent.[59] The world of the comfortable three was shaken.

Independent Stations and the Growth of Syndication

While the cable revolution and the parallel infusion of VCRs into 80 percent of U.S. households received most of the attention, network-affiliated stations were finding more local competitors as well. The All-Channel Receiver Act of 1962, requiring all receivers to come equipped with UHF tuners, meant that, as televisions were replaced in the 1960s and 1970s, new UHF stations could find a growing audience. The strong growth of cable also leveled the playing field between new UHF and established VHF stations by reducing the differences in signal quality and channel location in homes with cable television. Between 1975 and 1986, the number of independent stations with no network affiliation grew from 94 to 316, a 336 percent increase.[60] Network affiliates in mid-size markets suddenly had an average of two other stations taking bites out of the same advertising pie.

The growing number of both cable and broadcast channels motivated a major boom in the sales of syndicated programming, that is, programs that are rented to stations or cable networks. Sales and prices for programs formerly or currently on network television *(off-network syndication)* shot up. The revenue from the national syndication of the top situation comedy reached $500 million in 1988.[61] Black-and-white series that had been on the shelf for years *(I Married Joan, You Bet Your Life, Dobie Gillis)* were resurrected by cable networks desperate for cheap programming. The strong demand stimulated increased production of *first-run syndication* (programs shown for the first time in syndication). Game shows *(Wheel of Fortune, Jeopardy!)*, talk shows *(Oprah, Jenny Jones, Ricki Lake)*, and reality programs *(Entertainment Tonight, A Current Affair)* were cheap to produce initially and delivered outstanding ratings. As the demand grew, greater production costs, often shared with international partners, allowed the syndication of a few situation comedies *(She's the Sheriff)* and many new action shows *(Star Trek: The Next Generation, Baywatch)*. Although networks were still the major purchasers of new programming, they no longer were the only buyers.

More Webs, More Gold

With hundreds of new local stations, many more program producers, and an increasingly international market for programming, the time was right for a fourth network. Australian media magnate, Rupert Murdoch, obtained the U.S. citizenship necessary to purchase major *group owner* Metromedia's stations in five major markets. Combining the resources of a major Hollywood studio, Murdoch launched the Fox Network in 1986 and by the fall of 1987 had a lineup of four Saturday and five Sunday evening programs. Throughout the latter half of the decade, Fox added additional programming nights, reaching seven evenings per week in 1993. Although two attempts at late-night programming *(The Joan Rivers Show, The Chevy Chase Show)* failed, Fox made successful inroads into weekend sports programming with NFL Football in 1994, and Major League Baseball and the National Hockey League in 1996. However, Fox has limited daytime programming and has avoided surpassing the FCC minimum hour requirements for full network status. This strategy has allowed Fox to syndicate some of its most successful programming *(Married with Children)*, while the big three were restricted by the FCC's *Financial Interest and Network Syndication* and *Prime-Time Access* rules (see Chapter 4).

In the mid-1980s, Fox practiced a variant of the ABC 1960's youth strategy. By emphasizing youth-oriented and unconventional comedy programs *(Beverly Hills 90212, Melrose Place, The Simpsons, Married with Children)*, Fox targeted the viewers most interested in new programming on a new network. The gradual inclusion of additional program nights allowed the new Fox affiliates, formerly independent stations, to use up the syndicated programs already under contract, while the new network built its young, offbeat image. Although Fox has had more than its share of failures, its ratings have steadily improved. With the addition of twelve stronger affiliates in 1994, many switching from CBS after Fox won its rights to NFL football, the upstart was poised to compete on even terms in the prime-time and weekend time periods.

Fox's success encouraged more network proliferation. In the fall of 1994, *United Paramount Network (UPN)*, owned by Viacom and Chris-Craft Industries, and *The WB* network, owned by Time Warner and the Tribune Corporation, began a one-night-a-week schedule. The WB focused on youth comedies *(Sister, Sister; Parent Hood),* while UPN built on the success of Paramount's *Star Trek* series. Both networks have operated with substantially fewer affiliates and less national coverage than the four established networks. Rumors of a merger between the two that would strengthen the affiliate lineup have circulated periodically since their creation.

Maintaining and Segmenting the Mass Audience

Competition from cable and independent stations has forced networks to move in two seemingly contradictory, but actually compatible, directions. They have become more targeted to specific demographic groups (Fox, The WB, and UPN) while investing heavily in mass appeal programming. Despite declining shares, network television is still the most effective way to reach the mass consumer audience. Mass appeal programming, particularly hit series and major events, is especially attractive to advertisers because such programs deliver large audiences and the prestige that is associated with success. Networks need strong exclusive programming that stands out in an increasingly cluttered television environment. As a result, the broadcast networks and the advertisers that support them have paid more for major events and the top series. The Summer and Winter Olympics are superb examples of the increasing value of exclusive programming. The rights fees for the summer games increased over 1,800 percent between 1976 and 1996, from $25 million to $456 million.[62] The Fox Network paid $265 million per year for rights to the National Football Conference, ending a forty-year relationship with CBS.[63] Fox used its NFL clout to attract new affiliates, strengthening its network's national coverage. The cost of an average television series is now over $1.5 million.[64]

While the value of the most popular mass appeal programming soared, networks also began to target more carefully desirable demographic groups. Beginning with CBS's dumping of several popular, but demographically weak programs *(The Red Skelton Show, Jackie Gleason, The Beverly Hillbillies)* in the early 1970s, networks have increasingly courted urban, upscale viewers. In the 1980s, programmers began to schedule programs with similar demographic appeal during the same evening. Instead of blocking programs exclusively by genre, programs were blocked by demographic appeal. Action shows followed by *Monday Night Football* made the kickoff to the work week a male haven. Thursday became family comedy night on NBC with *The Cosby Show* and *Family Ties,* and later an urban, singles comedy night anchored by *Friends* and *Seinfeld.* By stringing together similar programs and reducing or modifying program breaks, networks successfully maintained audience flow among adjacent programs for many nights. Expensive mass appeal programming and demographic *targeting* were successful ways to fight both cable and its accomplice: a six-ounce piece of plastic known as the "clicker."

Controlling the Remote

Television remote-control devices were conceived as a reaction to advertising's support of television. In the early 1950s, Zenith's president, Eugene McDonald, saw the remote-control device (RCD) as a stimulus to better programming and advertising. Viewers would no longer be captive during commercial breaks. Advertisers would have to move from hard-sell to audience-centered advertising, or better yet, to pay television, which had no advertising at all.[65] The first generation of ultrasonic remote controls, packaged with deluxe receivers, was very costly and not very reliable. And before the multichannel cornucopia of cable television, they were not particularly necessary. As the number of available channels increased and the costs of production decreased in the late 1970s, the stage was set for an RCD boom. During the 1980s, the percentage of homes with remote-controlled televisions went from 16 to 77 percent.[66]

The rapid increase in remote controls did not pose as alarming a threat to broadcast television as cable and VCRs did, but the device did make both cable and VCRs easier to use. It also did exactly what McDonald had thought it would do: It changed the nature of television commercials. Advertisers had to match commercials more carefully to program content and audience. Commercials became faster paced and more imaginative. Many wrapped their pitch in an entertainment/information package (IBM's "you make the call" sports commercials, or Taster's Choice and MCI's mini-dramas). RCDs did not kill television advertising, but they did change it. However, the 1980s was a period of large-scale change on many fronts.

Merger Mania: Round One

The policy of reducing federal regulation of broadcasting that began under the Carter administration was pursued with vigor in the 1980s by the Reagan administration. It would lead to two major television networks and hundreds of stations changing ownership during the decade. Although many changes made under the label *deregulation* would have little impact on ownership, the FCC's 1985 decision to increase television station ownership limits would be the catalyst for what became known as "merger mania." The limits were raised from seven to twelve, and any one owner's stations could cover up to 25 percent of U.S. households. Within two years, all three major networks would change control. It was the first change in the sixty-year history of NBC and CBS. For ABC, it was the first change since its merger with Paramount Theaters in 1951.

The change in ownership limits that stimulated mergers was well timed for ABC. In the early 1980s, long-time chairman Leonard Goldenson began searching for his successor. To the surprise of most observers, on March 18, 1985, Goldenson turned to a much smaller company, Capital Cities Communications. It was a company with $2 billion in assets, including seven television and twelve radio stations in predominantly medium-sized markets.[67] The deal was for $3.5 billion. The press called Capital Cities Communications "the little fish company" that swallowed the whale.[68] Although Capital Cities could not tout its size, it was widely regarded as an efficient, tightly managed company, and it was a broadcast company. The merger eventually gave the new Capital Cities/ABC eight owned and operated stations reaching nearly 24 percent of the country, and a new corporate attitude. Network staffs that had expanded with little check in the era of the comfortable three were quickly "downsized." Reductions in the network news staff were soundly criticized. But Capital Cities/ABC's reductions were the precursor of 1980s network television: new owners with new debt, looking to "trim the fat."

For the next network merger, history would repeat itself. NBC had been created as a radio network by RCA in 1926, and RCA had earlier been formed by General Electric and several other partners. GE had sold its interest in RCA in the mid-1920s. On December 12, 1985, GE reversed that history, obtaining RCA and its subsidiary NBC for $6.28 billion. GE was interested in RCA's defense contracts as much as its rebounding television network. NBC's network ratings had improved dramatically since the late 1970s under the successive programming leadership of Grant Tinker and Brandon Tartikoff. While ABC had benefited by gaining new leadership from Capital Cities, NBC received a strong financial base from GE. NBC also endured the downsizing that ABC had suffered. At GE, Chairman John F. Welch, Jr. was known as "Neutron Jack"; like the neutron bomb, when he entered the picture the buildings remained but the people disappeared.[69]

The final ownership change was more a coup than a merger. In 1985, Loews Corporation Chairman, Laurence A. Tisch, joined the CBS board, after acquiring 25 percent of CBS's stock. He was viewed by CBS management as a corporate "white knight," someone who would strengthen CBS against a takeover threat from cable magnate Ted Turner. Turner's bid was weakly financed and his corporation had already incurred heavy debt in purchasing the MGM film library and in developing new cable networks (TNT). In October 1986, CBS's white knight turned "black," at least as far as current CBS chairman Thomas Wyman was concerned. By then, Tisch had invested $800 million in CBS stock, enough to control major decisions. At his command, Wyman was fired as chairman of CBS by the octogenarian acting chairman, William S. Paley. Paley was CBS's hallowed founder, but was now only a figurehead. Tisch was clearly in control.

The new ownership at ABC and NBC continued a policy of diversifying broadcast networks by investing in cable television networks. ABC eventually took controlling interest in the most successful cable sports network, ESPN, and at times offered expanded coverage of its own sports events on ESPN (The Masters' Golf Tournament). ESPN later developed a second service aimed at younger sports fans, ESPN–2, and has added a sports news network, ESPNEWS. NBC also invested in cable, creating a business and news network, CNBC, that later focused on talk programming. In the summer of 1996, jointly with Microsoft, NBC launched MSNBC, an all-news competitor for CNN.

Instead of buying into cable, Tisch recouped his investment in CBS by selling some of its assets. CBS Records brought in $2 billion from Sony Corporation. After an early failure in cable (CBS cable), the network refrained from joining its competition, remaining a broadcast-only company. Thus, while both ABC and NBC were diversifying their distribution systems, CBS seemed committed to the technology of television's first generation.

Merger Mania: Round Two

Anticipating regulatory changes and seeking strong partners with complementary interests, Capital Cities/ABC and CBS reentered the merger game in 1995. On July 31, 1995, Capital Cities/ABC announced a $19 billion merger with family entertainment giant Walt Disney Company.[70] It was a marriage between distribution (ABC) and software (Disney) providers. Since 1993, the FCC had been phasing out the financial interest and syndication rules that restricted network ownership and syndication of television programming. The ABC/Disney deal was designed to take full advantage of the new rules by fusing the "most watched network" (according to ABC promotions) with the most prestigious and successful name in family entertainment.

The day after the ABC/Disney deal, CBS strengthened its financial muscle and distribution system in a $5.4 billion merger with Westinghouse Electric Corporation, a diversified conglomerate with a long broadcast tradition. (Indeed, the first commercially licensed broadcast station was Westinghouse's KDKA in Pittsburgh.) Anticipating a loosening of ownership restrictions in the pending Telecommunications Act, CBS increased its owned-and-operated stations to fifteen, reaching one-third of U.S. households and adding long-term stability to its station lineup. CBS's sale had been anticipated for some time due to Tisch's advancing age and his earlier attempt to acquire home-shopping network owner QVC Inc. with the intent of turning CBS's leadership over to QVC's chairman Barry Diller. Some industry analysts were critical of the merger because neither CBS nor Westinghouse had a substantial record of entertainment program production. But the move was consistent with CBS's history of investing in strong broadcast properties and developing the strongest possible broadcast network.

A THIRD GENERATION OF TELEVISION?

Television can be readily divided into two generations. The first was characterized by three dominant networks and their affiliated stations and by limited competition. The second has been characterized by the emergence of cable, videocassette recorders, and remote-control devices, producing a host of new competitors and future partners. But a third generation is at hand. The changing regulatory picture prompted by the *Telecommunications Act of 1996,* the increasing internationalization of media industries, and the digitalization of print, audio, and video production facilities point to a changing future for broadcast television. For seventy years, broadcasting has prospered by developing strong local stations that could be linked together for the national distribution of entertainment and information programming. There is no indication that this approach will be replaced. As we noted in Chapter 1, broadcast television has certain competitive strengths that cannot be duplicated easily by other television distribution systems. However, with new owners and new partners, and with a new regulatory environment, the stimulus for change will be greater than ever.

The rewiring of existing cable systems, the expansion of digital satellite systems, and the use of digital technology to compress video signals should promote a sharp increase in the number of available channels. What has been called the "500-channel" future of television is already here for digital satellite owners who own systems capable of receiving 1,000 channels. New cable/satellite channels (MSNBC, ESPNEWS, CNNSI, MTV2) are announced monthly, and that rate will increase as channel capacity increases.

However, new channels do not mean new competitors. The reduction in ownership restrictions both within and across media means that one company can own more broadcast and cable channels. We likely will see more channels but about the same, or even a reduced number, of major owners. The major television industry players are shrinking rapidly. The mergers of Capital Cities/ABC and Disney; CBS and Westinghouse; Paramount, Viacom, and Blockbuster; Rupert Murdoch's NewsCorp and New World; and the $7.5 billion merger between Turner Broadcasting System and Time Warner are prime examples of the move to increasingly larger media corporations, each with an eye on international distribution.

Advertising-supported broadcast television will also compete with an increasing array of direct pay options, including *pay-per-view (PPV)* and video rentals and purchases. Newer conglomerates do not share the earlier bias of broadcast television for "free" (advertiser-supported) television. Most cable and all digital satellite systems already allow for pay-per-view options. If newer broadcast systems are developed, using digital compression to send several different signals over the same spectrum space, broadcasters may also benefit from direct fees. Channel 2 may bring you local news, a syndicated situation comedy, national news, and a pay movie at the same time. In Chapter 10, we will examine these and other options that broadcast television will pursue, and we believe, will continue to exploit in the near future.

CONCLUSION

The history of broadcast television is much more expansive than is popularly imagined. Beginning with experiments using a mechanical system in the 1920s, television experienced a volatile period of technological development that lasted for three decades. Not until 1953 was the national plan for station allotments complete and technical standards solidified. Then the medium grew rapidly, and by decade's end, nine in ten U.S. households had receivers. The 1950s was also a period of considerable experimentation in programming and critical acclaim for live television drama. But by 1960, anthology drama had disappeared and programming genres had begun to narrow. The next decade saw the stagnation of the first generation of television: Entertainment production moved to Hollywood but was controlled by three profitable networks in New York. With regulatory change and cheaper satellite distribution, cable television expanded in the 1980s and seized, along with increasing numbers of independent stations, over a third of television's audience.

As Hollywood initially resisted television, television resisted cable, reacting like "three blind mice." Later, new ownership commanding greater financial resources pushed for more expansion into cable and, with the end of the financial interest and syndication rules, for more participation in program production and syndication. As the millennium approaches, the dominant networks of radio and television (CBS, NBC, ABC) have become partners in diversified conglomerates, facing competition from newer broadcast competitors (Fox, UPN, The WB) and newer technologies (cable, VCRs, digital satellite systems). The future seems to present newly configured media oligopolies that will integrate television production and distribution, both nationally and internationally, as part of a larger array of entertainment and information "products," including motion pictures, newspapers, magazines, books, recorded music, and theme parks. However, it is difficult to see a near future without advertising-supported broadcast television. The wide coverage and low direct costs to consumers make it too attractive, but the medium will never return to the secure, insular competition of its first generation.

NOTES

[1]For a more detailed discussion of the three generations of television, see Robert V. Bellamy, Jr. and James R. Walker, *Television and the Remote Control: Grazing on a Vast Wasteland,* (New York: Guilford, 1996).

[2]"Television Trends in Ownership," *Time Almanac of the 20th Century,* CD–ROM, (Time, Inc., 1995).

[3]Christopher H. Sterling and John M. Kittross, *Stay Tuned: A Concise History of American Broadcasting,* 2nd ed., (Belmont, CA: Wadsworth, 1990), pp. 632–633.

[4]Gerald Mast, *A Short History of the Movies,* 2nd ed., (Indianapolis, IN: Bobbs-Merrill, 1976), p. 315.

[5]Jay Pridmore, "From 1860 to 1968, Chicago Was the Political Convention Capital," *Chicago Tribune Online Archive,* July 26, 1996.

[6]Erik Barnouw, *Tube of Plenty: The Evolution of American Television,* 2nd ed., (New York: Oxford University Press, 1990), pp. 4–7.

[7]Joseph H. Udelson, *The Great Television Race: A History of the American Television Industry 1925–41,* (Tuscaloosa, AL: University of Alabama Press, 1982), p. 18.

[8]Sterling and Kittross, op. cit., p. 100.

[9]Ronald F. Tiltman, "Television in Natural Colors Demonstrated," *Radio News,* October, 1928, pp. 320 & 374.

[10]Irvin Harris, "Scanning Devices: What They Do and How to Make Them?," *Popular Radio and Television,* May 1928, pp. 389–90, 431.

[11]James R. Walker, "Old Media on New Media: National Popular Press Reaction to Mechanical Television," *Journal of Popular Culture, 25* (1991), 21–29.

[12]David T. MacFarland, "Television: The Whirling Beginning," in *American Broadcasting: A Source Book on the History of Radio and Television,* ed. Lawrence W. Lichty and Malachi C. Topping (New York: Hastings House, 1976), p. 51.

[13]Udelson, op. cit., p. 38.

[14]Sterling and Kittross, op. cit., p. 100.

[15]Walter Davenport, "Face to Face by Radio," *Collier's,* July 23, 1927.

[16]MacFarland, op. cit., p. 50.

[17]Walker, op. cit., pp. 25–26.

[18]Sterling and Kittross, op. cit., p. 100.

[19]Andrew F. Inglis, *Behind the Tube: A History of Broadcasting Technology and Business,* (Boston: Focal Press, 1990), pp. 170–173.

[20]Ibid., p. 176.

[21]Ibid., pp. 177–178.

[22]*Television's First Year,* (a pamphlet published by National Broadcasting Company, 1940).

[23]Inglis, op. cit., p. 178.

[24]Udelson, op. cit., p. 152.

[25]Ibid., pp. 155–156.

[26]Sterling and Kittross, op. cit., p. 152.

[27]"Super Bowl Ads Again Go for Record Price," *Chicago Tribune,* January 8, 1997, Sec. 4, p. 2.

[28]Sterling and Kittross, op. cit., p. 297.

[29]Ibid., p. 657.

[30]Ibid.

[31]Ibid., p. 658.

[32]Ibid., pp. 353–354.

[33]Ibid., p. 398.

[34]Bruce C. Klopfenstein, "From Gadget to Necessity: The Diffusion of Remote Control Technology," in *The Remote Control in the New Age of Television,* ed. James R. Walker and Robert V. Bellamy, Jr. (Westport, CT: Praeger, 1993), p. 33.

[35]"Television Trends," op. cit.

[36]Klopfenstein, p. 30.

[37]*Broadcasting and Cable Yearbook,* 1996, p. C–243.

[38]Frank Sturcken, *Live Television: The Golden Age of 1946–1958 in New York,* (Jefferson, NC: McFarland, 1990), p. 13.

[39]Inglis, op. cit., pp. 128–129.

[40]Joseph R. Dominick, Barry L. Sherman, & Gary A. Copeland, *Broadcasting/Cable and Beyond,* 3rd ed. (New York: McGraw-Hill, 1996), p. 56.

[41]Sydney W. Head, Christopher H. Sterling, & Lemuel B. Schofield, *Broadcasting in America: A Survey of Electronic Media,* 7th ed. (Boston: Houghton Mifflin, 1994), pp. 58–59.

[42]Erik Barnouw, *The Golden Web: A History of Broadcasting in the United States, 1933–53,* (New York: Oxford, 1968).

[43]Tim Brooks and Earle Marsh, *The Complete Directory to Prime Time Network TV Shows 1946–Present,* 5th ed. (New York: Ballantine Books, 1992), pp. 1125–1128.

[44]Sterling and Kittross, op. cit., p. 636.

[45]Ibid., p. 251.

[46]Sturcken, op. cit., p. 147.

[47]Ibid.

[48]Sterling and Kittross, op. cit., p. 651.

[49]Pat Weaver with Thomas M. Coffey, *The Best Seat in the House: The Golden Years of Radio and Television,* (New York: Knopf, 1994), pp. 9–10.

[50]*The World Almanac and Book of Facts 1995.*

[51]Sterling and Kittross, op. cit., p. 364.

[52]William Boddy, *Fifties Television: The Industry and Its Critics,* (Urbana, IL: University of Illinois Press, 1990), p. 218.

[53]Ibid., pp. 218–219.

[54]Sterling and Kittross, p. 399.

[55]Sterling Quinlan, *Inside ABC: American Broadcasting Company's Rise to Power,* (New York: Hastings House, 1979), p. 233.

[56]Ken Auletta, *Three Blind Mice: How the TV Networks Lost Their Way,* (New York: Random House, 1991).

[57]Bellamy and Walker, op. cit., pp. 71–72.

[58]Sterling and Kittross, op. cit., p. 633.

[59]Ibid., p. 661.

[60]Ibid., p. 637.

[61]Rick Kogan, "WFLD Rolls Dice on Cosby Magic," *Chicago Tribune,* September 30, 1988, Sec. 5, p. 4.

[62]Kenneth R. Clark, "NBC Wins Olympics for $456 Million," *Chicago Tribune,* July 28, 1993, Sec. 4, p. 3.

[63]Richard Sandomir, "Dumb like a Fox? 4th Network Wins Rights to NFC Games," *Chicago Tribune,* December 18, 1993, Sec. 3, pp. 1–4.

[64]Dominick et al., op. cit., p. 385.

[65]McDonald's desire to reform commercial television was consistent with his financial commitments. Zenith invested heavily in a pay television called Phonevision in the 1950s.

[66]Klopfenstein, op. cit., p. 33.

[67]Walt Hawver, *Capital Cities/ABC The Early Years: 1954–1986,* (Radnor, PA: Chilton Books, 1994), p. 2.

[68]Ibid., p. 1.

[69]Auletta, op. cit., p. 79.

[70]Diane Mermigas, "Colossal Combos," *Electronic Media,* August 7, 1995, pp. 1 & 30.

3

The Economics of
Broadcast Television

INTRODUCTION

Most television stations in the United States are businesses. Most consumers view
their television set as a source of diversion, information, and entertainment. The
average viewer probably does not think much about the cost of programs or commercials. As a cultural force, television is a teacher, a companion, a baby-sitter, a
means to procrastinate, and a steady stream of amusement. But to the people who
create the content, television is a business. Business is concerned with money and
television needs an abundant supply of money. Understanding television economics
is essential to understanding broadcast television.[1]

In this chapter, we address both the ordinary and unique aspects of television
broadcasting industry economics. In order to understand these economic facets and
the role they play in broadcasting, it will be necessary at first to take a look at some
basic economic concepts that apply to all businesses: resources, value, and allocation. Next, we will examine the differences between broadcast programs as cultural
products and other goods or services in society. Many of the peculiarities of broadcast economics can be traced back to the unique nature of program segments that are
shown over television. Unlike consumers of other goods and services in the marketplace, audiences are typically not charged for watching programs; consequently, the
revenue for the producers must come from other sources.

The third section of this chapter contains more detail on the particular nature of
broadcasting in the United States. Other countries have adopted the U.S. system and

their situations are comparable. The common underlying element is, of course, advertiser support of the cost of programming. This section is key to understanding television economics, but it is delayed until the economics of television programming is explained.

Finally, this chapter will look at various *stakeholders* in the television broadcast industry. Fully understanding broadcast economics requires knowledge of the current condition of the industry with regard to its competitors and the outlook for the future.

WHAT IS ECONOMICS?

Economics is the study of how limited or scarce *resources* are allocated to satisfy competing and unlimited needs and wants. Economics traces the market forces (principally *supply* and *demand*) that alter the choices that influence that activity. The producer of goods and services expects to charge a price that exceeds his or her cost of production, but the price is largely determined by external demand from consumers and also influenced by the supply of functional alternatives.

According to media economist Robert Picard, the media serve the wants and needs of four groups.[2] The first group is the owners. Their economic goals include the following: preservation of the firm and its assets, high rate of return on investment, company growth, and an increase in the value of the firm.

The second group is the audience. Collectively they are looking for high-quality media products and services, low cost, and easy access.

Picard's third group is the advertisers, who seek access to target audiences, low prices for commercial messages, and high-quality service from the advertising medium.

The fourth group is comprised of the employees of the media organization. They are very interested in good compensation, fair and equal treatment, safe and pleasant working conditions, and whatever psychic rewards they can derive from their jobs.

Each stakeholder approaches the same system of broadcast television economics in different ways. Viewers want information and entertainment, advertisers want viewers for their commercials, and broadcasters want viewers in sufficient number to generate a profit. The common consideration among all of these entities, however, is how they use resources to generate profit by maximizing revenue and minimizing expenses.

Resources

In any economic system, decisions have to be made about the allocation of scarce resources. With broadcast television companies, scarce resources include the following: electricity to operate the transmitting equipment, the specialized broadcast equipment, skilled labor, news information, and the programs sought by the viewers.

The *scarcity* of resources from the viewers' standpoint is also important. The list of viewer resources is much shorter: time and money. Consumers only have so much discretionary time to watch television and only so much money to pay for programming that is not shown free. In the U.S. system of broadcasting, viewers are not required to pay for programs, but many do choose to bear the cost of basic program services such as MTV and CNN (basic cable service), premium channels such as HBO (pay-per-channel), or live sporting events (pay-per-view).

Picard notes that, as with any economic system, media companies must examine the wants and needs of their viewers.[3] Some of the basic decisions involve what programming should be produced, in what manner it will be shown, and who will pay. Government plays a role in the decision, depending on the particular system. In the United States, where there is a system of mixed decision-making, even public broadcasters must make basic decisions about wants and needs.

For example, a television broadcaster seeks money from advertisers who may need to reach men aged eighteen to forty-nine. That particular audience is difficult to reach with most television programming, but men are disproportionately attracted to professional sporting events. The *demand* for football is met when television stations *supply* a game such as the Super Bowl.

Public broadcasters are much less interested in advertisers because donations from the public pay for the programs (either directly or through the government). Even so, the public stations avoid supplying shows for which the demand is too narrow. Some programs with a small target audience must be balanced with other shows that appeal to larger groups of viewers. For example, do-it-yourself programs appeal to a handful of viewers interested in oil painting or ethnic cooking, while nature documentaries on public television appeal to larger numbers of viewers.

Value and Allocation

Several underlying value assumptions play a role in any understanding of broadcast economics.[4] Basic or fundamental analyses of markets deal with products that are homogeneous and undifferentiated. However, television programming does not fit this particular mold because individual shows are less easily reproduced than common commodities like corn and refined gold.

To some extent, information and entertainment on television are a social good beyond any economic value. Certain televised events like moon landings and Olympic contests have a value to viewers and society beyond the price paid for the service. Nevertheless, television remains a business, and economic decisions are necessary for the allocation of scarce resources. For broadcast television, allocation decisions are made in several markets.

First, there is a competition for audience and programs among sources of television broadcasting, usually among the networks and stations but also with nonbroadcast forms of programming. This macrolevel involves an industry that seeks an optimal system of resource allocation to benefit the greatest number of producers and consumers. Broadcasters compete with premium services such as cable television by offering major events through support from advertisers (e.g., the Super Bowl) and by declining to carry lesser events (e.g., soccer). On the other hand, some events with high revenue potential (e.g., title boxing matches) are supplied by pay-per-view channels.

The second market concerns the internal efficiency of the television station or program producer, both of whom are interested in holding down the cost of making a television show. Large companies take advantage of *economies of scale* (full-time utilization of expensive studios) and *economies of scope* (the producer and the distributor comprise the same organization).

In the third market, the consumers (viewers) of broadcast products look for their own cost–benefit goals. The television audience seeks the channels to satisfy its needs and wants at a reasonable cost. In the case of advertiser-supported broadcasting, the consumer pays very little direct cost, but does pay in the form of leisure-time allocation. This latter cost (lost time for other activities, like sleeping or studying) is sometimes trivial to the individual because it is not usually measured like money.

Finally, the fourth market is where stations and other programmers sell audience attention to programs. The buyer is the advertiser who wants access to those audiences. Noncommercial television broadcasters do not compete in this market, although they compete with other receivers of public funding.

As Collins and his associates note, the structure of choices in television broadcasting is under two pressures. One is the competition of distribution technologies, including cable television, direct-to-home satellites, Multichannel Multipoint Distribution Service *(MMDS),* home video (VCRs), and digital interactive television. Broadcasters also are pressured to broaden their market base to pay for the increased cost of competing with others.

This final point cannot be overemphasized. In the recent past, television broadcasters comprised a small oligopoly of stations for each market. The competition was fierce but self-contained. Stations benefited from a predictably certain zero-sum game among a small number of players. If NBC had the best shows on Thursday, another network was the winner of the three-way race on a different night. As other sources of video entertainment have appeared, however, the television broadcasters continually need to attract more revenue to pay for more desirable products—at the same time that their audience is segmented into less valuable pieces in an advertiser-supported scheme. The advertiser who bought a commercial in the last-place program was assured a goodly portion of the potential viewers when only three choices competed. Today, an advertiser in the first-place program may only reach a fourth of the viewers.

HOW BROADCASTING DIFFERS
FROM OTHER PRODUCTS

Despite its crucial importance to most broadcast economists, advertising revenue is temporarily deemphasized in this section. Understanding the economics of television begins with a fundamental understanding of the programming itself. Following this section, the reader is exposed to a more comprehensive picture of television economics.

With any economic analysis, the typical object of attention (unit of analysis) is the produced product or service, which in the case of television broadcasting is the program segment.[5] Two other appropriate units of analysis are the channel on which the program is distributed and the "total broadcasting service."[6] For the purpose of explaining the basics of broadcast television economics, however, the program segment, which is defined as that segment which *occurs between two successive commercial breaks,* is the easiest unit of analysis to understand, although the commercial broadcaster is equally interested in access to the audience as a product.[7] The program segment possesses a number of characteristics that distinguish it from nonmedia products, such as pizza, and from other media products, such as magazines.

Collins and his associates identify eight economic characteristics of the broadcasting commodity:

1. Immateriality
2. Novelty
3. Nonrival
4. Nonexcludable
5. Near-zero marginal cost
6. Instantaneous reproduction
7. Rapid product innovation
8. Short shelf life[8]

The most important distinction, represented by numbers 3, 4, and 5, is that the program segment is not a private good, but instead a public good. A public good is one whose cost of production is independent of the number of consumers. Unlike either pizzas or magazines, one person's consumption of a television program does not preclude consumption of the same product by another customer. If I watch *Roseanne,* so can you, without either of us being aware of the other.

On the other hand, the broadcaster's ability to market "access to audience" represents a private good. There is only one opportunity for an advertiser to be the last commercial preceding the kickoff of the Super Bowl. If Pepsi buys the commercial in the most favorable position, no other advertiser can consume the opportunity. Thus, broadcasters market public goods in order that they can profit through private goods.

The uniqueness of the broadcasting commodity can best be conveyed by briefly examining each of these eight economic characteristics.

Immateriality.   The aspect of a broadcast product that provides the basis of its value is not a physical thing. In the case of a program, the main value is the informational or entertainment content, not the electronic signal produced by a live camera or a recorded reel. In the case of the audience, the value lies in their immaterial "attention" to the advertiser, not their physical bodies. Television broadcasts thus derive their value from the content or potential attention rather than the channel. Although 1960s media guru Marshall McLuhan might disagree, the message is more important than the medium in providing value to the consumer.[9]

Novelty.   Consumption is a one-time event. Each new value then requires a new product. Even when a viewer chooses a rerun, the consumption is a reconstruction of an event in competition with new events. With pizzas, the new pizza is pretty much the same as the old pizza. On the other hand, the *degree* of novelty for each new broadcast commodity varies. In the case of news stories or a comedic surprise, novelty is everything. In the case of music videos, repetition is warranted.

Nonrival.   As a public good, the broadcast program is not destroyed by the act of consumption. Because a separate pizza must be supplied for each consumer who desires one, the price directly reflects the economic value as determined by supply and demand. The consumer's access to media products, on the other hand, is not constricted by the existence of other consumers, although the amount of leisure time for each viewer acts as a constraint. The consumer is constrained, however, not the product. The showing of a program like *Roseanne* involves a fixed cost that does not escalate as more viewers "consume" it, although the producer of a program has the incentive to spend more to attract more viewers.

Nonexcludable.   Because advertiser-supported television programs are given away, they are available to one and all. The only cost to the viewer, aside from buying a receiver and an antenna, is the lost opportunity to do something else instead of viewing. The value to the advertiser requires that no audience member be excluded, though some viewers are targeted more than others. In systems supported by subscriptions rather than advertisers, the expected revenue greatly exceeds the cost of exclusion. For example, a title boxing match can generate $30 to $50 per viewing home. If only 1 percent of the approximately 100 million available homes in the United States pays for the program, the producer will receive a tremendous revenue, as much as $50 million.

Near-zero marginal cost.   Like a magazine, the cost of producing one more additional consumer is next to nothing. This is yet another characteristic that some public goods evidence. In the sense of a single program, the marginal cost is near zero. In the sense of a series of programs, of course, there is considerable cost in producing additional episodes.

Instantaneous reproduction.   Unlike the magazine, however, the low-cost reproduction of a broadcast commodity is accomplished immediately. The larger the scale of operation, the better. Strong television signals produce greater economic benefit. This benefit is offset, however, by the program's dependency on a specific time slot. It is a key concept for broadcast economics that television programs, especially news and sports, are locked in the rapid product cycle of nearly continuous redevelopment. A pizza maker can satisfy a consumer next week with nearly the identical product that is served today, whereas a television program producer cannot.

Rapid product innovation.   Many products, even pizza, require innovation to remain competitive. Sealing additional cheese in the outer crust of pizza attracted customers to Pizza Hut, for example. In television, however, innovation is more than a good idea. It is essential because demand for content and access to audience is voracious and because the value of programs declines over time as the audience grows weary of additional reruns. As a result, a substantial proportion of the cost of broadcast products is devoted to research and development (R & D). Some of the decline of television networks can be traced to their inability, or unwillingness, to develop new program ideas. As we noted in Chapter 2, every year, for example, networks make weak imitations of the previous season's successful programs.

Short shelf life.   A corollary, then, of the need for novelty and subsequent rapid product innovation is that media products, especially television program segments, have a very brief shelf life. While some programs (e.g., *Gilligan's Island* and *Star Trek*) can be rerun forever, the vast majority cannot.

Implications for Production Strategy

At least three strategies exist for those involved in producing television programs.[10] First, economies of scope dictate that distributors seek to maximize the range and flow of programming. Just as movie producers, such as Disney, develop merchandising tie-ins with clothing manufacturers and fast-food restaurants, the producers of television programs exploit complementary ventures. Media conglomerates get involved in several product avenues, not because of greed, but because the product is enhanced by maximum audience *reach.* If an original idea for a television program also can be spun into a book, a movie, a magazine, a video game, and so on, the value of the idea is increased to its full potential.

Second, audiences expect a steady flow of programs and channels from which to choose, across all media access points. Even programs and channels that target smaller audiences will seek to maximize the range of segments reached. For example, public television stations will show reruns of programs popularized by commercial stations (e.g., *Lawrence Welk*) in order to meet the audience demands of older viewers.

Finally, the key to reach and flow is the system of distribution. In the case of broadcast television, it is the transmitter of the broadcast signal, the individual station, that is the locus of market forces that control economic potential. But because media production is hugely collaborative and expensive, distributors often rely on outside producers (studios and networks) to create the raw materials. In some countries, the government coordinates the efforts of production and distribution. In the United States, the advertiser-supported system works in a much different manner.

ECONOMICS OF U.S. BROADCASTING

The U.S. system of television was not carefully planned. As we noted in Chapter 2, it evolved over time, largely based on economic influences that first developed with the radio industry. The powerful corporations that today control television in the United States grew strong by looking for the most profitable way to market their products. The early emphasis on receiving equipment (hardware) gradually gave way to the marketing of the broadcast content itself (software). In this section, we examine the economic underpinnings of the present system.

Of course, government regulation has also played a large role in the present system. Because of the scarcity of broadcasting spectrum frequencies, the economic goals of corporations have been restrained by the government's concern for "the public interest, convenience, and necessity." The unplanned nature of broadcasting in the United States is primarily due to the competing forces of economics and government.

Regardless of the mix of government and economics, interest in economics has waned in recent years, as newer technologies have come along. Scholars who predict the future have found technology a more compelling predictor of where the system is headed. Even so, the issue of who pays for the new technologies is still a crucial one. Media practitioners have noted that there is a balance among three contributors to the U.S. system of broadcasting: distribution, programming, and funding.[11] Most of the attention recently has focused on distribution: how the programming will be delivered to homes in the future. But the fundamental question "Where does the money come from?" is rarely asked in these futuristic visions.

Although broadcast television economics extends beyond the realm of national networks, a basic understanding of network economics largely answers the question "who pays for broadcasting?" Efficiency is essential for any business and networks efficiently deliver a vast national audience. But, in television, a balance must be struck between the desirability of mass audience programs that maximize network efficiency and less efficient, but potentially more appealing, specialized programs. According to Owen and Wildman, "the production of mass media messages involves a trade-off between the savings from shared consumption of a common commodity and the loss of consumer satisfaction that occurs when messages are tailored to individual or local tastes."[12]

Affiliation

Understanding the economics of stations affiliated with broadcast networks is essential for understanding the new media landscape. As Jankowski and Fuchs point out, the only system delivering a programming signal to nearly every home in the United States, free of charge, is still the over-the-air station.[13] These stations, certainly the most important ones, are frequently affiliated with powerful broadcast networks, including ABC, CBS, NBC, and Fox. In 1995, other limited-service networks were introduced, including United Paramount Network (UPN) and The WB network, owned by Warner Brothers. In 1996, Barry Diller formed a small network of broadcast television stations affiliated with his growing home-shopping empire.

Despite early 1990s predictions of decline, and even death, for the television networks, there was a substantial revival in 1995. The Walt Disney Company paid $19 billion for ABC, and Westinghouse bought CBS for $5.4 billion. Fox further solidified its position by acquiring additional sports programming to compete with the primary networks, and subsequently Fox formed a merger with New World to get better affiliates. NBC remained in the hands of General Electric, which had purchased the network in 1987.

From the standpoint of supply, there are four important advantages of networking.[14] First, transaction costs are reduced because one network schedule takes care of 200 affiliates. Second, increased efficiency results from advertisers dealing with one network, especially because networks often compensate national advertisers when a program does not achieve its audience goals. Third, network programs benefit from being scheduled adjacent to one another; success breeds success in the case of new shows being placed between hit programs. Fourth, the cost of transmitting signals to affiliates is reduced if the same program is scheduled simultaneously.

Dual Clients

Broadcast economics appear unusual because the seller has two different customers operating in two different markets with two different products. The first customer is the consumer who watches the television programming (the first product). In the United States, the viewer pays nothing for this service beyond the intangible opportunity cost of not doing something else instead of viewing. Some direct costs are involved for the consumer (the TV receiver, the electricity to operate it, and perhaps the cable service to enhance the signal), but the supplier realizes no direct revenues from the mass audience.

The second customer is the advertiser who is interested in the huge audience for the programs produced or purchased by the network, or in some cases, the individual stations. The networks and their affiliated stations sell time in the form of commercial announcements (the second product). The revenues from the advertising more than cover the cost of the programming to the station or network. But, as profitable as broadcast television can be, some stations and networks lose money because their expenses are too high or their revenues are too low or both.

In their book, *Video Economics,* Owen and Wildman stress the importance of understanding that commercial broadcasters produce audiences, not programming:

> *The first and most serious mistake that an analyst of the television industry can make is to assume that advertising-supported television broadcasters are in business to broadcast programs. They are not. Broadcasters are in the business of producing audiences. These audiences, or means of access to them, are sold to advertisers. The product of a television station is measured in dimensions of people and time.*

The price of the product is quoted in dollars per thousand viewers per unit of commercial time, typically 20 or 30 seconds.[15]

ADVERTISING REVENUE

Advertising revenue is the fuel that drives the economics of broadcast television. The sale of local, regional, and national spot advertising announcements (commercials) accounts for nearly all of a broadcast station's income. The remainder, typically only 10 percent of total revenue, comes from any network compensation that flows from the network to the affiliate (see Chapter 5). *Independents* (broadcast television stations without a network affiliation) derive no additional income through compensation.

Compensation, as the name suggests, is revenue that compensates an affiliate for the lost opportunity to sell advertising during network time periods. For example, an independent television station may broadcast a two-hour movie and sell between twenty to thirty minutes of advertising. A network-affiliated station *(affiliate)* may simultaneously carry a similar film from a network but only receive three or four interior *station breaks* in which perhaps five minutes of "local" advertising can be sold. Most of the advertising revenue flows to the network.

On the surface, it appears that an independent has greater revenue potential because of increased *inventory* of time. In reality, the network can usually exploit its own scope and scale to provide more expensive programs that attract a far larger audience, which then delivers more value to the local station breaks. Broadcast stations are eager to affiliate with powerful networks that can provide programming that meets the wants and needs of a huge audience. In almost all cases, stations that are affiliated with networks have higher total revenue than independent stations in the same market. This fact helps explain why independent stations might want to be affiliates of networks.

The source of advertising revenue is influenced by cyclical events. For example, political advertising increases dramatically during presidential election years, such as 1996 when a record $500 million was projected by the Television Bureau of Advertising.[16] Ironically, some stations view political advertising as having a negative impact because regulations require it to be sold at the lowest rates, thereby competing with other advertisers willing to pay a premium. Another source of advertising revenue in 1996 came from the Olympics, which was expected to generate $700 million, although most of this sum would have been spent in some other promotional venue.

Advertising also depends on particular manufacturing sectors. When the automobile industry is robust, its advertising budgets for television broadcasting are substantial. As a general rule, however, television advertising is very healthy even during a recession. Advertisers seem more willing to fight harder to protect their share of the market during tough times, thus spending a larger share of their money on television commercials than during prosperous times.

Pricing

There is no direct price relationship between the production of broadcast programs and either the size or intensity of audience demand. As other media economists have observed, the centrality of non-price competition in broadcasting has "a profound influence on the structure and costs of production."[17]

As a result, the advertiser-supported model of broadcasting sets up commercial time as a product and the advertiser as buyer in a surrogate price transaction. Unlike the broadcast product, the commercial message is a private good. Commercials *do* compete on price because they *are* rivals for customers. Once a position between program segments is sold to one client, it cannot be sold to another. Like the seats that an airline sells, a commercial position is a perishable commodity tied to a specific event.

The cost of advertising is based on actual audience size, which is influenced by Nielsen Media Research. Potential audience size is influenced by the size of the market area in which the station broadcasts, and, to some extent, by the station's ability to affiliate with a popular network. The unit of comparison is *cost-per-thousand (CPM)*: the cost of reaching 1,000 viewers with an advertising message. Programs that attract large audiences are usually more cost-effective (unless the advertiser seeks a small, highly targeted audience), despite the higher cost of advertising. The average CPM for a commercial in a network program is about $6, whereas a similar commercial in the local news has a higher CPM.

Another measure used by buyers and sellers of television advertising time is the rating point. A rating point is a percentage of the potential audience tuned to a particular program. The cost of a commercial is calculated on the basis of the accumulated percentage points, a system known as *cost per point (CPP)*. Advertisers buy *gross rating points (GRPs)* to reach their target audience. For example, a local news program on the number one station may deliver 25 percent of the viewers in a particular market. If an advertiser buys eight commercials on that station for $1,000 apiece, the purchase achieves 200 GRPs (8 times 25) at a $5 CPP ($1,000 divided by 200).

The purchase, then, is for access to the audience for a program. The value of the program to the viewer is unaffected by the number of viewers, but the value of the commercial to the advertiser is directly tied to audience size. However, television stations do not necessarily seek out the largest possible audiences, for two reasons.[18] First, advertisers are interested in particular audiences, based on demographic characteristics. Second, the cost of a program that would reach the maximum audience in a competitive situation might exceed the profit potential. Broadcasters can only spend enough to maintain overall profitability. In some cases, like the grocer who loses a few pennies on some items *(loss leaders)* to get people into the store, television stations will lose money on some programs, especially major sporting events.

The higher price for local advertising is based on the needs of the advertiser. A used-car dealer is not interested in reaching viewers outside a driving radius of the dealer's car lot. Buying access to the right audience is more efficient than reaching too many viewers, even at a lower CPM.

In a very practical sense, the sales manager for a broadcast television station must carefully manage the price of commercials. It makes no sense to quickly sell a station's inventory at a given price. Transient business often comes in at the last minute in search of last-chance purchases of air time. If the station is sold out, this premium-priced business is lost. For example, a business that needs to run a sale on merchandise that is unexpectedly overstocked will need to run many commercial messages in a wide variety of time slots over a short period of time. If a station is "sold out," the advertiser sometimes is upset and refuses to come back again in the future when time is available. On the other hand, if commercials are priced too high, the advertising time may remain unsold. Typically, stations and networks aim for an 85 percent *sellout rate* so that they can accommodate last-minute buys.

Costs

The cost of a broadcast program cannot be scaled down to the price paid by the viewer, but it must be consistent with advertiser demand. The overall structure of the channel and its offerings is key. In the case of a full-service, network-affiliated television station, some programs are produced cheaply because the potential audience size is affected by the time of day. Those advertisers who cannot afford to spend huge sums to reach mass audiences are sometimes attracted to late-night programs for which there is a smaller audience, and therefore lower advertising rates. It would not make economic sense to produce expensive programs for these time periods.

A built-in, cost-inflation dynamic for broadcast programs results from non-price competition, peer-group rivalry among broadcasters, and an ideology of creativity.[19] According to research bearing the name, the term *Baumols disease* is attached to the rapid cost-inflation of television program costs over time. Advertising costs act as a downward pressure but the price of commercials has not had much of an influence on program costs. The simple truth is that networks try to outspend one another in order to procure the most attractive programming, at the same time that audience expectations escalate.

The result of the continuous growth in program costs is that the broadcasting industries grow larger and more consolidated, even though broadcast television networks have proliferated in the late 1990s. Like the automotive industries, among others, networks expand their activities to lower-level or higher-level distribution activities, something called *vertical integration.* To some extent, new technologies (e.g., cable television) and competition from new television networks (e.g., Fox) can shake up the economic near monopoly of program providers/distributors, but the upward pressures on costs are not abated because audience demand for more choice and better shows continues to rise.

The consolidation of media industries can be compared to similar conditions in the retail world. Some huge chain stores have become *category killers.* Local hardware stores struggle against Builder's Square, and regional electronics stores lose out to "superstores." Similarly, cable TV undermines some categories of shows on broadcast affiliates by offering a single channel dedicated entirely to one category of programming: news on CNN, sports on ESPN, and so on. With vertical integration within the broadcasting industry, however, the networks can own pieces of the category killers (e.g., Disney/ABC owns ESPN and NBC controls CNBC).

Controlling Supply

If economics is mostly "supply and demand," and if audience demand is difficult to predict or stimulate, then controlling the supply of both programs and commercials is the primary economic tool for broadcasters and their program suppliers. The main difference between the two controls is that program supply concerns the *conservation of resources* and commercial supply is closely related to *price determination.*

Controlling Program Supply

In their discussion of program supply, Owen and Wildman address the opportunities to exploit price by managing supply.[20] In particular, the release date of programs to various media is staggered to maximize revenue. This process of "windowing" schedules the broadcast product into a series of first-run, rerun, and other aftermarkets. Similarly, the motion picture industry releases its product first to theaters, then to home video, then to pay cable, and finally to broadcasters.

Windowing, accord to Owen and Wildman, is best understood as a form of price discrimination. The test is the consumers' willingness to pay. Broadcast audiences for motion pictures may have traded the psychic benefit of being the first to enjoy a movie for the economic benefit of seeing the film for free on a commercial television station. For the producer, there are many economic benefits from careful management of release dates for media products into the various distribution streams, including broadcast television.

Although affiliated stations get most of their programming supply from the networks, independent stations rely on syndicators of off-network and first-run programs; supply is controlled by competitive pressures among a very wide range of choices. Though the syndicator is often the original producer of shows to the network and the reseller of the same programs to individual television stations, sometimes the syndicator is just a distributor. For example, King World sells programs (e.g., *Wheel of Fortune, Oprah, Jeopardy!*) produced by other companies.

Controlling Advertising Supply

The television stations and their networks also control the supply of commercial time to the other half of their dual market: the advertisers. Interestingly, the number of competitors seems to have no effect on the price of advertising time sold in a particular area because stations primarily compete with other forms of advertising such as newspapers and direct mail.

Commercial time is sold as *spot* announcements or *participating sponsorships.* Spots are roughly interchangeable, whereas sponsorships involve a commitment to a particular program. Networks sell 75 percent of their time in the *up-front* market during late spring, when the new season's programming is announced. Stations sell their time either on annual contracts (like newspaper advertising) or on *scatter plans.* A scatter plan is a short schedule of spots covering a variety of time slots over a few weeks. The rates for the scatter market are less expensive, but the availability of spots can be somewhat limited.

An advertiser can buy early to ensure good placement, thereby paying a premium, or take the risk that there will be cheaper unsold time closer to the broadcast date. As the actual time of the commercial draws near, the network and the stations are under pressure to sell any unsold time. In most cases, however, the advertiser must purchase a *schedule* of spots to accomplish marketing goals rather than just one commercial.

Another complication with controlling advertising supply involves the program audience that supplies the value to advertisers. People often do not want to watch commercials. This is evident, as Owen and Wildman note, in viewers' decisions to pay a premium to commercial-free pay channels and to avoid commercials by using a remote control device, by flipping to other channels during commercial breaks or by fast-forwarding through advertising on recorded videotapes. Television broadcasters must weigh the viewers' willingness to pay for premium channels against their desire to view free over-the-air programming. A major consideration is the audience's tolerance for the number of commercials needed to produce a profit.

Control of Demand

It seems unlikely that the audience would ever demand television commercials in the same way that newspaper readers seek out print advertising. The difference is that television commercials interrupt the programs while printed advertising benefits from the reader's random-access searching, without much regard to time. That is, consumers of print advertising control their use of time, but audiences for television are at the mercy of the broadcasters' clock.

Control of program demand, however, is within the reach of networks, stations, and producers. It is to their collective economic benefit that audiences demand more programs and *different* programs, especially the type of shows that are inexpensive to produce. For example, inexpensive daytime talk shows have reached the point of saturation because broadcasters determined that viewers wanted to watch provocative shows. The ability to spice up the programming content can, at least in the short term, increase the viewers' demand for television programming. At the very least, creative programming content can reduce the exodus of mass audiences to specialized cable channels where provocative content is more common.

Impact of Regulation

Broadcasters must balance their economic goals against their legal commitments (see Chapter 4). Because the spectrum of frequencies available to over-the-air broadcasters is scarce, the federal government regulates stations, which promise to serve in the "public interest, convenience, and necessity." The station is the focal point of regulation. Even though the network often provides the programming, the individual affiliate is responsible to the Federal Communications Commission for the station's performance of promises made to serve the public. Special interest and pressure groups also can influence the programming policies of broadcasters. Even in a more relaxed regulatory climate in which the threat of license revocation is negligible, "stations must consider their relationships with local government and community leaders and with advertisers."[21]

The economic importance of government regulation is evidenced by the extent to which broadcasters attempt to influence legislators. Lobbying organizations like the National Association of Broadcasters exert powerful influence on Congress and the FCC. However, audiences for broadcast television also make their complaints about program content known to government regulators.

Although regulations are a concern, the public behavior of many television broadcasters is heavily influenced by economic interest: It is good business to offend the least number of viewers. With the growth of pay cable channels, however, broadcasters are in a bind. Some of their national audience, often those most desired by advertisers, is attracted to program content that is too adult-oriented for broadcasters. Viewers, for example, want motion pictures on television to be more like the films they see at theaters. The result has been a slow erosion of conventional standards of decency over the years. For example, of the original seven dirty words one can never say on broadcast television (as popularized by comedian George Carlin), only four remain. Advertisers serve as willing accomplices as long as their products are not targeted by pressure groups.

Not only is program content under constant scrutiny, some categories of broadcast advertising are severely restricted by government regulation or industry self-regulation. Legal products like cigarettes (prohibited by government regulation) and distilled spirits (controlled by self-regulation) are not advertised on broadcast television in the United States, although some stations in Texas began flaunting broadcasting industry guidelines in 1996.[22] Individual states occasionally restrict advertising of services by professionals like lawyers and doctors.

One interesting dynamic between government and television broadcasting involves political advertising. Broadcasters view elections as money-making opportunities. Legislators, on the other hand, exploit requirements for "equal time" to minimize the cost of advertising, under the guise of fairness. For example, candidates with less money than their competitors can sometimes demand television exposure at no or low cost. Other forms of advertising that compete with broadcast television are not subjected to regulations, but stations must sell political time at the lowest possible unit cost.

Importance of Technology

The entire system of television broadcasting is tied to existing technology, which is not likely to go away. Regardless of any optimistic predictions, there are 200 million television sets in the United States with features so basic that they limit the amount of change that can take place, short of either replacing every set, or adding expensive black-box equipment that would serve as the functional equivalent of replacing every set, in all nearly 100 million television homes.

Quite simply, every television set has a screen for the picture, a speaker system for the sound, and an antenna input. It is the antenna input that defines broadcasting, which in turn helps define the economic structure of television broadcasting. At its most basic level, the television set assumes an antenna-delivered signal.

Individual viewers may elect to connect a coaxial cable, a digital satellite cable, or a VCR cable to the antenna input, instead of the standard rooftop antenna, but the television set itself is designed to work very well without any external equipment. With a sufficiently strong local broadcast signal, the antennae (one VHF and one UHF) supplied with every television set will download the content that can attract an audience which a car dealer will want to temporarily distract with commercial messages.

As long as this basic technology remains ubiquitous, television viewers will expect a local broadcast signal: Why else would the manufacturer include the antennae? Networks will need their affiliates for the distribution system to work. Furthermore, there is not much indication that the television audience is dissatisfied with the arrangement, though viewers are often eager to supplement the limited choices available solely over-the-air. Universal service to all homes with television makes the broadcast television system "necessary, though not sufficient."

Nevertheless, there is a slowly growing love affair between many consumers, particularly the young affluent ones that many advertisers crave, and their computers. The networked computer competes with the TV set as a link between audiences and program sources for entertainment and information. To the extent that someone ties the schedule-based mass audience television system to the menu-based Internet computer system, the economics of television will be altered. Broadcasting's potential role in this transformation will be assessed in Chapter 10.

THE INDUSTRY

This section takes a look at the various stakeholders in the television industry. It is important to remember that the relationships among the different players is just as important as the individuals involved. Most importantly, the economic well-being of any sector is enhanced by its ability to coexist with (or even acquire) the competition.

The Producers

Although the networks and the individual stations produce their own programming, independent producers (usually motion picture studios) create the shows carried by television broadcasters. Program suppliers are less concentrated than the networks who buy from them, in the sense that suppliers are often smaller and greater in number. As a result, prices are very competitive for three reasons.[23] First, joint strategies among suppliers are more difficult with more suppliers. Second, price compliance is more difficult to monitor with more suppliers. Third, an abundance of suppliers triggers stronger temptation to cheat on price-fixing arrangements.

As with the networks, there has been considerable consolidation of control among program suppliers. The repeal of the Financial–Syndication (Fin–Syn) rules is expected to lead to more alliances among producers and their network distributors. Some producers (e.g., Disney) have made moves toward owning a major television network in order to influence their distribution channel.

There are only a handful of major studio producers: Fox, Columbia, Disney, Paramount, Universal, Warner Brothers, and smaller independent producers like Bochco or Cannell. The networks, freed from years of government restrictions, can now produce many of their own shows. As with any in-house activity, however, companies often benefit by having outsiders do the work when it concerns an area of expertise for the contracted firm. For example, in 1995 NBC lost millions of dollars producing its own miniseries *Gaijin,* which was eventually abandoned because of runaway costs. Independent producers are usually more frugal than the networks.

Producers rely heavily on the networks to distribute their programs. The economic arrangement involves some very creative financing, however. The network typically contracts for two showings of a particular episode of a series. After that, the studio retains the right to exploit its ownership by marketing the shows to foreign audiences for first-run exhibition or to cable networks and broadcast stations for rerun exhibition. As a result, networks exert pressure on the producer to assume a large share of the financial risk of producing the show, because the same producer retains the financial benefit of a successful series.

Assumption of risk takes the form of *deficit financing.* Under this arrangement, the producer charges the network less than the cost of producing the television program episode. The producer can actually make more money under this plan, even if only a few series ultimately become successful on the network, because *economies of scale* make it less costly per program to produce several programs. Of course, the size of the studio has an effect on its willingness to take a risk.

Another influence on risk-bearing involves *option periods.*[24] An option period is the amount of time during which buyers have to decide if they want to take a risk on a new program. Producers who prefer risk would rather have short option periods because the payoff is greater once the network success is determined. Usually the fate of a program is known within a few weeks. If the network must quickly renegotiate for future episodes, the potential for financial reward for the producer is greater when the option period is shorter.

The Networks

The outlook for the television networks' share of the prime-time viewing audiences is expected to show no gain or loss through 1998, according to an annual report by

Veronis, Suhler & Associates.[25] The same investment bankers' forecast predicted 1998 gross revenues for television networks to be $13.48 billion, up from $10.435 billion in 1993. Revenue from television stations is expected to be $21.23 billion, putting the sum for 1998 television broadcasting at $34.71 billion.

By comparison, cable television advertising should rise to $4.4 billion in 1998. Radio advertising is predicted to be $13.23 billion. Home video revenue will be close to $18.56 billion in 1998. Newspaper and direct-mail advertising are the major contributors to the total spent each year in the United States on advertising. Network advertising accounts for less than 15 percent of the total, despite any seeming prominence.

Predicting the continued health of the networks is complicated because of the way viewing estimates are reported. Observers who want to make the case that the networks are in trouble insist on citing a three-way race for combined share of viewing among ABC, CBS, and NBC. This made sense when there were only three networks, but Fox is clearly a fourth option. Although it is true that the multichannel environment helped whittle network shares from 90 percent in 1980 down to mid-70 percent shares in the 1990s among all four major networks, it is unfair to give cable channels all of the credit when the older three networks' combined share dips into the mid-50 percent range. Certainly the independent stations (affiliated with Fox, UPN, and The WB) deserve some credit, along with home video. Even so, the November 1995 Nielsen reports put average viewing of ABC, CBS, and NBC at only 53 percent of the available audience, down 10 percent from the previous November.

As noted earlier, there have been some ownership changes at the networks in the mid-1990s. Further consolidation and change is not unlikely. Television, particularly network television, continues to be a potentially healthy business.[26] The major challenge to its dominance lies in technological innovations like direct broadcast satellite (DBS) and fiber-optic cable, which may make obsolete the broadcast distribution of programs by affiliate stations. Most observers are content to predict eventual change, but short-term projections point to more of the same. In fact, the economic viability of networks is actually enhanced by government regulations that have increased ownership limits and eliminated rules designed to handicap the networks. For example, networks are permitted under the Telecommunications Act of 1996 to own as many stations as they want, as long as the total national reach is less than 35 percent of the entire population. One dark cloud looming on the horizon for television broadcasters is the cost of converting stations to a new digital TV standard (between $2 million and $10 million per station).

The Stations

Each of the three major networks has 200 or more affiliates, with Fox not far behind. About 75 percent of the nation's 1,500 television stations (not counting the additional 1,800 "low-power" stations and 4,800 translator transmitters) sell advertising. Over 98 percent of all households in the United States have at least one television set, with daily viewing averaging seven hours per home.

The number of independent television stations grew dramatically in the 1980s, from about 100 in 1980 to nearly 350 by the end of the decade. This growth has spurred the development of the Fox network, among others. For all the talk by economists about *barriers to entry* in broadcasting, there are many stations operating.

But the number of television stations per market is still limited when compared, for example, to the number of radio outlets in the same area. Because there is a *relative* scarcity of *good* broadcast signals in a market, greater demand exists for stations when there is an available supply. Owen and Wildman describe the license as "a valuable asset that commands a considerable price in the market."[27] This became particularly evident in 1994 when the Fox network bought a group of New World stations. The network affiliation switched to Fox, often leaving an incumbent network affiliate like CBS without a station in that market. For example, CBS affiliate WJBK in Detroit switched to Fox, leaving CBS with few viable options. Eventually CBS settled for a UHF signal on Channel 62. This affiliate upheaval was repeated in many other markets across the country.

Several factors influence the revenue potential for stations. First, the nature of the broadcast signal can significantly alter the value of the license. As noted in Chapter 1, VHF stations broadcast on channels 2 through 13 and are generally desirable for their signal propagation characteristics. UHF stations operate on higher channel numbers that require more expensive antenna systems operating at higher cost for electricity. Furthermore, UHF signals are less reliable. To the extent that a community is wired for cable television, this signal factor is mitigated.

A second factor is the network affiliation. Most stations desire such an arrangement because of the economies of scale involved. Because stations are responsible to the FCC for their programming, the agreement with a network to carry programs is not ironclad. Thus, the station affiliate gets the best of both worlds: It can offer high-budget programs from the network at minimal costs, but still occasionally preempt the network for a program of greater interest to the local community or a local advertiser.

The Advertisers

Advertisers can purchase advertising (called *spot advertising* or *spots*) on the networks to reach a national audience. If the target audience is local, the spots may be purchased instead on individual stations. There are three distinct spot marketplaces: network spot, national spot, and local spot.

The difference between network and national spot is that, with the latter, the advertiser may decide to buy only those stations that reach a geographic or demographic target. It is less expensive to buy spots on the network but it is frequently more efficient to purchase advertising on a smaller number of stations in specified markets. These ad hoc spot networks are usually assembled by *national sales representatives ("reps")* like Katz or Petry.

In the case of local advertising, merchants deal directly with the stations, sometimes through local agencies, to purchase spots that will be seen only on that station. A substantial portion of a station's *revenue* is determined by local advertising, especially in small markets.

Broadcasters compete with other media for both advertising and audiences. Television advertising has many advantages over other forms of media advertising: like print, it has pictures; like magazines and billboards, it has color; like radio, it has sound. Unlike its main competitors, however, it has full motion. Advertisers pay a premium for sight, sound, and motion. To some extent a combination of other media is not only substitutable for television advertising, but is also a worthy addition toward a "marketing mix." Cable television also sells advertising, but its audience for individual channels is very tiny and the marketing effort is less intense because of the steady stream of revenue from subscription fees.

A corollary to advertiser competition is audience competition. The same media that compete for advertisers also lure away potential audience. In this situation, cable television has its largest impact on broadcasters. A cable operator does not need to realize maximum benefit from each individual channel that is carried. A broadcast station, on the other hand, cannot appeal to diverse viewers at the same time: There is only one channel available to the local station. Because cable programming is subsidized by subscription fees, it can aim for smaller audiences that siphon away tiny segments of the potential broadcast audience.

Future plans by the government to supply a second channel to existing television broadcasters may change the competitive picture. If, for example, a second channel designated for high-definition television (HDTV) is used to provide compressed-and-multiplexed *additional channels* for a portion of the day when HDTV is not shown, broadcasters may become multichannel providers like cable.

Relationships among the Players

Understanding the relationships among producers, networks, stations, and advertisers requires some attention to their ultimate customer: the audience. Without viewers, the creation of value is impossible. Obviously, if no one is watching, there is no point in putting on shows. It is the attention of a mass audience that the advertisers are trying to distract to their products and services.

The various economic players are in a loose partnership to keep the system working. For example, the advertisers have an unspoken agreement with the networks to accept at face value a flawed system of audience measurements from Nielsen (see Chapter 7). It is widely known that the CPM cost of a commercial is based on a rating that is imprecise, but everyone accepts the number because there is no other starting point for negotiation.

Producers and networks have an uneasy alliance. Networks would prefer to own the productions, but often cannot do so for legal or practical reasons. The marketing arrangement is typical of all production–distributor relationships, except that inventories are electronic and transportation is nearly instantaneous.

CONCLUSION

Broadcast television economics is a dynamic subject. It is concerned with efficiency and balance, based on prices and costs as well as supply and demand. The structure of the industry in the United States is advertiser-supported, which puts broadcasters in the business of producing audiences, not programming.

If the industry is defined by advertising support, the system of national advertising is defined by network economics. There are few substitutes for large-scale network entertainment and news programs. Even the programming supplied by cable, home video, and other multichannel providers is based on programming originally produced (or intended) for the networks. Only the motion picture industry rivals the networks because both have a long tradition of creating programming and it is not clear that either could survive without the other. In fact, the studios have created alliances to exploit the potential for network broadcasting and cross-marketing (e.g., the Disney–ABC merger).

The future points to continued dominance by the major players, but it is not clear what form network broadcasting will take. If technology brings about a system of direct-to-home satellite distribution of national programs, individual stations will most likely evolve into specialized channels of local and regional programs, not unlike the transformation effected by radio stations when the large radio networks withered. Finally, the possibility of menu-based program systems could threaten the mass audience and its advertising base, if the audience ever becomes an active participant in program choice. Programs and commercials will not vanish, but they will change.

NOTES

[1]In addition to quoted sources, these authors were particularly helpful in writing this chapter: Alison Alexander, James Owers, and Rod Carveth (eds.), *Media Economics: Theory and Practice.* (New York: Lawrence Erlbaum Associates, 1993); Alan B. Albarran, *Media Economics: Understanding Markets, Industries and Concepts.* (Ames, Iowa: Iowa State University Press, 1996); Bruce M. Owen, Jack H. Beebe, and William G. Manning, Jr., *Television Economics.* (Lexington, MA: Lexington Books, 1974).

[2]Robert G. Picard, *Media Economics: Concepts and Issues.* (Newbury Park, CA: Sage Publications, 1989).

[3]Picard, op. cit., p. 9.

[4]Richard Collins, Nicholas Garnham, & Gareth Locksley, *The Economics of Television: The UK Case.* (Newbury Park, CA: Sage Publications, 1988).

[5]Many broadcast economists consider the audience and the advertiser's desire to gain access to the audience as the primary focus of television economics. Advertising is explored in the third section of the chapter, after a foundation is laid for the unique attributes of the program segment.

[6]Collins et al., op. cit., p. 6.

[7]Noncommercial television broadcasters are rarely interested in the economics of the audience because, unlike commercial broadcasters, they derive no substantial revenue from the size of the audience.

[8]Collins et al., op. cit., pp. 7–9.

[9]Nowhere is this more true than in the *promotion* of television viewing. The television broadcaster can successfully promote the specific scheduling of a program. Promoting loyalty toward the channel itself is less likely to succeed. Audiences choose to watch programs, not channels, in most cases.

[10]Collins et al., op. cit., pp. 11–12.

[11]Gene F. Jankowski and David C. Fuchs, *Television Today and Tomorrow,* (New York: Oxford, 1995), p. 53.

[12]Bruce M. Owen and Steven S. Wildman, *Video Economics.* (Cambridge, MA: Harvard University Press, 1992), p. 151.

[13]Jankowski and Fuchs, op. cit., p. 188.

[14]Owen and Wildman, op. cit., pp. 53–54.

[15]Owen and Wildman, op. cit., p. 3.

[16]Steve McClellan, "TVB Sees Ad Growth in '96," *Broadcasting & Cable,* October 2, 1995, p. 36.

[17]Collins et al., op. cit., p. 15.

[18]Owen and Wildman, op. cit., pp. 3–4.

[19]Collins et al., op. cit., p. 16.

[20]Owen and Wildman, op. cit., pp. 26–38.

[21]Owen and Wildman, op. cit., p. 5.

[22]The advertising of hard liquor on television had been forbidden by self-regulation until 1996. The distilled spirits industry attempted to regain its loss of market share, which declined at the hands of the beer and wine makers, who have been able to advertise their lower alcohol products on television. Ironically, the controversy may actually serve to limit the appropriateness of beer and wine advertising, rather than expand the opportunity for the distilled spirits industry.

[23]Owen and Wildman, op. cit., pp. 54–55.

[24]Owen and Wildman, op. cit., pp. 180–186.

[25]Geoffrey Foisie, "Higher Network Revenue Gain Projected," *Broadcasting & Cable,* July 25, 1994, p. 79.

[26]Although the weaker networks may periodically struggle to show a profit, the leaders can still do very well. At the end of 1996, NBC posted its fifth straight year of 20 percent operating–profit margin increases. Source: Steve McClellan, "NBC Posts $1 Billion in Earnings," *Broadcasting & Cable,* December 16, 1996, p.64.

[27]Owen and Wildman, op. cit., p. 15.

4

The Regulation of Broadcast Television

Although the day-to-day decisions at broadcast television networks and stations are largely determined by economic structures and constraints, broadcasting is a federally regulated industry, and regulatory decisions are of lasting consequence to that industry. Federal Communications Commission (FCC) rule-making, congressional action, and presidential influence have shaped broadcasting from the beginning. The profit motive may spark the competitive engine in commercial broadcasting, but the federal government has established the ground rules for that competition, largely determining the number and relative power of the contestants.

The last two decades have seen a decided shift in the philosophy of broadcast regulation in the United States. Instead of mandating general or specific program requirements, the Federal Communications Commission has consciously adopted a policy of *deregulation* that privileges competition among profit-making corporations as the key determinant of program decision-making. For strong supporters of deregulation, the requirement that stations broadcast in the public interest has become synonymous with the delivery of popular, and thus commercially successful, programs.

In this chapter, we will review rationales that justify some control of broadcast television by the government. Next, we will review the *Communications Act of 1934,* the law that still provides the regulatory basis for broadcast television. We will then introduce a model of the forces that influence the television industry. Next, we will examine the processes of license granting and renewal, and the rules limiting station ownership. Finally, we will review rules that have limited network control of the television industry.

APPROACHES TO GOVERNMENT CONTROL OF TELEVISION

Broadcast television has always been regulated. Despite great variation in the degree and type of governmental control, there is universal acknowledgment of the need to put some restrictions on the medium. Approaches to governmental control of broadcasting have been characterized as *authoritarian, paternal,* and *permissive.*[1] Totalitarian governments assume authority over broadcast operations, including television. The broadcast media are seen as agencies of the government whose primary responsibility is to advance the national agenda. The authoritarian model was dominant in the former Soviet Union and Eastern Europe, but has undergone considerable change since the decline of Soviet Communism. However, authoritarian regulation is still dominant in the Communist states of Cuba, North Korea, and China.

Paternal systems of regulation view broadcasting as a tool of social good, a means to making a better society. Broadcasting is financed by tax revenue, often through a tax on receivers, but decision-making is centered in a body independent of the government. The British Broadcasting Corporation (BBC) is the model of this approach. Paternal systems such as the BBC and the Canadian Broadcasting Commission (CBC) have been subjected to severe budget cuts in recent years, and the paternal approach appears to be on the decline.

Television in the United States follows a permissive approach to regulation that is characterized by a heavy reliance on advertising support to pay the costs of broadcasting, and a limited role for government in program decision-making. The permissive approach relies on market forces to determine programming choice. This generally means the programs that deliver the largest and most demographically desirable audiences (the key consumers of sponsor products and services) will remain on the air. The primary goal in permissive systems is audience attention as measured by ratings companies (see Chapter 7). Other effects of the medium (see Chapter 9) are generally of little economic consequence, unless they stimulate government regulation (e.g., the banning of cigarette advertising) or boycotts of an advertiser's products. Thus, most effects other than ratings are ignored or, if negative (e.g., promotion of aggression in children), denied by the regulated industry. The increasing globalization of the television industry is the direct result of an increasing use of the permissive approach in much of the world (see Chapter 10).

RATIONALES FOR REGULATION

Despite these varying political/economic orientations, at least three forces provide governments with a rationale to regulate broadcast television: technological necessity, economic competition, and the social impact of television. Governments with

authoritarian, paternal, and permissive orientations must all address the technological needs of the medium, while paternal systems have special concerns about the
social impact of the medium, authoritarian systems emphasize political control, and
permissive systems promote active competition.

Broadcast technology requires careful management to reduce interference
among stations and to mandate the adoption of universal standards that promote
investment in television systems. To make efficient use of a limited number of frequencies, many television and radio stations must share the same channel (band of
frequencies). For example, television Channel 2 located between 54–60 megahertz
on the very high frequency (VHF) band is used simultaneously by fifty-eight television stations spread across the United States.[2] Some authority, in this case the FCC,
must limit the number and power of stations using each channel in order to prevent
interference. This interference can be co-channel, between two stations of the same
channel, or adjacent, between two stations on abutting channels. In addition, if efficient use is to be made of the spectrum space, all stations need to use the same
transmission standards so that one receiver can be used to receive all available
broadcast television signals. The establishment of standards for black-and-white
television by the FCC in 1941, and for color television in 1953, was essential to
insure a future for the infant medium. The refusal by the FCC to set similar standards
for AM-stereo radio in the 1980s has been widely cited as major reason for that
technology's failure.[3]

In addition to technological limits, the capitalist economic system favored in
the United States requires some management of the balance among competing interests in the television industry. Backed by antitrust legislation, the federal government, through the FCC, promotes competition by limiting the number of stations
that can be owned by one company, the number of stations in a specific television
market owned by one company, and the cross-ownership by broadcast stations of
other media (radio, newspapers, cable television). Government action can also promote or retard the development of competing television distribution systems such as
cable and direct satellite broadcast, influencing the level of competition. In addition,
policies of the FCC sometimes enhance access to the medium by advertisers by
promoting diversity in both national and local ownership, thereby increasing competition among media outlets for advertising dollars.

Finally, because of the perceived and real social impact of television (Chapter
9), governments attempt to influence programming through direct mandate or persuasion. In authoritarian systems, the direct mandate means total control of all programming. In permissive systems such as the United States, the government does
not mandate specific programs, but may encourage specific types of programs (e.g.,
educational shows for children) or fair treatment of individuals (e.g., equal treatment of political candidates during a election campaign). The government may also
appeal to a more general need for programming to serve the "public interest." The
government sees its demands for responsible programming as evidence that a station
is operating in the "public interest, convenience, or necessity." In turn, stations get

the right to use the electromagnetic spectrum to make consistent, and at times spectacular, profits.

The need for government management of the scarce radio frequencies used in broadcast television is rarely disputed, although particular decisions are often fiercely contested. However, the government's role in promoting competition and socially responsible broadcasting is subject to perpetual scrutiny and is always subject to change. Each government action aimed at increasing competition favors one group, such as cable television, at the expense of others, such as broadcasters. Commercial broadcasters usually fight any attempts to impose specific program requirements, such as educational children's programming. The first few decades of broadcast regulation were characterized by regular debate about the social responsibilities of broadcasters. However, with the deregulation movement initiated during the Carter administration and vigorously pushed during the Reagan and Bush administrations, the federal government has adopted the belief that competition serves the public interest best by producing the programming that the public finds most appealing. Consequently, it has focused its attention on reducing regulation, particularly regulations that it believes inhibit competition.

THE COMMUNICATIONS ACT OF 1934

The legal basis for the regulation of broadcast television was created during the "Golden Age" of radio and later applied to the video medium. Although often amended or supplemented by other legislation, the Communications Act of 1934 still provides the foundation for the regulation of broadcast television, radio, and telecommunications in the United States. Although much of the Act concerns telephone regulation, the sections affecting broadcasting were taken with minor changes from the *Radio Act of 1927,* which was the first legislation to deal specifically and comprehensively with broadcasting. The landmark *Telecommunications Act of 1996* brought significant change to broadcast, cable, and telephone regulation, but the cornerstone provisions of the Communications Act of 1934 remained intact. We will briefly examine six key provisions of the Act: public ownership of the airwaves, the appointment and make up of the Federal Communications Commission, the FCC's authority to issue licenses for broadcasting in the public interest, procedures for rule-making and appeal, the prohibition against prior censorship, and Section 315, which regulates the use of stations during an election campaign.

KEY PROVISIONS OF THE COMMUNICATIONS ACT OF 1934

The Communications Act of 1934 established public ownership of the airwaves (electromagnetic spectrum) and the federal government's authority to supervise spectrum use in the United States. The judicial basis for governmental control of broadcasting is the scarcity of spectrum space. More groups requested the right to use it than can be accommodated within the available space. The right to use the airwaves can have great commercial value. The spectrum space used by a VHF television station in the largest markets would have a market value of several hundred million dollars if it were sold.

The government's decisions on *spectrum allocation* help structure media industries. The allotment of spectrum space is the essential first step for any new nonwired medium. AM radio, FM radio, VHF television, UHF television, and satellite transmission of radio and television were possible only after spectrum was provided for the new medium. In commercial broadcasting, the amount of spectrum allotted limits the number of potential stations and, thus, the degree of competition both nationally and in a particular local market.

The major vehicle for this spectrum supervision is the Federal Communications Commission (FCC), an independent regulatory agency created to regulate broadcasting and interstate telecommunications. The FCC currently has five commissioners, including a chairman. To discourage domination either by Democrats or Republicans, no more than three members can come from any one political party. Commissioners are appointed by the president and confirmed by the U.S. Senate; presidential appointments are routinely confirmed. The Commissioners' five-year terms are staggered to encourage the yearly introduction of new members, although because of resignations the cycle of appointments is far from regular. Commissioners can be and often are reappointed. Commissioner James Quello, for instance, served from 1974 to 1997.[4] The FCC is given considerable authority over routine technical matters, such as station frequencies, power, and hours of operation. Most major policy changes, however, are subject to challenge by the industry in federal courts or by congress.

The FCC is granted the authority to issue renewable licenses for the operation of commercial and noncommercial radio and television stations. Television licenses are granted for eight years. Licenses can be revoked during this time period, but this has rarely happened. When it has, the chief reasons given for revoking the license were misrepresentation (lying) to the Commission and engineering problems.[5]

Using a phrase borrowed from public utilities and transportation regulation, the stations are required to operate in the *public interest, convenience, and necessity* if they wish to have their licenses renewed. The FCC is charged with the task of determining if a station has served the public interest during its last licensing period. Stations are required by the FCC to solicit public comment on the operation of their station and to provide reasonable public access to that commentary. Station licenses are routinely renewed; only stations guilty of repeated technical violations, falsification on their application for a license, or other illegal behavior are likely candidates for nonrenewal or suspension. Rarely have stations not been renewed because of programming decisions that, in the judgment of the FCC, do not serve the public interest.

In the Communications Act of 1934, Congress granted the FCC the authority to create the rules necessary to enforce the Act. The FCC is required to make public statement of proposed rules, by publication in the *Federal Register,* and to allow for comment by interested parties before the FCC. The interested parties are usually the regulated media (broadcasters, cable companies, and so forth), represented by the communication law firms they retain. However, ever since the 1966 WLBT case, which we will discuss later, the public, through public interest organizations, has been granted standing before the FCC and can participate in the debate over proposed rules.[6]

New FCC rules can and frequently are appealed in the federal courts. The first appeal for challenges to FCC rules is to the U.S. Court of Appeals in Washington, D.C. If the FCC decision is upheld by the court, a second appeal may be granted by the U.S. Supreme Court, although the Supreme Court accepts only a small percentage of the cases brought to it.

Although the FCC can consider programming in its license renewal decisions, it cannot censor broadcasts prior to their airing (Section 326). Such *prior censorship* is practiced voluntarily by networks through their broadcast standards and practices departments (network censors), but the FCC can act only after broadcasters have aired obscene or indecent material. Based on the *Miller v. California* 1973 Supreme Court decision, obscene material is defined by three criteria:

1. an average person, applying contemporary community standards, must find that the work, taken as a whole, appeals to prurient interests;
2. the work must describe, in a patently offensive way, sexual conduct as defined by applicable state law;
3. the work must lack serious literary, artistic, political, or scientific value.[7]

The broadcasting of such material is illegal and is denied protection under the First Amendment to the U.S. Constitution.

Obscenity is rarely an issue in broadcasting, but the FCC also has successfully defended rules against a class of offensive, but not obscene, material defined as indecent. The FCC's rules on *indecency* have been the subject of repeated challenge in federal court. The FCC, sometimes at the direction of congress, has attempted a variety of bans on indecent material or restrictions on the material during hours when children are most likely to be in the audience. The most recent "safe harbor hours" for indecent material are between 8 P.M. and 6 A.M.[8] Although indecency rules have typically been enforced against radio "shock" jocks, a Kansas City television station was fined $2,000 in 1988 for airing an unedited R-rated movie.[9]

Finally, the Communications Act of 1934 requires the FCC to regulate the use of the public's airwaves for partisan political discussion during an election. *Section 315* requires stations offering *free* time and all other forms of benefits and access to candidates for office during an election campaign to offer the same opportunities to all legally qualified candidates for the office. These must be people who have publicly announced their candidacy and have met all requirements to run for and hold an elected office. Equal opportunity means, for free time, an equal length of air time and placement at a similar time of day, to ensure similar potential audience size. For paid advertising, equal opportunity means the same advertising rates for all candidates and that candidates must be allowed to purchase the same amount of time, although not all candidates will want to purchase the same amount. Candidates must be granted equal opportunity, regardless of their chances of winning the election.

However, stations are not specifically obligated to give candidates free air time, and most do not. A 1959 amendment to the Act provides exemptions from the requirements of Section 315 for regularly scheduled news and public affairs programming, including newscasts, news interviews, documentaries, and special news events coverage. This exemption allows stations to cover the campaign as a news event with little concern about providing equal opportunity. The many presidential, gubernatorial, and senatorial debates are exempt from Section 315 because they are special news events. Indeed, analyses of the content of most presidential campaigns reveal an imbalance in the amount of coverage of Republican and Democratic candidates and almost no coverage of the minor party candidates.[10]

To assure equal opportunity for time given on a broadcast station or network, Section 312 of the Act, as interpreted by the FCC and federal courts, requires stations to provide *paid* access during an election campaign to candidates for federal offices (president, senate, house of representatives). Commercial stations cannot refuse to accept paid advertising from qualified federal candidates, and stations must provide similar rates and access for all such candidates. To prevent station/network profiteering (Section 315) when demand for advertising time increases during an election campaign, candidates or authorized campaign committees must be charged the lowest rate regularly offered by the station to other advertisers (lowest unit charge). This requirement applies to commercials aired during the forty-five days before a primary or the sixty days before a general election.

MODEL OF BROADCAST TELEVISION CONTROL

Although the Communications Act of 1934, as amended, places the FCC at the center of broadcast regulation, major FCC decisions affecting broadcast television are subject to control and influence from groups that are more powerful or more persistent. In Figure 4-1, we present a basic model of control and influence over broadcast television in the United States. The model has been streamlined to include only government, industry, and consumer groups with a major role in decision-making. Although each of these groups may influence particular decisions affecting broadcast television, there is frequent tension among the groups. Major decisions that are perceived to affect the industry status quo are subject to a dynamic interplay among these forces.

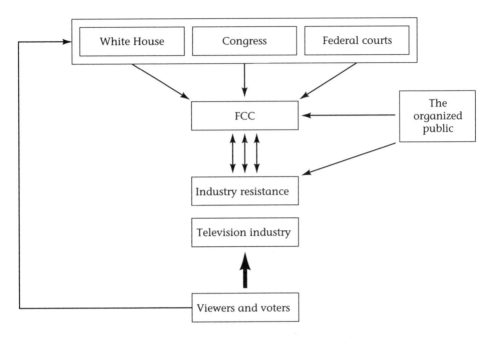

FIGURE 4-1   Model of Broadcast Television Control

The FCC

As an independent regulatory commission created by federal legislation (Communications Act of 1934), the FCC is subject to direct control through legislative action. It is one of many agencies, such as the Federal Aviation Commission and the Food and Drug Administration, that are given broad guidelines by congress and required to make specific policy. Independent regulatory agencies are an admission by the federal government that normal market forces in a capitalist economy generally promote their self-interests, and may not protect the interest of the general public. Issues of public health, safety, and use of public property, such as the airwaves, are particular areas of concern.

The FCC exercises control and influence over broadcasters in four ways. The most direct control is through the creation of rules and the imposition of penalties for violation of those rules. Most penalties start with written warnings, progress through increasingly severe fines, and end with the loss of license, the "death sentence" for any broadcast station. When the FCC refuses to renew a station's license during its eight-year license period, the reasons offered by the FCC for its action become a de facto rule for the industry. Thus, in 1966, when WLBT in Jackson, Mississippi lost its license for failing to serve its community's African American majority, the television industry was served notice that overt racism would have a price.[11] In addition to this overt control, the FCC produces position papers that state the current FCC position on issues of concern. These position papers are often seen as the first step in rule-making and may provoke strong reaction from the industry. Finally, the FCC can indirectly influence the television industry by promoting informal negotiations among conflicting parties. For example, in the mid-1970s, the FCC nurtured an agreement among the three major television networks to reserve the first hour of prime-time television for family-oriented programs.[12]

Congress

As its creator, the United States Congress has the clearest authority over the FCC. By amending the Communications Act of 1934, congress can change the makeup of the FCC, assign it new duties, and eliminate or curtail old ones. And congress does so with regularity. The Act has been amended many times in the six decades since its creation. Congress can also create entirely new legislation that places new responsibilities on the FCC. For example, the Cable Act of 1994 prescribed new duties for the FCC, including the regulation of the rates charged by local cable systems.

In addition, because congress has considerable influence over the FCC's budget, it can severely limit the FCC's capacity to investigate station conduct. In 1995, the Republican congress threatened to cut the FCC's budget by 20 percent. Limited resources mean limited regulation. Although appointed by the president, FCC commissioners must also be confirmed by the senate. Thus, congress has some control over the FCC's leadership.

By calling formal hearings, powerful congressional committees and subcommittees, such as the House and Senate Communications subcommittees, can focus industry and FCC attention on issues of concern, such as violence on television (see Chapter 9) or the quality and quantity of children's programming (see Chapter 5). Finally, the FCC officials receive regular pressure from congressional staff concerning complaints raised by stations and citizens in their home districts. Many stations have received improved service from the FCC after a phone call or visit to their representative's or senator's office.

The White House

The president and the executive branch of the federal government have influence over the FCC and the broadcast television industry by employing both coercion and persuasion. The president appoints the FCC commissioners, and this alone gives the president the greatest control of any individual. The president's appointment power is checked by the need for confirmation of these selections by the U.S. Senate and the requirement that no more than three of the five FCC commissioners can come from one party. Open FCC seats are usually thought of as Republican or Democratic seats. However, a nominee with the appropriate political philosophy can usually be found in either party. During any four-year term of office, a president can expect to make multiple appointments to the FCC. A two-term president usually will have an opportunity to appoint every commissioner.

The president also has considerable persuasive influence over the commission through direct consultation with the FCC chairman. Former motion picture actor, president of the Screen Actors Guild, and 40th President of the United States Ronald Reagan was particularly effective in supporting the competitive interests of the motion picture industry by urging the Commission to keep the Financial Interest and Syndication Rules. These rules limited competition faced by Hollywood studios in television program production and syndication. The president was successful despite the commitment of then FCC Chairman Mark Fowler, Reagan's own appointee, to eliminate regulations that reduce competition. In 1996, the Clinton administration brokered a deal with the networks to rate programs voluntarily for sex and violence.[13]

The executive branch of the federal government influences the television industry in ways beyond direct presidential influence. For instance, the Department of Justice enforces antitrust laws, the Federal Trade Commission regulates advertising, and the National Telecommunications and Information Administration (NTIA) develops telecommunications policy for the president. The Department of Justice's interpretation of antitrust laws, which promote competition by restricting monopolistic practices, sets the boundaries for mergers among media companies. Tight interpretation of these laws helped kill a takeover of ABC by International Telephone and Telegraph in 1967. Looser interpretation of antitrust laws has stoked the fires of merger mania in the mid-1980s and mid-1990s. Similarly, NTIA position papers written in the late 1980s have served as the guide for later Bush and Clinton administration policies that removed barriers to increased horizontal (ownership across different types of media) and vertical (ownership of both production and distribution units) integration in media industries.

The Federal Courts

As we noted earlier, the FCC's decisions are subject to appeal to the U.S. Court of Appeals and, when a second appeal is accepted, by the U.S. Supreme Court. Thus, the federal courts are the final authority for FCC decisions. In reviewing FCC decisions, federal courts cannot base their judgment on their interpretation of the wisdom or worth of the FCC's decision. Decisions can be overturned on three grounds: First, the decision was made without due process, which means that established policies of FCC conduct were not followed; second, the decision is not supported by the authority granted to the FCC by congress; third, the decision is in conflict with the U.S. Constitution and is unconstitutional. Because the development of specific policies is often delegated to the FCC by congress and is thus subject to interpretation, FCC decisions are often challenged on grounds of overstepped authority. Given the increasingly litigious nature of U.S. society, it is not surprising that most major FCC decisions are tested in the courts and full implementation of new policies is often delayed for years. Recent subjects of fierce litigation include the FCC's rules on indecent programming and the changes in the Financial Interest and Syndication rules.

The Broadcast Television Industry

The legislative, executive, and judicial branches of the federal government have the most direct control over the FCC, but the Commission is under constant scrutiny and pressure from the regulated industry. Networks, major group owners of stations, and industry trade associations (e.g., *National Association of Broadcasters,* Network Television Association, Association of Local Television Stations), as well as corporations and trade associations representing broadcast competitors (e.g., *National Cable Television Association*), all lobby the FCC for favorable treatment. High-profile and high-priced communications law firms are retained at substantial cost to represent the competing commercial interests. As indicated in Figure 4-1, members of the broadcast television industry offer a layer of resistance to any FCC action that they view as harmful. This resistance is so effective that, at least according to its critics, the primary activity of the FCC is no longer advancing the public interest, but deciding among the competing interests in the television industry (e.g., Hollywood producers versus broadcast networks). Millions are spent to influence the FCC and fight the court battles frequently pursued by the party that loses its FCC decision.

The Organized Public

Although certainly not as powerful or persistent as the regulated media, organized citizens' groups with legal representation do pressure the FCC on matters of public concern. Although the deregulatory approach of the last twenty years has made the FCC hesitant to add regulations to satisfy citizens groups, FCC actions on children's television in the mid-1970s were provoked and shaped by Action for Children's Television, originally a group of concerned Boston mothers.[14] The WLBT Case in 1966 established the right of citizens to petition the FCC to deny the renewal of a station's license, even if the group did not intend to operate the station. This decision touched off a brief frenzy of both actual and threatened license challenges by pressure groups in the 1970s. Gradually, the number of challenges diminished because of the FCC's tightening of petition to deny procedures and its granting of licenses for longer periods of time. In addition, major foundations reduced the funding for media reform that had supported some of the earlier challenges.[15]

Viewers and Voters

Virtually the entire U.S. population exerts some pressure on the television industry through its program choices. However, some members of this "unorganized" public are much more influential than others because of their value to advertisers. The regulated industry and increasingly the FCC have argued that the public and the public's interests are best represented by the collective decisions of television audiences, rather than by organized groups of citizens. Audiences do influence program decision-making by choosing among the available program options. Their choices are reflected in program ratings (audience size) and the demographic composition (gender, age, income groups) of the audience. On commercial stations, programs must draw the attention of an audience desired by advertisers. Although the target audience varies with the particular product or service sold, in general, consumers with more income are in greater demand. This market-driven approach to programming is the essence of the permissive approach to broadcast television in the United States. However, since only viewing, as measured by ratings services, is needed, this definition of serving the "public interest" is limited simply to watching television. It ignores any positive personal or social impact of the medium.

Most viewers vote with their remote controls, but many also vote each November. When viewers become voters, they also indirectly influence broadcast television. The election of a president and/or congress with a different economic philosophy can, in a relatively short time, change FCC policies, and these can change the industry. The 1980 election of Ronald Reagan, an economic conservative, set off a period of sustained deregulation by the FCC that continues today. The consequence has been an increase in the diversity of television channels (broadcast, cable, and satellite), but also a consolidation of ownership in the television industry. This consolidation includes mergers between Capital Cities/ABC and Disney, Westinghouse and CBS, and Time Warner and Turner Broadcasting.

LICENSING AND LICENSE RENEWAL

The FCC's power is most clearly evident in the licensing process. Stations must have FCC authorization to broadcast in the United States. The FCC manages broadcast uses of the electromagnetic spectrum, assigning portions of the spectrum for broadcast television. In the Sixth Report and Order issued in 1952, the FCC added channels 14–82 (later reduced to 14–69) in the UHF (Ultra High Frequency) part of the spectrum to the twelve VHF (Very High Frequency) channels it created in 1946. These channels contained over 2,000 allotments for the development of broadcast television stations across the country. At the time, only 108 of these allotments were active stations. The new allotment plan led to the building of nearly 500 new stations over the next decade.[16]

Although only about a quarter of the original allotments remain, new stations went on the air at a rate of about fifteen per year between 1991 and 1996.[17] The FCC requires that groups or corporations seeking a license must be financially sound and able to operate the station, and have no more than 25 percent of the corporation owned by non-U.S. citizens. In their applications, stations must outline their plans for providing programming that will serve the public interest, based on assessments of their local communities. Engineering reports must reflect little or no interference with existing television stations. If an application is successful, the FCC issues a construction permit, and when station construction is complete, it issues a license to broadcast. The license can be revoked if false information was given in the application. The FCC charges nominal fees to process license applications.

Once a license has been granted, stations must seek renewal of their license every eight years. During the eight-year period the station must keep files, available for public inspection, of public comment on its use of the broadcast license. During the months prior to submitting their license renewals, stations must solicit public comment about each station, through regularly scheduled announcements on the stations. The station must justify that its programming has served the public interest, convenience, and necessity. In general, license renewals are quite routine; broadcast stations rarely fail to be renewed.[18] However, the loss of a license is catastrophic. Stations give thoughtful attention to the renewal process and to the reasons offered by the FCC when any station has renewal difficulties.

PERSONAL ATTACKS AND POLITICAL EDITORIALS

Although the FCC as eliminated most of its earlier *Fairness Doctrine* that required stations to present reasonable opportunity to discuss conflicting views on issues of public importance, the Commission does require specific actions by stations when an individual is personally attacked or when it endorses or opposes a candidate for office.

Individuals or groups whose honesty, character, or integrity, or similar qualities are attacked by the station must be notified of the attack within one week, given a script, tape, or summary of the attack, and allowed reasonable opportunity to respond to the act, using the station's facilities. Attacks on foreign groups or public figures, or those made as part of newscasts, news interviews, and on-the-spot coverage of news events are exempt from this provision.

If the station endorses a candidate for office, it must notify all other legally qualified candidates for that office within twenty-four hours, provide a script or tape of the editorial to them, and offer reasonable opportunity for the candidates or their spokespersons to respond to the station. Candidates who are opposed by the station must be given the same opportunity to respond.

OWNERSHIP RESTRICTIONS

Throughout its history, the FCC has successfully argued that restrictions on ownership of broadcast stations serve the public interest, because these restrictions encourage greater ownership diversity and competition. Due to the greater scarcity of channels, the FCC has enforced greater restrictions for television than radio. However, during the era of deregulation, ownership restrictions have been loosened, allowing companies to own more stations. Again, the rationale for ownership restrictions is based on the desire to allow a greater variety of voices to use the spectrum, particularly at the local level. A diversity of ownership in a particular community should foster the competition among ideas that is crucial in a democracy. In addition, diverse ownership should promote competition among commercial broadcasters that might produce better or at least more attractive programming, and reduce the probability of advertising rate-fixing. We will review the restrictions governing ownership nationwide, and then examine the restrictions within local markets.

National Ownership Limits

As a result of changes included in the Telecommunications Act of 1996, no individual, company, or corporation can own television stations that reach more than 35 percent of the households in the United States. Ownership was previously restricted to 25 percent of U.S. households and a maximum of twelve stations.[19] Consequently, networks that buy enough stations can secure coverage of over one-third of the country, even without any additional affiliate station support. Because the largest group owners usually expand ownership to maximize the efficiency of their operations, the eased restrictions could well mean that a smaller number of larger companies will come to control the available television stations. A flurry of station sales followed the 1985 increase in station ownership limits from seven to twelve, continuing a trend toward increased consolidation of ownership.[20]

Other restrictions on national ownership have been eliminated by legislative or FCC action. The Telecommunications Act of 1996 eliminated long-standing restrictions on network ownership of cable television systems.[21] Earlier FCC rule changes, Congressional action, and the Telecommunications Act of 1996 removed restrictions that had prevented telephone companies from entering into competition with cable system operators.[22]

Local Ownership Limits

To avoid too much consolidation of owners, national ownership restrictions may be necessary, but, at the local level, restrictions are essential. Because most markets in the United States have five or fewer television stations, ownership of more than one television station in a market would greatly restrict competition. The *Duopoly Rule* restricts television station ownership to one station per market with a few exceptions. The Telecommunications Act of 1996, along with earlier FCC action, loosened restrictions on multiple radio station ownership, but the duopoly rule remains in effect for television.

Although duopoly is prohibited, stations can work together in the same market through *local marketing agreements* or *lease management agreements*. These are contracts between stations that allow one station to control the programming, operations, and advertising sales of another station.

In addition, the newspaper/broadcast cross-ownership rule restricts television station owners from purchasing newspapers in the same market. Because a local newspaper is usually the largest source of competition for the advertising dollar, this restriction is aimed more at reducing the probability of price-fixing than at increasing the diversity of opinion in the community. The newspaper/broadcast cross-ownership rule was not instituted until 1975, after newspapers in many markets had already launched television stations. Existing combinations of newspapers and broadcast media, such as WGN–TV and radio and the *Chicago Tribune,* were allowed to continue in markets with several competing sources of news. However, new newspaper/broadcast combinations generally have not been allowed. When Australian media baron, Rupert Murdoch, purchased five Metromedia television stations prior to launching the Fox Television Network, he was forced to sell either his station or his local newspaper in the two markets where he owned both. He opted to sell the *New York Post* and his Boston television station. However, Murdoch later received a waiver from the FCC and was able to reacquire the *Post* to prevent its closing. The FCC is increasingly willing to take such action when there is strong reason to believe a newspaper might shut down.

Finally, the Telecommunications Act of 1996 removed long-standing bans on new combinations of television and radio station ownership in the same market. The Act also allows a broadcast station owner to own a cable system, but not in the same market as the station.[23]

Consequences of Ownership Rule Changes

Changes in ownership rules have been prompted by changing perceptions regarding the degree of competition that exists in the television industry. In the first generation of television, the competition was restricted to three major networks, their affiliates, and a handful of independent (non-network) stations in major markets. Most ownership restrictions evolved during this period. As cable and independent broadcast television alternatives grew rapidly in the 1980s, the FCC concluded that increased competition had reduced the need for restriction.

In 1985, it increased the limit on station ownership from seven to twelve and this increase, combined with the loosening of antitrafficking rules, which prevented short-term ownership of stations, triggered a sharp increase in station sales. Within two years, all three major television networks had either new ownership (ABC, NBC) or new leadership (CBS), partially as a result of new ownership rules. In 1984, the year before the rule change, eighty-two stations were sold with a total value of $1.25 billion; the average figures for 1985 and 1986 were 114 stations sold with a total value of $3 billion.[24] The record prices of these network and station sales created extreme pressure to reduce costs and increase profits to pay back the large debt incurred. The results included substantial increases in advertising rates despite reductions in audience ratings, and severe reductions in personnel, especially in network news divisions.[25] The structural change touched off by the change in ownership rules shook the television industry.

The Telecommunications Act of 1996 may well have the same result. Anticipating passage of the Act, two major networks merged (ABC/Disney, CBS/Westinghouse). Media giant Time Warner, with substantial cable and broadcast holdings, merged with Turner Broadcasting System, the most successful developer of cable networks. Station sales have been brisk and prices are up sharply since the Act passed. In a corporate capitalist economy, the big, if given a chance, usually get bigger. The television industry is no exception.

CONTROLLING THE NETWORKS

As early as 1941, the FCC curbed the expanding power of broadcast networks by putting the ultimate control of programming in stations rather than networks. As part of the *Chain Broadcasting Rules,* the FCC forbade station/network affiliate contracts from forcing stations to carry any particular program. Stations must decide to clear (agree to accept) a network's program based on the merits of the program and not contractual obligation. Station *clearance* has become an unquestioned right in the television industry and an urgent need for networks. Although over 90 percent of network programs are cleared,[26] stations that fail to clear a program affect the program's potential audience, assuring lower national ratings. Thus, a network must first sell its affiliated stations on a program if it is to have a chance of succeeding.

The FCC further limited network power by enacting both the Prime Time Access Rule (PTAR) and the Network Financial and Syndication Rules (Fin–Syn). The 1971 Prime Time Access Rule limited network programming in prime time (7–11 P.M., EST) to three hours Monday through Saturday, creating one-half hour of *access time* formerly programmed by the networks. Network-owned or -affiliated stations in the fifty largest television markets were required to offer new programs, rather than network reruns (off-network syndication). Original programming featuring local talent was encouraged. PTAR was responsible for the rapid growth in new syndicated programming, some with local involvement *(PM Magazine).* However, most of the new access programs were nationally produced: familiar game shows *(Wheel of Fortune),* entertainment news *(Entertainment Tonight)* and reality shows *(A Current Affair).* Since PTAR restricted programming on network affiliates, it created opportunities for an increasing number of independent stations to offer popular network reruns in access time.

In July of 1995, the FCC reviewed PTAR and decided to eliminate it because it was no longer needed to promote program competition. The rule was set to expire in one year.[27] Although it failed to stimulate much local program production, the PTAR did help to increase the number of program producers and syndicators while aiding the growth of the independent television stations that became the bases of newer networks (Fox, UPN, The WB) in the last two decades. The half hour of access time it freed from networks has become so valuable that stations are unlikely to return it to their networks.

The Financial Interest and Syndication Rules (Fin–Syn rules) also have been phased out after more than twenty years. The rules had limited network ownership of its own programming and forbade networks from participating in program syndication in the United States. The rules were applied to ABC, CBS, and NBC, but the Fox Network, because it did not exceed fifteen hours of programming in prime time, was exempt. Indeed, Fox's competitive strategy was based on its exemption from these rules.

These rules promoted the development of new independent production companies (Carsey–Werner, Lorimar, Stephen J. Cannell, MTM) and secured the place of major Hollywood studios in the production of network programming. Because of the rules, the networks limited program production to news and sports and the occasional entertainment program. The rules stimulated the development of new syndication companies and turned existing syndicators into industry giants (King World Productions, Viacom). The Fin–Syn rules helped to create financially strong production companies and syndicators. This strength, coupled with the enlarged market for programming resulting from cable and independent television station expansion, convinced the FCC that competing interests no longer needed protection from the once all powerful networks. Accordingly, the last of the Fin–Syn restrictions were lifted in 1995.[28] The end of the PTAR and the Fin–Syn rules have led to a revival of vertical and horizontal integration in media industries, allowing a rapid increase in the complexity and power of the largest media corporations (Time Warner/Turner, Viacom/Paramount, Disney/ABC, Westinghouse/CBS).

CONCLUSION

Broadcast television in the United States operates under what has been termed a permissive approach to regulation. The dominant forces controlling programming are market forces. However, the federal government does exercise control over the use of the airwaves, which are considered public property. The rationale for regulation comes from the need to control interference among stations, the need for standardization in the technology used for broadcasting, and the desire to promote healthy competition among rival commercial interests.

Although the Telecommunications Act of 1996 instituted several significant changes, the most significant law governing broadcasting remains the Communications Act of 1934, as amended. The Act created the five-member Federal Communications Commission to regulate broadcasting and interstate telephone communications. It mandates public ownership of the airwaves, a stipulation that allows the federal government through the FCC to license individuals and groups to broadcast for an eight-year period in "the public interest, convenience, and necessity." The Act specifies how FCC commissioners are appointed and the length of their terms (five years). Prior censorship of broadcasts is prohibited. However, the FCC can fine stations for indecent programming and does consider programming, during the license renewal process, in deciding if the station has served the public interest. Section 315 of the Act requires broadcasters to provide equal opportunity for station use to all legally qualified candidates during an election campaign.

Because the FCC can make rules that affect broadcasters, it is the focal point of broadcast television regulation. However, the FCC's actions are strongly influenced by more powerful forces. The president appoints FCC commissioners, with senate confirmation, and has considerable persuasive power over the Commission. The congress can change FCC duties through legislative actions and controls the FCC's budget. Major FCC decisions are usually reviewed in the federal courts. Action by the U.S. Supreme Court is final. The competing segments of the television industry routinely confront the FCC on any significant policy, frequently appealing FCC decisions in the federal courts. Citizen groups have influenced FCC policy and station practices, but their influence has subsided during the past fifteen years. Through measurements of audience size and demographic composition made by ratings services, viewers directly influence program decisions by stations and networks. When viewers become voters, they can change the political environment through presidential and congressional elections, and, thus, the makeup and policies of the FCC. The FCC historically has been concerned about the diversity of broadcast station ownership. Rules have limited the number of stations that can be owned nationally and locally. Currently, no one can own stations serving more than 35 percent of the nation's homes, and locally ownership is limited to one station per market. The FCC has also, at various times, restricted the cross-ownership of newspapers and broadcast stations, and cable systems and television stations in the same market. Rules that previously restricted network programming in prime time, and network ownership and syndication of programming recently have been eliminated. However, FCC regulations still give stations control over their programming by reserving their right to refuse (not clear) any network program. The sometimes cooperative and sometimes competitive relationship between local station and networks will be discussed in the next chapter.

NOTES

[1]Sydney W. Head, Christopher H. Sterling, & Lemuel B. Schofield, *Broadcasting in America,* 7th ed., (Boston: Houghton Mifflin, 1994), pp. 542–543.

[2]*Broadcasting & Cable Yearbook 1996,* Vol. 1, (New Providence, NJ: R. R. Bowker), p. C–145.

[3]Bruce C. Klopfenstein and David Sedman, "Technical Standards and the Marketplace: The Case of AM Stereo," *Journal of Broadcasting & Electronic Media,* 1990, 34, pp. 171–194.

[4]"FCC Commissioner to Step Down," *Chicago Tribune,* January 1, 1997, sec. 3., p. 1.

[5]F. Leslie Smith, Milan Meeske, and John W. Wright, *Electronic Media and Government,* (White Plains, NY: Longman, 1995) p. 69.

[6]Christopher H. Sterling and John M. Kittross, *Stay Tuned: A Concise History of American Broadcating,* 2nd ed., (Belmont, CA: Wadsworth, 1990), pp. 424–425.

[7]Smith et al., op. cit., p. 358.

[8]Ibid., p. 364.

[9]Ibid., p. 366.

[10]M. R. Kerbel, *Edited For Television: CNN, ABC, and the 1992 Presidential Campaign,* (Boulder, CO: Westview, 1994).

[11]It should be noted that this action was forced on the FCC by court action. See Sterling and Kittross, op. cit.

[12]Sterling and Kittross, p. 434.

[13]Doug Halonen, "It's a Deal," *Electronic Media,* March 4, 1996, pp. 1 & 26.

[14]Sterling and Kittross, op. cit., p. 420.

[15]Joseph R. Dominick, Barry L. Sherman, & Gary A. Copeland, *Broadcasting/Cable and Beyond,* 3rd ed. (New York: McGraw-Hill, 1996), pp. 279–280.

[16]Sterling and Kittross, op. cit., pp. 632–633.

[17]*Broadcasting & Cable Yearbook 1996,* p. C–244.

[18]Smith et al., op. cit., p. 69.

[19]Fourteen stations were allowed with minority ownership of the additional two stations. Smith et al., op. cit., p. 174.

[20]Head et al., op. cit., p. 191.

[21]Doug Halonen, "Historic Rewrite Finally Passes," *Electronic Media,* February 5, 1996, p. 1 & 54.

[22]Ibid., p. 54.

[23]Ibid.

[24]*Broadcasting & Cable Yearbook 1996,* p. A–100.

[25]Ken Auletta, *Three Blind Mice: How the TV Networks Lost Their Way,* (New York: Random House, 1991), p. 477.

[26]Head et al., op. cit., p. 198.

[27]"Networks Freed from Prime-Time Rule," *Chicago Tribune,* July 29, 1995, Sec. 2, pp. 1 & 3.

[28]Doug Halonen, "FCC Votes to Kill Fin–Syn Rules Immediately," *Electronic Media,* September 11, 1995, p. 4.

5

The Local Television Station

BY *KEVIN SAUTER*
University of Saint Thomas

The local television station is the backbone of the national television system in the United States. Whether viewers receive the signal over-the-air, through a cable system, or via satellite, it is the local TV station that carries most of the shows that viewers want to watch. This chapter's examination of local stations will focus on the programming available and the forces that bring those programs into our homes. Although some of these topics are covered in other chapters of the book, the focus here is the local station's perspective. First, we examine the ownership of stations and the relationship between stations and networks. Second, we look at the organization and management of local stations. Next, we unravel the lines of program creation and distribution to see how the shows are brought from producers to viewers, and we also review the organizational and production components necessary for local stations to create their own programming. Finally, we review the role of advertisements and ratings, and their effect on the health and success of a local station.

In order to understand the way that programs are delivered through local stations, it is helpful to use an example of broadcast system organization and economics. One market that can serve as an example of all the various types of local stations and their programming is the fourteenth (of 211) largest TV market in the country, Minneapolis and St. Paul, Minnesota, known also as the Twin Cities. Of course, the stations in Minneapolis/St. Paul have their idiosyncrasies and are affected by local conditions, but this market demonstrates most of the elements found in local stations: ownership and affiliate relationships, programming and news operations, advertising and ratings, management and organization. There are eight local stations in the Twin Cities: a public station, affiliates of the big four networks (ABC, NBC,

CBS, and Fox), affiliates of the smaller networks (The WB and UPN) and an independent station. Most medium and large markets have these same local station forms, though a smaller market might have only a single station.

STATION OWNERSHIP AND AFFILIATE STATUS

By 1995, there were over 1,150 commercial TV stations in the United States, with slightly more on the UHF band of channels 14–69 (about 600) than in the VHF range of channels 2–13 (over 550).[1] There are also slightly more than 1,300 low-power TV stations, a special type of broadcaster whose station reach is limited to only a few miles' radius. Owners of the traditional UHF and VHF broadcast properties can be divided into several camps: O&Os, corporation or group ownership, and private, or "mom-and-pop" operators.

The stations that the networks actually own are called *O&Os (owned-and-operated)*. For example, in the Twin Cities, CBS purchased Channel 4 WCCO TV (as well as several other broadcast properties) in 1991 from a family trust for $195 million.[2] WCCO joins the CBS O&O stations in New York (WCBS), Los Angeles (KCBS), Chicago (WBBM), and other markets. As owners, the network can obviously make management decisions for all of its stations, move personnel and equipment among them, negotiate with unions, and apply leverage when purchasing syndicated programming. O&O stations can also use the network "stars" to promote local viewership, have direct access to video of local news events that might be of national interest, and control and shape the non-network *dayparts* of its stations. The profit from running local stations has been significant historically, but in these more competitive times, the "money tree" image of local stations has become more of a "money bush." The *profit margins* for O&Os can still reach an amazing 25 percent or more, which translates into yearly profits that can be in the tens of millions of dollars, a significant amount for networks struggling with decreasing viewership and increasing costs.

Corporate or *group ownership* is the most common form of television ownership, with nearly 90 percent of stations in the United States owned by some form of corporate group. In the Twin Cities, Channel 11 KARE, the NBC affiliate, is owned by Gannett, Inc., whose broadcast properties include nine TV stations located in Washington, D.C., Atlanta, Phoenix, and other markets, as well as the national daily newspaper, *USA Today*.[3] Like the networks, a corporate entity such as Gannett may manage its assets independently or as a group, sometimes swapping key people or providing similar on-air promotion packages for all its stations. In one unusual change, Gannett removed the call letters from its Minneapolis station (at the time WUSA), and gave them to its Washington affiliate, replacing the patriotic theme in Minneapolis with the community-friendly KARE. Other ownership groups may concentrate their properties in medium markets. For instance, Clear Channel Television owns a UHF station in Minneapolis, and seven other stations in medium-sized markets such as Mobile, Alabama; Jacksonville, Florida; and Wichita, Kansas.

Private ownership by individuals or families constitutes the third type of ownership in television, though the number of stations under the control of one person or family has dropped considerably as prices for stations have continued to rise. On rare occasions, wealthy individuals like Rupert Murdoch, Barry Diller, or Ted Turner come along to purchase a series of broadcast properties with financial support from others. Typically, groups of stations remain in the hands of large group owners.

Individual stations in major markets may cost hundreds of millions of dollars, and even a medium-sized market station can cost over $100 million. In the Twin Cities, Stanley S. Hubbard and his family have owned KSTP Channel 5, and several local radio outlets, since the early days of television (KSTP went on the air in April, 1948). The Hubbard family has broadened its base in the media industry by buying several other television properties (five are small stations in Minnesota), but also by developing corollary communications businesses, particularly in satellite systems that deliver programming directly to the viewer's home TV set. A second "family" operation exists in the Twin Cities on Channel 23, an independent station that had been through bankruptcy proceedings when purchased by the former general manager at another station in town, with her limited partners, for $3.5 million.[4] It is extremely difficult to maintain individual ownership in today's competitive and expensive market, with leveraged buyouts a constant threat to publicly held companies, but the "mom-and-pop" operations, like the Hubbard's and Channel 23, still exist and exert influence in several markets. However, most individual ownership is of *low-power television (LPTV)* stations.

In the era of corporate deregulation, broadcast properties have become just another trading commodity among corporate entities, a far cry from the stable TV world envisioned by the Communications Act of 1934 and long nurtured by the FCC. Critics see the shift of more television properties into fewer hands as eroding the bond between station and community, undermining localism. As new networks develop relationships with local stations, programming decisions become more centralized and the "look" of individual stations becomes less distinctive. Nevertheless, it is still the local station that delivers the programs to viewers' homes and, no matter who owns the station, the link between network and station is transparent to the audience. The next section examines the many intricate relationships between stations and networks that largely determine what appears on TV screens in homes across the country.

NETWORK AFFILIATES

The stations with which most of us are familiar are the affiliates of the national networks, ABC, CBS, NBC, and Fox. Of the 1,161 commercial stations in the United States, 833 are affiliates of one of these big four networks. In the most important aspect of the network–affiliate relationship, the local station agrees to run the programs supplied by the network during most portions of the day. Although the

FCC requires owners of local stations to be wholly responsible for what is broadcast over their assigned frequencies, in practice the affiliates have relatively little to say about what programming the network provides for them, and they generally run the programs they are given. Occasionally they may preempt a network schedule to insert a program of local interest, such as a locally-produced documentary, town meeting, or sports event, but the network still has considerable leverage to encourage the local stations to run its programs at the assigned time and day. For example, when an affiliate rejects a program (an act called *nonclearance*), the network frequently finds an independent station in that market to carry the program to compete head-to-head with the affiliate. As we note later in this chapter, such defiance by an affiliate can affect the amount of overall compensation paid by the network.

Networks provide stations with two rewards for clearing time for their national programs: *compensation* and advertising time. Network compensation ranges from several hundred to several thousands of dollars per hour in prime time, depending on the network, the popularity of the program, and the size of the potential audience. The yearly total of compensation funds rarely rises above 5 to 8 percent of total station income, but with over 200 affiliates, the total compensation outlay for a network can be over $100 million a year. The networks, as a budget-tightening measure, have periodically attempted to reduce compensation, hoping to offer successful programs with little or no money paid to the local station. The networks have argued that lost compensation dollars could be made up by the sale of the ninety seconds or so of advertising time that the local station is given in each program. Predictably, affiliates were not happy with any proposed decrease in compensation payments. With the upsurge in the popularity of Fox (and the always-present option for a station to switch its affiliation), the potential of newer networks (The WB and UPN), and the availability of syndicated programs as an alternative to network fare, networks in the late 1990s are under pressure to maintain happy and profitable relations with their affiliates. Thus, the continued use of network compensation is likely for the foreseeable future.

The second network revenue stream for the local affiliate comes in the form of advertising time in network programs that the local station sells on its own. The network will sell most of the network *spots* (also known as commercial positions or commercials) in a program to national advertisers, like Coke, Ford trucks, or Huggies diapers. But it also allows the local station to sell 90 to 120 seconds of advertising time, called *local avails,* in each network program. The local station can then sell its several commercial positions to businesses in the area, like car dealerships, restaurants, health clinics, or banks (local spots). The local station may also sell its local spots to a national advertiser who might want to target a specific market for a product or campaign (e.g., Toro snowblowers in the northern states).

Because of the large audience for prime-time shows, the money from the sale of these few slots can amount to a considerable income for the station. For example, during *Seinfeld,* the top-rated sitcom in the 1995 season, one thirty-second local spot cost about $12,000 in the Twin Cities, depending on the overall "deal" arranged with the buyer, and the strength of the ratings for *Seinfeld* in that quarter of the year. With the income generated through the sale of commercials in prime time, coupled with the network compensation revenue, the affiliate makes its money without encountering any direct costs for the program's production. Although the amount of advertising time given to the affiliate changes during the daypart and the program, and compensation varies by market and audience share, this arrangement is usually profitable for affiliates.[5] Thus, a good portion of an affiliate's programming day is given to passing on to the viewer the programs developed and paid for by the network.

Most people still watch network affiliates for many of their favorite programs, but this audience is being eroded by cable networks, satellite programming, and videotapes (see Chapter 2). Still, the networks' programs, offered through their local affiliates, generally attract a larger audience than those of any single competitor. For the 1996–97 television season, the highest rated program not originating from ABC, CBS or NBC was Fox's *The X-Files,* ranked number 35.[6] So even though there is a distinct decline in the network affiliates' audience share because of increased competition, the network programs are still the central component of the entertainment schedule.

If viewers watch programs in the early morning, such as *Good Morning America,* they are watching the network; soaps during the day, the evening national news, and prime-time shows are all offered by the networks. And finally at night, from *Late Night* to *The Tonight Show* to *Nightline,* the networks vie for audience attention. While the local stations are not completely passive in their delivery of network programming—most network affiliates produce local news programs, special interest, and sports programming—the bulk of their day is the same as every other affiliate's around the country. At 10:00 P.M. (EST) on Tuesday nights, for example, nearly every ABC affiliate in America will be running *NYPD Blue,* and nearly every NBC station will be showing *Dateline.* Though the stations are local, their programming is, by and large, a product of decision-makers in New York and Los Angeles. However, content sometimes determines acceptance of network programs. For instance, *NYPD Blue* is not shown by some ABC affiliates because of its adult material.

Fox Broadcasting Network offers a slightly different form of the network–affiliate relationship.[7] Like many in the early Fox network, Channel 29 was not a significant factor in the Twin Cities market, earning only a minuscule share of the audience on most nights and using its airtime for reruns of old network programs, movies, and cartoons. The addition of Fox programs provided the Channel 29 management with a fresh identity for the station and a new attraction to a group of viewers coveted by advertisers, the 18–49-year-olds. Anchored by the early success of such breakthrough programs as *Married with Children* and *The Simpsons,* Fox later added *Beverly Hills 90210* and *Melrose Place* to its youth-targeted lineup.

Fox is not a full-service network, however, offering programming only in prime time and leaving the rest of the day for its affiliates to schedule with shows of their own choosing. Channel 29 complements its Fox programming with a steady stream of reruns from the traditional networks, cartoons, movies, and other syndicated programs. The counterprogramming strategy that is employed by many Fox affiliates in their battle with the older networks runs throughout the day at Channel 29, with cartoons run as an alternative to the soaps, replays of the *Fresh Prince of Bel-Air* and *The Simpsons* opposite the early evening news block, and for viewers not interested in the local news following prime time, they offer yet another repeat of the original *Star Trek* series.

Fox's effect on its affiliates has been striking. In Minneapolis/St. Paul, the little UHF station on Channel 29 that only a few years ago could not be received clearly in many homes and that few people watched, has become home to a local passion, the Minnesota Vikings of the National Football League. Its nightly programming draws a significant audience and generates considerable revenue for its owners.

The example set by Fox has led to the development of two additional programming service networks in the Twin Cities and around the country. Warner Brothers Television (The WB) and the United Paramount Network (UPN) both launched as new networks in 1995 hoping to follow the success of Fox (see Chapter 6). While it is too early to tell whether these new networks will be as successful as Fox, the expansion of network programming into formerly independent stations further erodes the unique local qualities of local stations. By 1998, UPN and The WB plan to each offer four nights of programs per week. The new, smaller networks, then, provide some prime-time programming, but for the remainder of the broadcast week, day and night, their affiliates act as independents.

INDEPENDENTS

Stations without an affiliate agreement with a network are considered *independents* and must program their day according to what they feel is needed in the local market. While affiliates of the big three networks may only program a few hours in the early morning, perhaps a couple of hours just before the early news, and, of course, the all-important local news programs, the independent station must decide for itself what to put on the air twenty-four hours a day. The station generates its revenue by selling the advertisements in the programs to local businesses or directly to national advertisers. This contrasts with the network affiliates, which have only a few advertising slots to sell in any network program. On the other hand, the advertising revenue must be used to pay for the programs themselves, a burden not carried by those stations affiliated with a network. The ratings of most independent stations are generally lower than network affiliates, and advertising rates reflect that smaller audience. As discussed in Chapter 3, the key for the independent is to balance the costs for the programming with the potential for revenue generated by the advertising.

A station's ownership and its affiliate status are the prime determinants of the type and variety of programs it broadcasts. To the viewer, the ownership of the station is obscured, but the affiliate status is heralded at almost every break in promotional spots and through much of the programming by the ubiquitous, transparent network logo in the lower right-hand corner of the screen. In spite of this attempt to develop network loyalty in viewers, it is still the programs themselves that pull people to the channel, and it is to that programming that we now turn our attention.

SOURCES OF PROGRAMMING

Most of what comes to us via local stations are programs developed for the network and distributed through their affiliates. The big three networks supply an almost seamless flow of programs from the early morning news shows through the afternoon soaps to the national news. All of the networks provide shows in prime time, and some offer their affiliates late-night programming as well. But in the holes of the day where the networks are not giving them programs, the affiliates must determine for themselves what they will put on the air. They have two options: They may purchase programs through syndication or develop their own programs through local production.

SYNDICATED PROGRAMMING

We will examine the nationwide syndication industry in some detail in Chapter 6. In this chapter, we will look at how syndication helps local stations round out their program schedules. Most of the broadcast day for independents and some of the day for network affiliates is made up of *syndicated* programs. These are shows that are sold to individual stations for airing on that station alone, rather than the network arrangement in which all affiliates will show the same program at the same time throughout the country. A syndication company will attempt to sell in each of the 211 markets in the country, seeking to land the strongest affiliate but willing to settle for the smallest station if necessary. So as programs run in different markets, on different types of stations, they are placed in the schedule by the local programmer in response to the needs, and advertising dollars, of the community.

Off-Net Syndication

The most common type of syndication is off-net syndication, or the selling of network reruns to individual stations. When a popular program on the network schedule runs long enough to have a solid base of episodes, the producers of the program will attempt to sell the reruns to stations in individual markets. During the initial run of the program the producers receive a fee from the network, sometimes, but not always, making a profit. The big money in TV, however, is potentially in syndication. For example, *The Cosby Show* is estimated to have generated almost $5 million per episode when it went into syndication, with *Cheers* and *Family Ties* in the $1.5 to $2 million range per episode. A program that has staying power may run in syndication for years, continuing to generate revenue for program producers, and usually for the stars, with no additional money expended.

The local station must also be able to make a profit on its syndication buys for the system to operate effectively. For example, the hypothetical *College Follies* program may cost a station $1,000 per showing for 396 shows (in industry jargon, 66 episodes for six runs equals 396 *plays*). If scheduled five nights a week at the same time, a practice known as *stripping,* the buy will run for about a year and a half. The station uses two of the eight minutes available in the program for promotions and station IDs, leaving six minutes, or twelve advertising slots, for sale. At a cost of $150 per ad, the program generates $1,800 a day, or $800 profit.[8] Over the run of the show the station can expect to make over $300,000 profit from this property. These numbers indicate how syndication operates for the seller and the buyer of a program. Certainly there is a lot of guesswork in syndication, with considerable financial risk for the seller and the buyer, but when it works, the off-net syndicated property can generate profits for everyone.

First-Run Syndication

One alternative programming source that is particularly valuable for independents competing with network programs and for all stations during other time periods are programs created expressly for the syndication market, known as *first-run syndication.*

First-run programs are created by producers for the express purpose of selling them directly to stations in local markets, thus bypassing the networks altogether. The advantage to the station is that they now have new programs not seen elsewhere to combat the repetition of off-net shows. Most of the successful first-run programs are talk and game shows, like *Jenny Jones* and *Jeopardy!* Reality shows, though, like *Rescue 911* and *Real Stories of the Highway Patrol,* and tabloid programs, like *Hard Copy* and *A Current Affair,* are also successful first-run offerings. One change in the 1990s was the development of successful hour-long dramas in first-run, led by a show very popular around the world, *Baywatch,* and followed by such unusual, but successful, programs as *Hercules, the Legendary Journeys* and *Xena: Warrior Princess.*

Local stations purchase first-run programs as a way to combat network fare or to fill a spot against other syndicated properties. Because the job of the independent station is to counterprogram the networks and build a niche audience it can sell to advertisers, first-run programs that appeal to more narrow constituencies can often run against established network or off-net offerings and bring to the station a smaller audience share but sufficient revenue to cover the costs of the program and still generate a profit. The audience for *Coach* will probably be similar to the group that watched it the first time through its network run, and it will most likely gain solid ratings. However, first-run shows that are more unusual and less costly may bring a more narrow, but loyal, viewership.

Regulations Affecting Syndication

With the recent demise of the prime-time access, and financial interest and syndication rules (see Chapter 2), *syndication exclusivity (syndex)* remains the last major regulation affecting syndication. When a property is sold to a station in a local market, there is an assumption that it will be shown only on that station in the community. With the advent of cable, the importing of distant stations (called *superstations*), and the proliferation of basic cable networks, it became possible for a single syndicated property to be seen several times a day on different stations in the same market, thus reducing the value of the program to the holders of its rights. The reinstatement of syndication exclusivity in 1990 closed this loophole, with the FCC ruling that a cable system is responsible for monitoring the showing of syndicated shows whose rights are held in a community and blacking out that material. In response to this order, superstations and basic cable networks have become exclusive outlets for some syndicated properties to eliminate potential conflict.[9] *Thirtysomething,* a popular hour-long drama of the late 1980s, was sold directly to the Lifetime Network and is available only through that distribution channel. No sales were made to local markets. Clearly, a range of influences affects what appears on the TV screen, where it appears, and when. The viewer may not see the impact of the government's influence, but to the local station, regulatory limits are part of the ebb and flow of programming decisions.

Children's Programming

With the passage of the Children's Television Act in 1990, stations in the United States are obliged to offer programs that address the educational and informational needs of children ages sixteen and younger. Congress also set limits on the number of commercials per hour: twelve minutes on weekdays and ten and one-half minutes on weekends.

In 1996, the government set the standard for the minimum number of hours per week that a television station schedule "educational and informational" programming for children sixteen and younger: three hours each week between 7 A.M. and 10 P.M. The requirement went into effect with the Fall 1997 season.

The actual impact of these government rules is not great because most stations had already followed informal guidelines on the number of shows and commercials. But the codifying of practice made local programmers aware of their responsibility to special audiences, such as children.

LOCALLY PRODUCED PROGRAMMING

Localism would dictate that programs be produced with the interests and needs of the community as the principle that guides the creation of what we see on the screen. As discussed above, however, many other factors account for the programs that actually end up reaching the home television set. Whether it is the dictates of the FCC regulations that affect program purchases, or the economics of the marketplace that determine the value of syndicated shows, what is watched is often not a function of what the audience wants to see on television, but rather what programming is available and affordable to the stations. Nevertheless, local stations produce several types of programs that are designed to meet the needs of the local audience and, of course, to make money.

The most prominent of these local productions are the various newscasts at most of the network affiliates and at some of the larger independents. In addition to news, some local stations produce children's programs, talk shows, religious newscasts, and sports broadcasts of local teams. The news, though, is by far the most important, costly, and often lucrative component of local productions.

THE LOCAL NEWS

There are four slots in the programming day where locally produced news is a mainstay in most *major markets:* the early morning, mid-day, early evening, and late night. While some stations will produce many hours of news (KCNC in Denver schedules seven hours of locally-produced news a day), other stations may opt for only two newscasts, one between 5 P.M. and 6:30 P.M. and the other immediately following prime time.

The news at the local level developed partly in response to the dictum of the Communications Act of 1934 to operate in the "public interest, convenience, and necessity." As a way to demonstrate their responsiveness to the local community, and as a way to ensure their license renewal, local stations created the half-hour news program to keep viewers abreast of events in their neighborhoods as well as to provide glimpses of national and regional news. In the 1970s, however, the perception of the news department as a public service changed as news began to be seen, not as a drag on the economic bottom line, but rather as a profit center. The news program, when controlled effectively, can generate significant direct revenue through sales of advertising time, and can act as *lead-in* for access and prime-time network programming, thus pushing up advertising rates throughout the evening (unless the newscast ranks third or fourth in the market). Also, as in *nonbarter syndicated* programming, the local station can sell *all* of the advertising time in the newscasts rather than the minute or two they receive during network programs.

But the cost of news production is also high, with personnel and equipment in the news department demanding an extensive budget. During the heyday of local station profits in the seventies and eighties, the news was a great contributor to a station's overall financial health, often producing a third of all revenue. As the nineties economic realities became apparent, and as audiences found alternatives to local television, news became less resistant to layoffs and decreases in budget. Still, at most affiliate stations in the country, the value of the local news is seen in its financial performance, its perceived contribution to the community (both positive and negative), and the simple historical standard of the local station providing its viewers with news. To better understand the dynamics of the news program, it is helpful to examine its component parts: people, equipment, and influence.

Producing Local News

The news division can often be the single largest entity at a local station, with an estimated 28,000 people staffing newsrooms nationally in 1996.[10] Among these staffers are the highly visible anchors and reporters, the unknown *videographers* and editors, and the technical support crew for the show. Also helping to guide the production process are producers of the news, news directors, vice-presidents of news, and independent consultants. If sales representatives who market the news program to the local business community are counted, the people associated with the news can constitute well over half the staff of any local station. At WCCO TV in Minneapolis/St. Paul, 90 people out of a total station workforce of 190 work directly in the newsroom with another 60 or so intimately involved with the news operation. In medium- and small-market stations the average newsroom employs 36 people.[11]

In the case of on-air talent, salaries can reach into the hundreds of thousands of dollars a year. Crew members and support staff make more moderate salaries, and eager young members of the news team, especially in small and medium markets, may be barely making more than minimum wage. But the total costs incurred for the people needed to run a news operation can be enormous and place pressure on the entire station to support the hour or so of news generated each day. Nevertheless, news operations make money for their stations. A study of the economics of local stations concludes that "about 83% make money, 4% losing and 13% coming out even. . . . Newsrooms have truly become profit centers."[12] In addition, the news division is the component of the local station with which the local community is most familiar and often acts as the public persona of the station itself. In many ways, local TV news is the most visible element of the local station in U.S. broadcasting.

The hierarchy of the news department is led by the station manager or an executive in charge of the news. This person usually is responsible for the administration of the department and has influence on the staffing and "look" of the newscast. Independent consultants are hired by top management to review the on-air product and may recommend changes as significant as a reconsideration of news judgment and perspective or as apparently trivial as the dress code or hairstyles of the reporters and anchors.

It is the news director, though, who has the hands-on job of creating the daily newscasts. From the early morning "news huddle," where potential items for the news are discussed, to forging initiatives in the overall handling of the news, the news director has a busy day. It was probably a news director, for example, perhaps with advice from consultants, who began to place additional emphasis on "live shots" for the newscasts, giving the station a slightly different look and rhythm compared to the competition. But good ideas travel fast in television news, and a quick survey of local newscasts will frequently find many reporters standing in front of unlit buildings or burned-out houses in the middle of the night to report "live" from the scene of something that happened earlier in the day.

News directors are frequently innovative in overall approach to the news. Occasionally, a unique brand image results from stylistic changes in a newscast. For example, John Culliton, as a news director at WCCO in Minneapolis (and later the general manager at KCBS in Los Angeles), received national attention for declaring the 5:00 P.M. news program a "family-friendly" program where news video is monitored for its possible negative impact on children in the audience.

While the news director makes these larger decisions, each individual newscast may also be guided by a *producer.* The producer works with the news director to select the events that will be covered in that newscast, assigns reporter and crew to cover an event, and makes the call on sudden newsworthy events that may require the high-tech equipment of the newsrooms: the satellite uplink truck, a helicopter, or microwave relay van. The producer may also write the copy for the newscast read on-air by the anchors, though the "intros" and "outs" for pretaped segments may only be a line or two for each story.

Reporters are the legs of a newsroom, sent out to gather the information and create the stories that make up much of the newscast. Stories are generated for the evening news in much the same manner that they originate in print journalism. The usual *beats* that are covered in the news include: the courts, the police and fire stations, and the state legislature or city council. Feature stories may come from organizational press releases, phone calls from the public, or the enterprising hustle of a videographer or reporter.

Once the stories are determined for an individual newscast, the assigned reporters and videographers will set out to gather the news. Some limited events, like a car crash or snowstorm, may require only a videographer to be sent to the scene for an hour or so, while an analytic or investigative story may require a reporter and field producer, and could take several days or even weeks to complete. At some stations in small and medium markets, a "one-man band" approach has been adopted, in which a single person (usually the reporter) will gather the pertinent information, shoot the video, and ask the questions while taping interviews.

After the news crew, large or small, returns to the station, the length of the piece must be determined, the accompanying copy must be prepared, and the videotape edited. Finally, it goes on the air. The amount of time devoted to news during the program, called the *news hole,* may be anywhere from twelve to eighteen minutes, with the remainder of the newscast allotted to weather, sports, chatter among the "news team" and, of course, advertisements.

The actual airing of the news requires yet another set of people to run the cameras, monitor audio, and be sure the *graphics* are ready on time and in order. The person responsible for the pace and flow of the newscast is the director, a different job than the news director discussed earlier. The director decides which camera will be "live" at any given time, when the videotaped segments will be rolled in, and when the show will go to commercial.

The anchors are, of course, the most visible component of the live news program and, because of their notoriety, they are usually the most generously compensated of the personnel in the newsroom, sometimes commanding salaries that are higher than the general manager or the head of sales. The anchors are the ones with whom we identify a newscast, and the search to find personalities who strike a chord with viewers can be the key to a local station's success.[13] In the top twenty-five markets, the median salary for anchors is $233,000 a year, seven to eight times the median salary of $31,000 for those in the bottom sixty markets. Local news is a business in which a considerable salary can be earned, but the job slots are few and the odds are long of reaching lucrative financial heights.

News Technology

The technical side of the local news has propelled this format forward as surely as audience demand. In the 1960s, cameras in the studio were large and unwieldy, limited field reporting was shot on 16-millimeter film stock, and lighting was intense and hot. In the 1990s studio cameras sometimes operate without studio crew through robotics,[14] all field visuals are captured on lightweight and increasingly smaller video cameras (put directly onto computer disks in some markets, bypassing tape altogether), and the studio is a comfortable environment where sets are often created as much with electronic gadgetry as they are with wood and paint. In every station where production is done, there are three types of necessary equipment: capturing equipment, processing equipment, and transmission equipment.

The ability to capture visual and aural images is at the heart of all production, a vital first step in the production process. The switch from film to video cameras for field production came to the networks in 1965 and trickled down to the affiliates over the following ten years. Cameras in the 1990s are generally of the *camcorder* variety with the ability to capture the image and store it (usually on tape) in one unit all weighing in at less than fourteen pounds.[15] Cameras are usually mounted on tripods for steady shooting, interviews are videotaped and then edited into new sequences, tape is shot in as efficient a manner as possible, and lighting is used for basic illumination rather than for artistic effect. Expensive studio cameras are also used to capture the live portion of newscasts, which are then sent to the control room to be blended with the prerecorded segments from the field.

In the processing phase of news production, field footage captured on tape must be edited into the news reports, or packages, that viewers see as the final product. In the age of computers, many stations are moving to a system in which all of the material is digitized into a computer and then manipulated with the familiar point-and-click methods from word processing *(nonlinear editing)*. The final processing step is to put all of the disparate elements together into a newscast. The most crucial piece of gadgetry necessary to pull together the individual images is called the *switcher,* a piece of routing equipment that selects the input called for by the director, whether live shots, video, or remote feeds, and puts it on the air.

The third and final phase of the local news is sending the images to our homes. Once the newscast is shot, it is immediately processed through the central system at the station for monitoring everything that goes on the air *(master control)* and then transmitted over the electromagnetic spectrum to the antennas on top of homes and either microwaved to, or received by, local cable systems. In a few markets, the signals of the local TV stations are beamed up to satellites where they can be picked up by distant cable systems and given regional or national coverage.

Local Competition

Because the local news is one of the very few programs on TV that originate in the community, it is a regular viewing habit for almost half of the population in the major markets. The news is often a source of significant revenue for the station, and the success of the local newscast in securing viewers can add to the *flowthrough* of audience share into programs that follow, thus increasing revenue for the entire evening. The local news performs an agenda-setting function in the community (see Chapter 9), telling the audience what and who is important, as well as helping viewers monitor their world by telling them what the weather might be like tomorrow and who won the game that night.[16] TV news can also be a galvanizing component for the community, providing everyone with a similar view of the world and community, giving viewers common experiences to share with others and a perspective, though subtle, on how to interpret the events and forces that swirl around them.[17] Having the top newscast in the market enables a station to charge higher prices for the commercials inserted into the program, but it also gives the station influence and "bragging rights" about its stature in the community. The struggle to be number one can be vicious and intense.[18]

To win top station status, a newscast must court viewers. Using attractive anchors, employing a *happy news* approach to their on-screen presence and adding soft-news endings to the newscast have been staples of past news wars,[19] but such simple changes as a faster pace, different set, and brighter graphics might also lead to increased viewership. More ominous to traditionalists in journalism, however, is a change in the type of news selected for broadcast. In Boston, for example, WHDH Channel 7 developed what some called a *tabloid news* approach, patterned after fellow Sunbeam Corporation station WSVN in Miami and featuring a rapid-fire pace to news stories and a decided emphasis on violence and the unusual. While still third in the ratings, Channel 7's news clearly has energized the Boston market.[20] A less dramatic approach to increasing audiences is to do on-air and print media promotions for a newscast, calling it "Action News" or "News 4 You." But in the end, it is the number and type of people watching a newscast—the ratings—that ultimately determine what kind of news is found on local television.

OTHER LOCAL PRODUCTIONS

A look at the TV schedule will reveal very few programs that are locally produced beyond the newscasts. Logic would dictate that with the technical expertise to create programming, with the equipment to produce it, and with the possibility of generating revenue through advertising sales, local programs would be an attractive alternative to network or syndicated shows. The reality, however, is that television is expensive to produce, requires extraordinary effort on the part of the station personnel, and may not be able to compete successfully for audience attention against syndicated properties. Nevertheless, several types of programs are locally produced, though they represent a very minor portion of the programming schedule.

Perhaps the most common form of local production other than news is the talk and entertainment program. These shows are usually shot in a studio with a minimal set, feature talent and crew often shared with the news department, and their stock-in-trade is the interview. Whether the focus of discussion is events in the community, a cooking segment, or a celebrity on tour, the format dictates a lot of "talking heads" and limited action.

Another locally produced talk show is the public affairs program, in which the content of the program is serious discussion of the political issue *du jour.* Much like the nationally syndicated *Washington Week in Review,* these programs are often roundtable discussions of politics and economics on both a local and national scale.

The magazine-style program is another form of local production that can still be found in some markets, though it is an endangered species. *Chronicle* on WCVB in Boston, a nightly half hour, has the highest profile of these shows, though it is still second in its access time slot behind *Jeopardy!* In Philadelphia, *The Bulletin* began as an hour-long afternoon magazine, was shortened to a half-hour lead-in to *60 Minutes* and finally was canceled in 1996.[21] Much like network versions, locally produced magazine programs are often a mixture of features, interviews and investigative stories about the local area. Occasionally, consortium efforts are used to provide a more regional and even national flavor to the programs, by exchanging stories with other stations around the country via satellite. Ironically, as equipment is developed that makes these programs even easier to produce, their popularity and availability on local stations is in decline. However, as syndicated programming becomes increasingly expensive to purchase and advertising time dips because of barter syndication deals, perhaps locally produced news and information programs will make a comeback.

One form of local programming that is growing in major markets is the Sunday-night sports talk show. Stations run a half hour or more of highlights, analysis, and player interviews after the late news on Sundays. In markets with professional or college sports teams the show might be hosted by a coach or popular player with the local sports announcer given a strong on-air presence. These shows have a ready and stable agenda, entail relatively low direct costs, and can garner a fairly large share of the audience. Because the audience is *skewed,* heavily male 18–49, the demographics are attractive to certain advertisers, making this style of program a successful moneymaker for the station.

A larger and more difficult sports production is the broadcast of local teams' games. In the sports-crazed 1980s and 1990s, most professional sports are produced by network or regional companies, but the occasional contract is offered to the local stations for coverage. The Minnesota Twins baseball team has a contract with a local station to produce all of the telecasts of their games, though they occasionally broadcast some of the games on other channels in the Twin Cities to accommodate the needs and contractual demands of the networks, advertisers, teams, leagues, and the public. All professional football teams are under contract with the NFL for broadcasts of the regular season, but preseason games are open for bidding among local stations.

Once a contract is agreed on, the local station must make arrangements for the on-air talent, the production facilities, the staff and crew for the telecast, and sell advertising time to local and national advertisers. College sports teams might have similar arrangements with the local stations. Even high schools find their way onto the local airwaves. In many states the high school football, basketball, or hockey tournaments might take one or several days of the local station's schedule, draw considerable audiences, and provide many hours of advertising time for sale. Local sponsorship is high for these events, and profits are reasonable, in spite of significant costs to rent on-location production equipment and hire freelance personnel to supplement full-time staff.

A few other forms of local production can be found among the network reruns, movies, and game shows that dominate local television. In order to meet the FCC demands to operate in the public interest, some larger stations generate an occasional hour-long documentary or will dovetail with a network offering by producing a "town meeting." Some stations will produce or assist in the production of a religious program to be aired on Sunday mornings when network offerings are few. Another locally produced form, the children's show, is undergoing a resurgence through the development of *Kids' Clubs,* during which an on-air host introduces cartoons and offers special events or merchandise for the club's members at reduced cost. Finally, the "novelty" local show is represented by *Hawaii Stars,* a karaoke-based program that aired on KHON in Honolulu and won a 19 rating and 38 share. If the ratings continue, look for a similar version on local stations everywhere.[22]

ADVERTISING AND THE LOCAL STATION

Though the casual viewer probably is not aware of the difference, several general types of advertising can be found on local television. As mentioned earlier in this chapter, network spots are those commercials that are sold directly by the network, embedded into their programs, and shown to all parts of the country simultaneously through their local affiliates. Whether the commercials are for products available in stores, like Nike shoes or Miller Lite beer, or whether they are promoting the store itself, like McDonalds or JC Penney's, the advertiser must have the need and financial resources to take advantage of the tremendous reach of a network program.

A second type of ad, the national spot, is similar to the network commercial, though it is distributed through the local station rather than via one of the networks. A national advertiser might want to focus its efforts in a particular market rather than, or in addition to, buying the expensive network spots, so it will purchase advertising time on local TV stations. The commercials are often the same ones we will see in network programs, are noticeable for their high production values and feature the products and services with which we are probably already familiar. Their place in the broadcast is unrestricted. They might be placed in the minute or two of local advertising time made available in a network program, they could be shown during the evening newscast, or inserted into syndicated programming. No matter where they appear, the revenue from the sale of this time goes directly to the local station.

The third type of advertisement on local stations is the local spot, a commercial created for a company in the community and shown mostly during the programs purchased or produced by the station. Television time is expensive, and most of the advertising done on local stations is for restaurants, banks, car dealerships, and other large, prosperous businesses that need exposure and name recognition. The spots can be produced by an advertising agency or might be developed and produced cooperatively by the local merchant and station account executive. In many smaller markets, videographers for the news might use part of their time to shoot and edit commercials for a business that buys time on their station.

Infomercials

A hybrid form of advertising and program has developed in the last decade, the program-length advertisement, or the *infomercial*. Infomercials are enjoying a growing popularity at many local affiliates and independents. The practice of making long-form commercials began in earnest in 1984, after the FCC relaxed its regulations on commercial time in any given hour. Since then, the same listing has appeared in many TV guides for the early morning and the late-night shifts: *Paid Program*. The industry has developed into a billion-dollar-a-year business with some of that cash flowing into the local stations, supplying them with an additional revenue stream and a new form of programming.[23] What may have started as a cheap device to sell perfume and exercise equipment has rapidly caught the attention of Fortune 500 companies, with infomercials in the late 1990s on the air for Lexus, Nissan, Fidelity Investments, Upjohn, Apple Computers, and Microsoft.

LOCAL RATINGS

The final element in the health of a local station is the tally of people watching a program at any given time: the ratings (see Chapter 7 for more a more detailed treatment of audience measurement). The programming we have discussed is determined, in large part, by how many and what type of people will watch it, and the audience size and composition then serves as the basis for setting the rates charged to advertisers.

Ratings are most often associated with network shows, with the audience size for particular programs often published in the daily newspaper so even viewers can see what they, as a group, are watching. At the local level, however, advertising rates must be established by determining the size of the audience for the program in that market. Four times a year the most prominent of the ratings businesses, the Nielsen Media Research company, conducts a *sweep* of the local TV markets in the country to measure audience size and composition for all of the programs carried by local stations. The networks endeavor to support their affiliates during sweeps by scheduling special programs, and by running lurid or investigative news segments, big-budget movies, and new episodes of hit shows. Local newscasts deliver their most important stories, often in several parts, promote their locally produced programs, and develop station ties to community events. The size of the audience counted during sweeps then sets the advertising levels for the following three months until the next sweeps period.

Rating points, the percentage of all potential viewers watching a particular program, are important because the size of the audience will help determine the advertising rates for the newscast. On the other hand, *share,* the percentage of people with their sets on who are watching the newscast, provides the competitive information of how the station stacks up against the other newscasts in town. The sales and public relations people at the station will "spin" the numbers that estimate ratings and share to make them more attractive to advertisers and to gain an edge over the competition. In the Twin Cities, for example, a commercial on one local newscast with a slightly larger, but older, audience runs about $1,500 for a thirty-second spot. In contrast, on a competing station with a lower overall number of viewers, advertisers are willing to pay up to $2,500 per spot to reach the younger audience comprised of more men than women.[24] The ratings game in local television begins with numbers provided by the Nielsen company, but in the true tradition of salesmanship and persuasion, a rating is just the starting point for negotiations about how much a spot will cost.

STATION ORGANIZATION

The essential function of a commercial television station is to produce a profit for its owners, and so it needs to be managed in an effective, efficient manner. All local station management must oversee four primary divisions: administration, sales, programming, and engineering. Subsumed under these umbrella divisions are the positions that account for most of the non-news jobs in the television industry. In addition to the divisions in general, two of these positions, *traffic* and promotion, are also of particular interest here.

Administration

At the top of the management hierarchy at TV stations is the general manager. The GM is responsible for the overall performance of the station, represents the station to the community, the network, and the owners, and oversees the administration of the station: developing and administering the budget, hiring station personnel and outside consultants, beginning initiatives in programming and sales, directing the news division, and so on. The overriding concern for the general manager, however, is to ensure that the station is a profitable, well-run business and an asset for the owners and the community.

Sales Department

A handful of vice presidents assist the general manager by managing the major divisions at a typical station. The sales division, by virtue of its function as the revenue generator at the station, is often considered the most important part of any station's existence. It is not atypical for the GM to come from the sales department because the financial security of the station is so dependent on the sale of the station's central product, its advertising time. The programming product is important, but the advertising product is central.

Local stations have three general types of commercials to sell: national spots, local spots, and program-length commercials. The first two of these have their own salespeople, often with their own manager. The search for national spot buys is coordinated by "rep firms" that represent the stations to the large national corporations who purchase this time in local markets. The local station's "national sales" staff must be aware of how many viewers there are, what type of viewers watch each program, and how valuable those viewers are to different advertisers. Often, program-length commercials, better known as infomercials, are handled by the national sales department as well.

The local sales force must look for businesses in the community that can afford to buy the expensive television time, usually in fairly large numbers of spots. Sometimes the local account executive will help to coordinate a purchase of time called a *co-op buy,* which involves several similar businesses selling the same product buying time together. Often, the manufacturer of the product, perhaps a washing machine or television set, will supply the advertisement and pay part of the cost of the air time. Co-op ads often identify local businesses where the product is available at the end of the commercial. Because there is stiff competition for local advertising dollars among TV stations, newspapers, radio stations, direct mail and other marketing outlets, the local sales force must be creative and aggressive.

Programming Department

The programming department is separate from the news division, even though both are responsible for putting shows on the air. While the news division is responsible for the production of the local news, the programming division is responsible for everything else that appears on the station's channel. Affiliates of the three largest networks have little time to program themselves, but independent stations and Fox, The WB, and UPN affiliates have considerable time during the day to place programs. The primary function of the programming division is to get the largest or most desirable audience possible for the station. The program director will monitor the other stations in the market to determine what to program against the competition. Sometimes this will involve scheduling a similar type of program to go head-to-head with the competition, or it might involve a counterprogramming strategy. But acquiring programs is just as important a programming function as scheduling them.

As noted in Chapter 6, programming must also be responsible for negotiating with syndicators for their shows, an aspect of the business that has become increasingly leveraged in the last decade. While a straight cash purchase is still an occasional option, more variations of the purchase exist than ever before. There is negotiation over how many runs a program will be allowed, what other properties of the syndicator might be purchased with the original buy, where in the day the show will be scheduled, and what the level of exclusivity in the market will be. There are also considerations for the number of barter advertising slots in the program. When "hot" new properties come on the syndication market, like *Friends* or *Mad About You*, stations must also determine whether they should purchase a program simply to keep it out of the hands of the competition. The programming of a local station is a minefield and success requires planning, diligence, and a little luck.

Promotion

In station organization, the department that markets the station and the programs to the viewers is promotion. The job of this department is to develop a "look" for the station, from logos and artwork to slogans and advertisements for its news and entertainment programs. The promotion department might be asked to generate a campaign for its evening newscast by creating spots for the show, arranging for billboards, or producing direct-mail brochures. Community events might be sponsored by the station in support of its programs or network celebrities can be brought to town for appearances.

Engineering

Simply put, the engineering department keeps the station on the air. The distribution of the station's signal is the first responsibility of this department, though the task is much more complicated in the new era of multiple input and distribution systems. A station must be sure to receive the programs of the network coming in via satellite, must monitor the programs that run on videotape, and must be sure that the microwave links with the news trucks out on live shots are working properly. The technical experts must also maintain the equipment and be sure that the station's signal is sent to the local cable system by microwave, satellite, or coaxial cable link. There is nothing worse than "dead air" at a TV station, and it is the job of the engineering department to be sure that programming is on at all times.

Traffic

Although the job of *traffic* is usually under the supervision of one of the major divisions, it is a vital link in the station's success, for it is traffic's responsibility to make sure that the right programming element goes on the air at the right time. The number of different elements that appear on the air is considerable: advertisements, promotional announcements, public service announcements, news inserts, and the different types of programs. Each of these elements must be scheduled and then logged as they appear, so that the programs flow seamlessly to the viewer and, more importantly, so that billing can be accurate. If a local advertiser buys commercial time during the sports segment of the newscast, it is up to traffic to be sure it appears. If, for whatever reason, the commercial is not shown in its entirety, then the station is liable for a "make good," another showing of the commercial at an appropriate time, or a refund of the cost of the spot. Television operates on many small units of programming running at exactly the right moment in order for the viewer to stay interested, and it is up to the people in traffic to ensure that programming scheduled is what appears on the screen.

CONCLUSION

Local television is still the dominant delivery system for programming in the United States. Whether they are over the air or carried on a local cable system, the television programs most people watch are brought to the viewer through the conduit of a local station. That local presence, however, may only be felt in the newscasts or other occasional local productions that occur at most stations. The rest of the schedule is dominated by network fare for affiliates, and syndicated programming available to any station in the country. In spite of the sameness of programming across the country, the local station is still the most prominent element of localism in U.S. broadcasting and the mainstay of the industry.

NOTES

[1]*Broadcasting and Cable Yearbook,* (Providence, RI: R. R. Bowker, 1995).
[2]John Culliton, General Manager, WCCO-TV. Personal interview, Minneapolis, MN, Feb. 16, 1996.
[3]*Broadcasting and Cable Yearbook,* op. cit., p. C41.
[4]Donald O'Conner, General Manager, KTMA Channel 23. Personal interview, St. Paul, Minnesota, November 10, 1995.

[5]It might be a better idea for an affiliate to run a local or syndicated show instead of an extremely weak network program, because there is more local advertising time to sell in local shows. Because of this threat, networks are quick to cancel programs with disastrous ratings.

[6]"Season-To-Date," *Electronic Media,* July 14, 1997, p. 43.

[7]Laurie Thomas and Barry Litman, "Fox Broadcasting Company, Why Now? An Economic Study of the Rise of the Fourth Broadcast 'Network,'" *Journal of Broadcasting & Electronic Media,* 35, (1991), pp. 139–156.

[8]In this example, the cost of the show ($1,000) is an average cost. Actually, a station charging only $150 per commercial would only pay about $300 per play over six runs, or $1,800 per episode, and keep an even bigger profit than $800. To keep the average cost per showing at $1,000, larger stations must pay more per play. Typically, the daily cost of a program is equal to the price of two commercials on the station's rate card.

[9]Sydney Head, Christopher Sterling, & Lemuel Schofield, *Broadcasting in America,* 7th ed., (Boston: Houghton Mifflin), 1994, pp. 310–311.

[10]Vernon Stone, "News Operations at U.S. TV Stations," jourvs@showme.missouri.edu, 1995.

[11]Vernon Stone, "Paychecks and Market Baskets: Broadcast News Salaries and Inflation in the 1990s," jourvs@showme.missouri.edu, 1995.

[12]Ibid.

[13]Kathleen Hall Jamieson and Karlyn Kohrs Campbell, *The Interplay of Influence,* 3rd ed. (Belmont, CA: Wadsworth, 1992), p. 71.

[14]Keith Wright, "Robots in the News: Camera Robot Navigation in Television Studios," *Industrial Robot,* 21, 1994, pp. 17–19.

[15]Ed Rosenthal, "Latest Sony News Gear Aims for Flexibility," *Electronic Media,* March 18, 1996, p. 24.

[16]Hans–Bernd Brosius and Hans Mathias Kepplinger, "Linear and Non-linear Models of Agenda-setting in Television," *Journal of Broadcasting & Electronic Media,* 36, 1992, pp. 5–24.

[17]Ed Fouhy, "The Dawn Of Public Journalism," *National Civic Review* 83, 1995, p. 259.

[18]Angela Powers, "Competition, Conduct and Ratings in Local Television News: Applying the Industrial Organizational Model," *Journal of Media Economics,* 6, 1993, pp. 37–51.

[19]Dolf Zillmann, Rhonda Gibson, Virginia Ordman, & Charles Aust, "Effects of Upbeat Stories in Broadcast News," *Journal of Broadcasting & Electronic Media,* 38, 1994, pp. 65–78.

[20]Ed Siegal, "TV Wars: Has Local TV Gone Tabloid," *The Boston Globe Magazine,* February 12, 1995, pp. 18–26, 29–31.

[21]Gail Shister, "Philly Stations Overhaul Local News," *Electronic Media,* February 26, 1996, p. 44.

[22]Eliot Tiegel, "'Hawaii Stars' Singin' Along," *Electronic Media,* January 8, 1996, p. 52.

[23]Steven Cole Smith, "Infomercials Flourish Everywhere Since Deregulation," *Minneapolis Star Tribune,* August 1995, p. 8–E.

[24]Susan Kief, Sales Department, KARE Channel 11, Personal Interview, St. Paul, March 22, 1996.

6

The National
Broadcast Industry

Broadcast television at the national level encompasses the four major networks and their nearly 800 affiliated stations, along with about 400 nonaffiliated, or independent stations, some of which are affiliated with fledgling national networks. Although stations provide television service in their local markets, these national television networks and syndication companies deliver most of the programs viewed in those markets. In this chapter, we will examine the distribution system for national broadcast programming, including the broadcast television networks, the development and scheduling of network programming, and nationwide syndication industry.

THE BIG 4: ABC, CBS, NBC, AND FOX

Four major broadcast networks presently dominate the national television arena. Their combined share continues to decline with the advent of newer distribution technologies such as coaxial and fiberoptic cable, direct satellite, and interconnected computers. In 1996 the four-network share for prime-time viewing stood at only 68 percent. Yet, the future of networks seems bright and newcomers are clamoring to form additional broadcast networks.

In order to understand where the broadcast industry is today, it is helpful to briefly review how it evolved into a system of affiliated television stations. Many of the factors that constrained the development of more than three or four major networks are still influencing the future evolution of major broadcast networks. The paramount variable is distribution: Only broadcast networks consistently reach nearly every home in the United States through hundreds of affiliated stations. Another factor is the possible number of healthy television stations in the average broadcast market. Although there are more than ten stations per market in the major metropolitan areas, most large cities have six or fewer viable stations. Finally, there is an ecological influence: As with the major automakers, systemic constraints may limit the big successful companies to a small handful.

Television networks originally emerged in the 1940s from broadcast radio networks. As we noted in Chapter 2, when television first became widespread in the late 1940s and early 1950s, only NBC and CBS had the financial reserves to put together expensive, large-scale network programs, often featuring the same programs and personalities that had achieved radio fame. Though it began operating in 1948, ABC gathered momentum as a television network in the late 1950s when two of the smaller motion picture studios broke ranks with the general boycott of the networks and began providing content for ABC.

It was partly the struggle between major suppliers (movie studios) and the major networks (ABC, NBC, and CBS) that eventually led to regulations limiting the financial participation of networks in their own programming. The Federal Communications Commission in the early 1970s ruled that networks could not retain financial interest in the entertainment shows that it rented from the producers who made them and later profited from the syndication of rerun episodes. The FCC's justification was the utter dominance of the big networks: They held an iron grip on nationwide distribution of programs. Even an attempt by Overmyer/United to start a fourth television network in the late 1960s was thwarted by the relatively small number of stations unaffiliated with the Big 3.

With the rapid growth of cable television in the late 1970s and 1980s, however, the power of the networks diminished, and they were finally were deregulated in the 1990s. In the 1980s one of the major studios (20th-Century Fox) was acquired by Rupert Murdoch, an international media mogul who saw an opportunity in the many unaffiliated television stations that signed on in the late 1970s and early 1980s. Starting with just a few programs in 1987, Fox eventually grew into a full network.

Who are the Big 4, then, and how is their dominance felt by the rest of the television industry? The next few sections examine each network in greater detail.[1]

NBC

NBC (National Broadcasting Company) is the original broadcast network in the United States. It was purchased for $6.28 billion in 1986 by the General Electric Corporation, which was, in the 1920s, one of the original founders of the Radio Corporation of America (RCA) that spawned NBC. GE is a multinational corporation that manufactures aircraft engines, medical systems, power systems, household appliances, lighting and wiring devices, and silicone sealants.

NBC began as a television network in 1940 and was an early innovator with such programs as *The Today Show* and *The Tonight Show*. After being mired in third place from 1976–1977 to 1983–1984, NBC had a short reign in the last half of the

1980s as the number-one network, a status that it managed to recapture in the mid-1990s with its popular programs and "Must See TV" promotional campaign.

CBS

CBS began as the United Independent Broadcasters in 1927, before a rapid series of ownership changes. It finally became the Columbia Broadcasting System when cigar-maker William S. Paley purchased the network in 1928. Under his guidance CBS became the "Tiffany" network, with many of the most popular radio and television programs for decades. In terms of audience ratings, the CBS network was number one for many years, with NBC in the number-two spot. An unsuccessful bid to start a cable network hastened Paley's stepping-down as chairman in 1983. After more turbulent years in the early 1980s, an unfriendly takeover attempt in 1985 by Ted Turner triggered substantial confusion after which Laurence Tisch began buying up enough shares to become the major stockholder and new leader of CBS. An attempt to focus on the core broadcasting business led to Tisch's dismantling of CBS ancillary publishing and music recording divisions. In 1991, CBS finally landed back on top of the ratings for three years, until being outmaneuvered by Fox, the upstart network that outbid CBS for NFL Football and then purchased New World Communications, which cost CBS eight key affiliates. In 1995, CBS was purchased by Westinghouse Electric for $5.4 billion, thus ending a stormy Tisch era that left the network in fourth place at the beginning of the 1995–1996 season.

ABC

The number-three network from its inception in 1948 until 1976, ABC (the American Broadcasting Company) was widely regarded as the weakest of the Big 3 networks. In 1952 ABC merged with United Paramount Theaters. During the lean years, ABC survived by making exclusive deals with Disney and Warner Brothers for programming. By 1972 the network finally became profitable and in 1976 was able to capture first place among the networks. In 1986 the network was bought by Capital Cities Communications for $3.5 billion and its corporate name was changed to Capital Cities/ABC, although the network still promoted itself as ABC. In 1995 the Walt Disney Company purchased the network for $19 billion and the official name was changed back to ABC in 1996.

Fox

The origins of the Fox network date back to 1977 when Paramount tried to launch a fourth network, under the direction of Barry Diller. When Diller became chief executive officer of 20th-Century Fox in 1984, he was in a better position to try again because international media mogul Rupert Murdoch took control of the company in 1985. Murdoch had tremendous resources from other media operations that helped bankroll the huge expenses needed by the fledgling Fox network.

Fox began in the fall of 1986 with a late-night talk show featuring Joan Rivers. From a single night of programming in 1987, Fox grew to five nights by 1990 and seven nights by 1993. Two strategies helped the network attract the attention of audiences. First, it debuted its shows in the summer months when the other networks showed reruns. Second, it targeted younger, ethnic male audiences that were disenfranchised by the Big Three's quest to deliver ideal demographics (18–49 white women) to advertisers. Advertisers were eager for Fox to succeed because of the power held by the established networks.

Fox benefited when the FCC ruled that the network was not really a network because its total number of prime-time hours did not exceed the arbitrary, government-set level of fifteen hours per week. Some observers at the time speculated the government was eager to see more competition for ABC, CBS, and NBC.

The Hollywood writers' strike in 1988 also indirectly assisted the growing popularity of Fox programming. The other networks were severely handicapped by the strike, while Fox had built up a supply of original programs.

The Fox network pulled off its biggest coup when it outbid CBS for the rights to NFL football. It was able to parlay this success into the purchase and re-affiliation of several key stations.

THE NEW NETWORKS

The success of the Fox network encouraged other motion picture studios to venture into network programming. Some had already formed temporary consortia, such as Operation Prime Time, to distribute programming, but most were seemingly content to have their product distributed by the networks and then reap the rewards through syndication of off-network programs.

Having a distribution arm such as a national television network, however, is better than just being a producer. Producers who are also distributors can create rather than supply programming markets. Paramount, in league with BHC Communications, and Warner Brothers both decided to get into the national network business in January 1995 by forming UPN and The WB.

Before examining each of these two fledgling networks, it would be beneficial to look at the factors that influenced the scramble for studios to form networks. First, the cable systems were nearly at capacity. The best way to get a cable channel was to buy into a media conglomerate. In 1994 Paramount merged with Viacom, which owns MTV, VH–1, Nickelodeon, The Movie Channel, Flix, Blockbuster Home Video, USA Channel, Nick at Nite, Spelling Entertainment, TV Land, and part-interest in Comedy Central, Sundance Channel, and All-News Channel. This opportunity for producers coincided with demand on the station side because many large markets had unaffiliated television stations in need of first-class prime-time programming.

Second, the studios can better use their total investment in television production if they stay busy. Studio space is expensive, technical staffs are scarce, and unproduced scripts tend to pile up. The sheer excess capacity of motion picture studios leads them to look for new profit areas.

Finally, the financial benefits of becoming the third- or fourth-rated network are tremendous. Although the initial costs are great, a new network can slowly grow, like Fox, into a seven-night schedule. Moreover, the cyclical nature of the network business leads to major shake-ups from season to season, and anyone has a chance to put lightning in a bottle.

Unfortunately, there are drawbacks to being UPN or The WB or another "wannabe" network. As noted earlier, there is a practical limit to the number of profitable stations in a given television market. To use a fast-food analogy, there may easily be consumer demand for a fourth restaurant at an exit along the interstate highway, but the going is very tough for the two newcomers who vie to be the fifth, especially if the number of restaurants is somehow limited by regulation, as station allocations per market are regulated. Nearly 20 percent of the nation's households were unable even to sample the two new networks.[2]

A second problem relates to the entertainment industry's capacity to produce programming. There is a finite number of writers, producers, and production staff who can handle the demands of network-quality programming. The existence of a fifth and a sixth networks could easily stretch the limits of first-run production.

UPN

BHC Communications is the parent company for the United Paramount Network (UPN). Its subsidiary, Chris-Craft, owns several large-market television stations. When UPN was first formed by Paramount and the United/Chris-Craft stations, Viacom, the parent company of Paramount after a mega-merger in the mid-1990s, held an option to buy into the network. Instead, the stations and Paramount later went their separate ways, although Paramount retained rights to supply programming. The first notable success was *Star Trek: Voyager,* a *spin-off* of the science-fiction series owned by Paramount through its other television and motion picture incarnations.

UPN was the early favorite among the new networks. UPN had 156 stations in 1996, many more than The WB. Hour-long dramas were an early staple on UPN to counterprogram the major network's sitcoms, but none of the first season shows survived, except for *Voyager.*

UPN launched several African American sitcoms in the 1996 fall season. Some research shows that black viewers watch 50 percent more television than white viewers,[3] but UPN President Lucie Salhany denied any ulterior motives.[4] The WB also received some criticism for exploiting black stereotypes in its entertainment programming.[5] The strategy, however, was very successful in attracting urban viewers for both fledgling networks in 1996.[6]

Just as Fox had lost money in its early years, UPN was not an overnight success. In 1995 BHC lost $128.7 million on UPN.[7] Chris-Craft's 1995 fourth-quarter earnings fell 67 percent, to $4.6 million from $14 million a year earlier, due to start-up losses at UPN.[8] By the fall 1996 season, Chris-Craft was reporting $38.9 million third-quarter losses, compared to a negative $28.7 million for the same period in 1995.[9]

The WB

Owned by Warner Communications and subsumed by the merger of Time Warner and Turner in 1996, The WB had operating losses of $102 million by the middle of 1996, with $66 million lost in 1995 alone.[10] In the third quarter of 1996, The WB lost $27 million, compared to a $7 million loss for the same period in 1995.[11]

The WB's distribution system is characterized by many more *secondary affiliation* deals with stations, with a total of ninety-three stations by the start of the 1996–1997 seasons. It has more hours of weekly programming, largely due to children's programming, such as *Animaniacs.* Both The WB and UPN moved from two to three nights of prime-time programming effective with the 1996–1997 season, and then to four nights the following year. In addition to its list of affiliates, The WB receives national distribution from superstation WGN in Chicago. Until the end of 1996, UPN reached markets where it has no affiliation through former superstation WWOR in New York. The WB, however, has attracted huge ratings from WPIX in New York, sometimes outdrawing the NBC flagship WNBC in prime time. Both UPN and The WB received a ratings boost in the 1996 fall season because neither network carried the low-rated presidential and vice-presidential debates.[12]

Warner Brothers and Paramount still produce programming for the networks. Similarly, ABC may own a program that winds up scheduled on CBS, but not very frequently. Thus, one essential difference between the original three networks (ABC, CBS, NBC) and the newer networks (Fox, UPN, and The WB) is that the latter challengers are more likely to produce shows that are distributed on a competing network.

Keeping affiliates is as big a concern as holding onto viewers for UPN and The WB. Rumors surfaced in 1995 and again early in 1996 that UPN and The WB would merge, but secret talks stalled when it became apparent that the affiliated stations in the largest and most profitable markets were reluctant to give up their network status.

NETWORK PROGRAM DEVELOPMENT AND ACQUISITION

Television networks constantly need new programs to replace failed or aging shows. The audience eventually tires of even the most popular programs. Producers bring their ideas for replacements to the networks, but the networks frequently initiate the search for fresh material. Each year, over 6,000 ideas must be considered.

The cost of developing a new television show is enormous. Each network spends on the order of $100 million each year, counting all of the network's annual purchases of undeveloped concepts, unscripted ideas, unproduced scripts, and rejected pilots.[13] The cost of producing a single pilot for a half-hour sitcom is $1 million and ranges up to $3 million for other series. It is therefore no wonder that made-for-TV movies are used to test the viability of dramatic shows.

The idea stage of program development arises from a network's particular needs. Like a coach building a team, the programmer looks for strengths and weaknesses in the existing lineup and tries to address specific needs for counterprogramming the competition. Beyond that, however, the program executive must spot viewing trends and viewer demographics. One prime criterion is finding an idea similar to *concepts* that have proven successful in the past. Also, the programmer looks for producers, like Aaron Spelling and Steven Bochco, who have strong reputations for creating winning shows. Finally, the casting of a particular actor with star appeal can make the difference between success or failure.

Programs described as *"high-concept"* often serve as attention-getting devices for broadcast schedules. Each year, networks inject their schedule with unusual concepts, such as space aliens, superheroes, or supernatural powers, to stimulate innovation. Most high-concept programs fail, but the networks need the attention these shows bring, regardless of viability, to generate excitement. The idea must have some chance of surviving, but every network needs to experiment with occasional high-risk concepts.

Recycling old ideas is virtually assured, given the number of programs that have already been on the air over the past fifty years. Often the programmer will take an idea from two or more shows and combine the elements into a new show. Appealing characters and situations complete the mix.

An important element in the development of concepts is research. Once a concept is conceived, the networks will test it on potential audiences. If the idea survives, a pilot or made-for-TV movie is produced and shown to test audiences in specially-wired auditoriums where viewers can press buttons to register their approval or disapproval. The researchers use focus groups to refine the audiences' opinion of a particular concept or pilot.

Although the prime goal of program development is to attract a wide audience, programmers inevitably encounter public and critical appeals to the nebulous standard of "quality." It seems that everyone knows what quality is, but most have difficulty defining it. When pressed, most people describe quality as the key characteristic of the shows that they enjoy. Rather than acknowledge that their tastes are personal, viewers prefer to believe that the program itself contains some intrinsic feature, called *quality*. If the public wants more quality shows, and if quality merely means "shows we like," can anyone wonder that the networks gauge the success of a broadcast schedule by audience size in the form of ratings and shares?

A competing notion of program enjoyment argues that comfort, not quality, is the real issue. Television is a low-impact, passive activity for many people. Audiences often seek escape and relaxation from television. Comfortable characters in predictable situations leads to bland television, but it is entirely possible that most viewers want to relax with something familiar, punctuated occasionally with something unexpected.

Once the programmer decides on an idea for a show, several decisions have to be made before a deal can be finalized with the producer. Negotiations center on several deal points: number of episodes, program duration, number of plays, commercial format, and price. For example, the network will frequently order six episodes with an option to renew, up to twenty-four total episodes per year. Each episode is typically contracted for two showings. In the case of a one-hour show, the program will be formatted for twelve minutes of commercial time. The episode costs the network $800,000, but it costs the producer over $1 million to produce. As we will see later in this chapter, the producer runs a deficit in hopes of substantial profits in syndication following the episode's network run.

SCHEDULING PRACTICES AND STRATEGIES

Programmers have learned specific strategies for maximizing and maintaining audience size. Most of the techniques originated in a simpler time when there were only three or maybe four competing stations in the typical market. Cable was in its infancy and would not become a major force until the 1980s. The VCR appeared in the mid-1970s, but did not become an influential force until the mid-1980s.

Audience flow is the underlying basis for programming strategies. It is a simple idea: Keep the audiences you already have by enhancing the compatibility of each program's appeal. The most basic strategy is called *blocking,* which is the grouping of similar shows together. If the first four half-hour programs are sitcoms, the network or station is using a comedy block. Another station might compete with an action–adventure block featuring three one-hour thrillers. Aside from format blocks, programmers also use demographic blocking to maintain audience flow. Thus, a male-appeal block competes with a female-appeal block. Sometimes the block is based on age appeals rather than gender.

The elements within a comedy block frequently alternate between old and new shows, with the newer show sandwiched between the older, established programs. This technique is known as *hammocking* because the popular shows are the solid posts between which the hammock is hung. New shows sometimes are temporarily placed in hammocks between two strong programs and then moved to another time period once the audience has had a good chance to sample them. When the network does not have enough "posts" (popular programs) on a given evening, the programmer might surround a single hit show with new or weaker programs leading up to and following it. This strategy is called *tent-poling,* and is usually less effective than hammocking because the weaker shows tend to pull down the ratings of the tent-pole program.

Strong programs, whether they are tent-poles or hammock posts, are scheduled at even time periods like 8, 9, and 10 P.M., because viewers are accustomed to a "break-point," when viewing in a half-hour comedy block can mesh with an hour-long drama block. One reason why half-hour comedies play well in the early portion of prime time is that competing one-hour dramas cannot easily pick up any new viewers at the "bottom" of the hour. One strategy for maneuvering around a strong competing show scheduled at a break-point is to extend the preceding program well past the start of the hit show. Networks, particularly PBS, will schedule two ninety-minute specials from 8 to 9:30 and 9:30 to 11 P.M., which effectively discourages viewers from jumping to either the 9 or 10 P.M. break-point shows. This tactic is called *bridging*. The cable channel TBS has also used bridging for many years, by starting its programs five minutes past the usual break-points, although the original reason behind this scheduling practice was to get a separated listing for TBS in printed guides.

One way to disguise the break-points is to eliminate the break altogether between a strong show and a new show. Such *seamless transitions* are accomplished by rearranging the local station breaks and advertising *adjacencies* to make one program's split-screen credits and closing program material blend right into the cold-start of the next show, eliminating the opening credits that were common in the glory days of broadcast television.

Other scheduling strategies center on habit formation. Except for prime-time programs, most shows on the networks and on stations appear five and sometimes six days in a row at exactly the same time, a practice known as *stripping*. A stripped program is easy to remember, thus promoting habitual viewing. In the alternative strategy, *checkerboarding*, different programs are scheduled at the same time on different days of the week. Thus, the program grid resembles a game board, rather than unbroken strips. Outside of primetime, checkerboarding is typically used when not enough syndicated episodes are available for stripping a series.

Finally, programmers distinguish their shows by offering something different from the competition. This *counterprogramming* attempts to attract an audience that is not well served by competing networks. For example, one network might successfully compete against a top-rated comedy block on another network by appealing to a different audience, offering an action–adventure program or a news magazine. The alternative to counterprogramming is called *blunting*, whereby one network matches the program type of the competitors. However, as more and more channels compete for the same total audience, networks have a harder time countering and blunting.[14]

During the ratings sweeps, when ratings are measured in local markets across the nation, networks may put their weaker programs on *hiatus* and *double-run* their more popular shows. More often, programmers will bring out the high-power entertainment specials and miniseries during measurement periods, a practice called *stunting*. Advertisers dislike stunting because it distorts the ratings for many time periods.

Regardless of the size of the station or network, the broadcast programmer has the same set of responsibilities. She or he must keep a track record of the current schedule and help target the appropriate demographics for advertisers. Like traditional products, each program has its own life cycle. Networks and stations need to have programming in reserve that can be taken off the shelf in order to plug a weak time period or to provide a needed *rest* for a show that has been running for a long time.

Finally, the networks must promote the programs to potential audiences. In 1996, the television networks and stations spent over $400 million (some of it on their own air time) to put together a promotional blitz to advertise the new fall shows. Networks realize that promotion is a key component of attracting and maintaining viewers. Even the closing credits of television shows succumbed in the early 1990s to a split-screen treatment, where the names of the production staff are squeezed into a nearly unreadable typeface so that promotional announcements can appear in the other portion of the screen. If these network promotions are successful, a program will continue to be aired by the network for many years and its old episodes will contribute to a second national source of programming, syndication.

SYNDICATION

When networks assemble a schedule to distribute programs, each "show" usually represents one original plus one repeat (rerun) telecast.[15] In essence, the network "rents" the program from its owner (the producer) at a hefty fee. Assuming that networks will preempt each show a few times for special events, network series typically produce twenty-two to twenty-four episodes per year. Because the program holds some residual value for future showings, the producer charges less than the full cost. As a result, each program loses upfront money in the hopes of making a big profit on the backend. The whole arrangement is known as *deficit financing*.

If the program stays on the network long enough to accumulate a sufficient number of episodes—usually 120, or five years' worth—the producer can license the program rights to stations or cable channels, which will most often show the episodes daily (Monday through Friday) instead of weekly. The reselling of successful television programs that typically originated on a broadcast network is called *off-network syndication*.

Syndication also describes programs that bypass network distribution, such as *Oprah* and *Entertainment Tonight*. These programs are *first-run syndication* and get their initial exhibition on individual television stations. The show may air at 4 P.M. on an ABC affiliate in one market and at 4:30 on an NBC affiliate in another.

As we noted in Chapter 2, until recently the FCC restricted network affiliated stations, in the top 50 markets, from using off-network shows during 7 to 8 P.M. EST and prohibited networks from holding any financial interest in shows that originated on networks. With the repeal of these restrictions, the syndication environment was altered. First-run syndicated programs, like *Wheel of Fortune* and *Jeopardy!,* which flourished in a regulated access time period where off-network shows were prohibited, began to compete with off-network fare.

Syndication involves several type of programs: sitcoms, dramas, talk shows, magazines, reality-based programs, game shows, children's programs, and feature films. The *sitcom* (or *situation comedy*) is the most prevalent form of prime-time network series program and also the staple of syndicated programs. In the fall 1996 season, there were sixty-four different sitcoms among the six networks in prime time. One reason for the sitcom's success as a format is its length. Half-hour shows give programmers more flexibility in scheduling. Another factor is the sitcom's self-contained story. In most cases, the episodes need not appear in any particular order, unlike such serialized dramas as *ER* and *NYPD Blue*. Sitcoms have a simple structure that audiences appreciate, particularly when the main character or star is appealing.

Dramas typically last one hour and are scheduled later in the evening on prime time, although family dramas may appear in the *lead-off* position to counterprogram against competing networks running sitcoms. The chief benefit of one-hour dramas is that the audience, once attracted, will stay viewing longer, allowing the network or station to maintain its competitive edge longer against the other channels. Dramas also allow writers to cover more story elements and develop characters more fully. At one time, the Western was a popular genre, with such shows as *Gunsmoke* and *Bonanza,* but the crime or mystery format became more popular over the years. Another dramatic format is the serialized prime-time soap opera, like *Melrose Place* or *Dallas,* but it was later replaced by a subtle imitator, the medical show set in a hospital.

Regardless of the general format, one-hour dramas in syndication do not attract large audiences, largely owing to their length. Syndicated programs often run at transitional time periods like early afternoon, when viewers are less likely to watch for a full hour than they are during prime time. Running five reruns at the same time each day, called *stripping,* works better for sitcoms and other half-hour formats than for hour-long dramas. Attempts to reedit one-hour dramas into half-hour shows have proven unsuccessful in the past.

As a result, most dramas are syndicated to cable channels rather than to television stations. Whereas the latter must maintain maximum audiences through the day, cable channels are an incremental part of a general service to the subscriber. Because the cable system operator can justify a fifty-cent-per-month subscription increase for an additional channel that only costs ten cents per subscriber, it is not necessary for programs on most cable channels to attract a very large audience.

The talk format is an inexpensive alternative to sitcoms and dramas. Because there is no story, the producer saves $40,000 to $60,000 per episode right off the top. Because many of the participants appear for the lowest possible fee in order to promote their book or new movie or latest song, the cost of talent is limited, except for the host. Talk shows have the added benefit of seeming live and current, even when they are taped a few hours before, as is the case with late-night talk shows. The topical nature of talk shows does present a limitation for rerun syndication; syndicated and network talk shows are first-run. Cable channels that show reruns of old talk shows prove to be the exception rather than the rule.

Another type of first-run format is the *magazine format.* Networks produce these programs, such as *20/20* and *60 Minutes,* through the vast resources of their news divisions. The cost of a prime-time hour of information programming in a magazine format is low compared to the expense of sitcoms and dramas. As with talk shows, magazine programs do not work well in reruns. Consequently, individual stations schedule magazine shows that are produced directly for first-run syndication. While the network versions are frequently an hour in length, the first-run syndicated versions, such as *Entertainment Tonight* and *Hard Copy,* last only a half-hour in order to maximize their scheduling flexibility.

Another type of syndicated program is the *reality show,* based on the successful prime-time genre in which real events are presented for entertainment value. Examples include first-run syndicated programs such as *People's Court* and *Real Tales of the Highway Patrol.* Reality programs have become increasingly popular because they earn respectable ratings and are inexpensive to produce. The extensive use of news footage and amateur videos, simple production formats, and low talent fees contribute to a strong bottom line.

However, among the first-run syndicated formats, the most enduring genre is the game show. In the early days of television, many of the popular prime-time programs (e.g., *What's My Line* and *I've Got a Secret*) were celebrity game shows. At one time, daytime television was littered with game shows, primarily because they generated solid ratings but had very low production costs. Companies donated prizes in exchange for promotional considerations and the contestants often received only a few consolation prizes, including the "home version" of the game. In recent years, the two most popular syndicated programs have been *Wheel of Fortune* and *Jeopardy!*—both of which are distributed by King World.

Another syndicated format is the children's program, frequently based on entertainment rather than education. Public television still devotes a large portion of its day to educational programs for children, and the FCC in 1996 passed regulations requiring all television stations to carry three hours per week for children's education. But the main type of children's programming in syndication and on networks is the animated cartoon, with a heavy dose of "action" (or violence, depending on one's point of view). The proliferation of cable channels, which can program longer blocks devoted to children's programs, thus attracting greater loyalty, has led many broadcast television stations to limit children's programming to the weekends or early morning hours. The primary exception has been for affiliates of Fox and The WB, whose networks provide children with lengthy daily offerings that compete with syndicated programs.

The final type of syndicated program is the feature film or motion picture. Movies are the oldest form of filmed entertainment, and television stations have a long tradition of carrying motion pictures, either from the networks or via syndication. Feature-length films come in two varieties: *theatricals* and made-for-TV. Theatrical exhibition is traditionally the first *window* for movies, followed by release to home video, *pay-per-view* cable, pay-per-month cable, network television, and local syndication. Successful films occasionally go directly to the networks, but most films produced for movie theaters are cycled through the usual sequence.

Made-for-TV movies are produced for television and cable networks. Many such films are based on stories recently taken from headline events, and the topics are commonly sensational. Although these "made-fors" are not accorded much respect by serious film critics, the networks that schedule made-for-TV movies opposite theatrical releases often attract larger audiences because viewers have not had dozens of opportunities to see them on cable or home video. The fresh appeal of a movie never-before-seen is the primary reason for the relative success of made-fors.[16] Beyond the audience appeal, the networks also schedule made-for-TV movies to test ideas that can be turned into series. Producing a one-hour pilot for a new drama series is not much less expensive than making a two-hour movie. If the idea succeeds, the network will develop the concept as a series for the coming season. If not, the made-for-TV movie at least fills a two-hour movie slot.

Television stations are not limited to one of these types of syndicated programs. Most stations produce their own local news programs, and some carry locally-produced entertainment programs (see Chapter 5). In the early days of television, virtually all stations had a local host for movies and children's cartoons. Local talk shows were commonplace until the ready availability of syndicated versions. It is less expensive to share the production costs with other stations that carry a syndicated program, and national shows can attract big name guests far more easily than most local stations can.

Dayparting

Most syndicated programming is segregated by daypart: talk shows in the morning and afternoon, game shows and hit sitcoms in the early evening, movies and other types during late night. The reason for this *dayparting* is simple: Different demographic groups are available at different times of the day. Adults who work at home are more likely to enjoy daytime serials (soap operas) and talk shows, while children are more likely to watch during the afternoon and early evening hours.

The television industry uses terminology for dayparts that is usually descriptive and occasionally arcane. The morning daypart is what it seems, the 7 A.M. to noontime period, and is subdivided sometimes into early morning and late morning dayparts. The afternoon daypart runs from noon to 6 P.M., when the evening or early evening daypart begins. Other terms stem from the way advertising is bought, with prime time being the most desirable daypart when most people have the opportunity to or are in the habit of watching television. The early evening hours were traditionally reserved for local (6 to 6:30 P.M. Eastern time) and national (6:30 to 7 P.M. Eastern time) news programs. Before and after prime was originally known as *fringe* time: early fringe from 4 to 6 P.M. and late fringe from 11 P.M. to 1 A.M. Regional variations exist and time zone differences are common.

In the 1970s, the FCC, as part of the Prime Time Access Rule, gave network affiliates "access" to the first half-hour of prime time, which had previously begun at 7:30 P.M. Eastern time. The additional block of time expanded into *access,* and signified the time period between the network news and the beginning of network prime time, usually (but not always) from 7 to 8 P.M. Eastern time.

Syndication Payments

As we noted in Chapter 5, the station pays by one of three methods: cash, *barter,* or *cash-plus-barter.* The cash method is the most simple arrangement. The station simply pays the syndicator for the program, and all of the nonprogram time (commercial *avails*) is available for sale by the station to advertisers. The only source of revenue for the program producer is the station's cash payment of a negotiated price. With barter, however, there is no payment from the station to the syndicator. Instead, a number of advertising minutes, usually 50 percent, are held back by the syndicator for sale to national advertisers, with the remainder available to the station for sale to local advertisers. One problem is that stations also sell local time to national advertisers, which puts them into competition with the syndicator for spot sales.

A hybrid approach to program sales is called *cash-plus-barter.* In this scheme, the show is also sold to the station for cash, except that one minute is held back (in the case of a half-hour show) by the syndicator. Talk shows like *Oprah* have two minutes retained by the syndicator. Cash-plus-barter originally came about when syndicators sought ways to offer increasingly expensive first-run programs at prices that the station could afford. Since that time, the cash-plus scheme has been used for programs hotly demanded by stations.

Negotiating for Syndicated Programming

Individual television stations negotiate with syndicators over the rights for syndicated programming. First-run syndication often includes 160 original episodes and 100 reruns. Off-network shows vary according to the number of years that the particular program ran on the network, which is typically four or five years. Negotiation usually involves a representative of the program's producer visiting the television market and making a sales pitch. This method involves travel and is time-consuming. The syndicator can also lose control of a program's price when a station plays one syndicator against another. In recent years, the practice of *bidding* has replaced standard negotiation for highly popular off-network shows that are new to syndication. Bidding is simpler for the syndicator and leaves the stations fighting one another. When a hit network show first becomes available to stations, the syndicator contacts stations by fax, in the largest markets first, asking for a license fee proposal from the station within forty-eight hours. Travel costs and time are eliminated or compressed, and the syndicator is in control. Stations want the best programming and will sometimes overbid for shows, forgetting that sometimes one bad deal can ruin a station's bottom line.

Another wrinkle in the negotiating process is the *futures* market for syndicated off-network series. Because a program may not be available in syndication for a few years, the future rights are sold while the show is still riding high on the network. The station must gamble that the show will maintain its popularity. However, stations must realize that not all network hits are successful in syndication. Similarly, some mediocre network shows have attracted far larger audiences in syndication than during their prime time run (e.g., *WKRP in Cincinnati*).

CONCLUSION

The majority of television programming in the United States is contracted by national television networks and program syndicators. Programming is delivered to local stations by satellite and broadcast in over two hundred local markets (see Chapter 1). Although cable television has flourished as a competing distribution system, its role in program creation is still secondary. Cable programming is heavy on sports, news, and talk, programming that can be produced at lower costs. Expensive new programming, such as made-for-television movies, situation comedies, dramas, and action programs, are usually purchased and initially distributed by networks. As the cable television and digital satellite services continue to develop, this disparity may narrow, but for now most popular programming is the province of broadcast networks and national syndicators.

NOTES

[1]Historical and business background is derived from Howard J. Blumenthal and Oliver R. Goodenough, *This Business of Television,* (New York: Billboard Books, 1991); Barry Monush, ed. *International Television & Video Almanac,* (New York: Quigley Publishing, 1996); Anthony Slide, *The Television Industry: A Historical Dictionary,* (Westport, CT: Greenwood Press, 1991).

[2]Frederic Biddle, "Two Giants Enter Network Fray, *Boston Globe,* January 9, 1995, p. 2.

[3]Chuck Ross, "Blacks Drawn to Indy TV, Cable," *Advertising Age,* March 4, 1996, p. 8.

[4]Jefferson Graham, "UPN: Funny Has No Color, *USA Today,* July 3, 1996, Sec. B, p. 9.

[5]John Carman, "TV in Black and White," *San Francisco Chronicle,* August 26, 1996, Sec. E, p. 1.

[6]Bill Carter, "Two Upstart Networks Courting Black Viewers," *New York Times,* October 7, 1996, Sec. C, p. 11.

[7]Lynette Rice, "Round Three: UPN vs. The WB," *Broadcasting & Cable,* August 26, 1996, pp. 5, 10.

[8]Eben Shapiro, "Chris-Craft's 4th-Period Net Fell 67% on Start-Up Losses at UPN," *Wall Street Journal,* February 15, 1996, p. B-7.

[9]Marla Matzer, "Contented Kingdoms," MediaWeek (Superbrands Supplement), October 7, 1996 pp. 28–35.

[10]Rice, op. cit.

[11]Matzer, op. cit.

[12]Brian Lowry, "Debates Offer Opportunity for UPN, WB," *Los Angeles Times,* October 4, 1996, Sec. F, p. 26.

[13]This amount pales in comparison to the total amount spent by the major networks during the 1996 fall seasons merely to promote the new lineup: $400 million, according to the *New York Times,* September 20, 1996, p. D–1.

[14]Carolyn A. Lin, "Network Prime-Time Programming Strategies in the 1980s," *Journal of Broadcasting & Electronic Media,* 39(4), 1995, pp. 482–495.

[15]Some information for this section came from William J. Adams and Susan T. Eastman, "Prime-Time Network Television Programming," in *Broadcast/Cable Programming: Strategies and Practices* (5th ed.), ed. Susan T. Eastman and Douglas A. Ferguson (Belmont, CA: Wadsworth, 1997), pp. 99–139.

[16]Although some theatrical releases perform very well in prime time, the average Hollywood retread does not do as well as a highly promoted adaptation of a tawdry novel or a "Don't Steal My Baby" melodrama that is made for television.

7

Audience Measurement: Viewer as Commodity

INTRODUCTION

The discussion of broadcast economics in Chapter 3 noted the unique dual nature of television marketing. The programming on broadcast television is designed to attract an audience, and the attention of the audience is then sold to advertisers. The common element in each transaction is the viewer. Viewers' attention is thus sold as a commodity to the advertisers who target their attention to commercial messages.

In this chapter, we examine two key areas in the transaction: (1) the nature of the audience's attention that is being sold, and (2) the currency by which a transaction is measured, that is, the value indicated by the ratings. The value of the audience's attention is directly linked to audience measurement. The word *ratings* has a specific meaning but denotes a more general interest on the part of advertisers and broadcasters in how much attention the viewers presumably give to commercial messages on television. The link is tenuous because program ratings attempt to measure the mere presence of the audience at the time that the commercial airs, without directly gauging the effectiveness of the persuasive message.

For example, the program rating for a particular program may indicate that 20 percent of the potential audience was tuned to a broadcast channel. The advertiser and the broadcaster, who wants the advertiser as a customer, make a good-faith assumption that the same audience that watched the show also watched the commercial breaks within it. As anyone who has left the room during a commercial knows, however, not everyone pays close attention to advertising. Nevertheless, viewers do see many commercials, and they recall the selling points of advertised products and services. Even when they fast-forward past a familiar commercial on a home-recorded program, viewers are still exposed to some of the original message.

Except for channel surfers, viewers only watch one show at a time, so each program and its commercials are in competition with other programs and commercials. As the number of program options grows, so too does the competition among the choices, and because the amount of time available to watch television is finite, television shows must compete with other leisure activities.

VIEWING LEVELS

The amount of leisure time spent viewing television is staggering. The average U.S. home has the television turned on for over 7 hours per day. The average adult between 24–54 watches 4.3 hours a day; the typical child between 2 and 11 watches 3.3 hours a day.[1] The worldwide average for television viewing is 2.7 hours per day.[2] One reason Americans pay so much attention to the tube is the relatively generous amount of leisure time they have. Leisure time in America is growing rapidly[3] and is most often associated with "easy" activities, like watching television.[4] Television claims 30 percent of all leisure activities,[5] particularly among older people[6] and the less educated.[7]

Of course, not all viewing is devoted to over-the-air broadcasting. As nonbroadcast options grow in popularity, the share of viewing to over-the-air sources continues to decline. By the first week of the 1996 premiere season, when the total amount of money spent by the networks to promote their new fall shows approached half a billion dollars, the six-network share in prime time was only 66 percent, down from 71 percent in 1995. When one considers the year-round average viewing of the three major broadcast networks, the combined share has slipped from 90 percent in the 1970s to about 55 percent in 1996.

Demographic factors also influence viewing.[8] For example, watching television is positively related to adult age and family size, but negatively related to education. Individual factors that increase viewing are race (black), occupation (blue-collar), residence (urban), and gender (women). Even so, virtually everyone watches television at some time during each day, and the total time spent viewing either broadcast or nonbroadcast programming shows no sign of decline.

Of course, time spent viewing is not the same as time spent viewing *at full attention.* The broadcast audience is busy with other activities during viewing: reading, playing, working, and dozing. At one level, the audience has an opportunity to watch a given commercial, an activity called *exposure.* At a different level, viewers actually process the information to which they are exposed, called *cognitions.* Presumably these cognitions lead to changes in attitudes, though not necessarily, depending on the persuasiveness of the message and the receptivity of the viewer. Even more tenuous is the link between attitude change and behavior modification— in this case, buying a product or service. Without exposure, there cannot be attention. Without attention, there cannot be attitude change and potential influence on buying behavior. Broadcasters sell exposures and advertisers seek attention.

ATTENTION RESEARCH

The burden of making the commercial message persuasive falls entirely on the advertiser, but to the extent that viewers pay different amounts of attention to various media (e.g., magazines, newspapers, radio), television broadcasters are sensitive to how attentive their audiences are. Some observers have even speculated that extremely popular programs are *less* effective vehicles for commercials because the audience is frequently too involved in the programming to have residual attention for the commercial breaks. A bland show may maintain a more even-handed low level of attention that continues into the adjacent advertising.

At least two studies have examined the program environment in which commercials are placed. One study found that high arousal programs that are pleasant enhance the viewers' evaluation of a commercial, while unpleasant high arousal programs depress evaluation.[9] Low arousal programs, on the other hand, create a contrast whereby unpleasant programs enhance the viewer reaction to commercials and pleasant programs undermine viewer appeal of the commercial. Another study found a similar contrast with regard to viewer *involvement*.[10] Low involvement commercials (i.e., ones not using attention-getting devices) create positive cognitive activity when placed in high involvement programs. Commercials that do use attention-getting devices perform best in low involvement programs. But when high involvement commercials are scheduled in high involvement programs, the viewer is distracted from the advertising message.

In addition, researchers have studied viewers' attention to commercials and have found that audiences remain visually-oriented 33 percent of the time. Viewers, however, maintain eye contact with programming 62 percent of the time.[11] The 33 percent is contrasted with much earlier studies that reported 55 percent of viewers paying full attention to commercials. The researchers concluded that the multichannel viewing environment, coupled with remote-control flipping in the later study, had "reduced the opportunity for commercial exposure."[12] With regard to partial attention to television, the data showed that the mean eyes-on-screen time (52 percent) for men viewing commercials was greater than for women (40 percent). For program content, the gender difference was reversed (64 percent versus 70 percent). The researchers concluded that attention to programs was consistent with earlier studies but attention to commercials had diminished significantly.

How do these findings compare to newspaper advertising? Only about 19 percent of readers read a newspaper thoroughly from front to back. Fifty-eight percent read certain parts thoroughly and skim others. Ten percent just skim and another 7 percent fail to read the paper at all. A key difference between print media and television programs is that the latter denies random access: It is more difficult to skip around a real-time television show and avoid commercials than it is to select portions of a newspaper and avoid advertising.

Perhaps because they fear a loss of advertiser support, broadcasters do not seem very interested in talking about attention to commercials. First, it is something that is not easily measured; it is easier to count exposures than cognitions. Second, as mentioned earlier, broadcasters feel that it is up to the advertisers to make their messages attention-gaining. In fact, network executives have occasionally suggested that audience measurement extends to the commercial breaks themselves, so that advertisers might be penalized in some way for running dull or offensive messages that cause viewers to switch channels in search of something more interesting.

Specifically, advertisers are concerned about how many viewers fail to watch the commercials that the sponsor buys. Sophisticated audience measurement devices have been proposed to measure such activity, but presently the methods used by Nielsen and other companies primarily measure program ratings. However, special reports can be generated by the data that is collected minute-by-minute.

Two kinds of commercial *avoidance* have been identified: passive viewer avoidance and active viewer avoidance.[13] Passive avoidance entails physical action: leaving the room, talking to others, or reading a magazine. One study found that 32 percent of the viewers physically avoid commercials, far greater than the percentage of viewers who avoid programming content.[14] In active avoidance, the viewer employs mechanical devices to interrupt attention to the screen. Another study found that commercial avoidance was one primary use of the remote control device.[15]

The technology of video recorders and remote control devices has altered the audience's attention to recorded commercial messages. For example, *zipping* is fast-forwarding through commercials in shows taped at home. A closely related phenomenon is *zapping*, which is deleting commercials on shows at airtime rather than playback. The key difference is that zipping can only be performed with the VCR. Adhoc zapping can take place in real time (live) or with VCR use.

Despite "ad-killer" devices built into VCRs,[16] most viewers who want to avoid commercials merely change channels (zap) or fast-forward through them (zip). Advertising agencies are fully aware of the problem and attempt to produce zap-proof commercials by making them more interesting and attention-getting.[17]

Virtually all research findings have found that younger viewers are more likely to *zap* (avoid) commercials. Men are by far the heaviest zappers, and sports is the most zapped form of programming.[18] The average household zaps once every 3:42 minutes, and affluent viewers are more likely to zap.[19]

Despite the common belief that commercial zapping is so prevalent, the majority of household channel-switching occurs during actual programming.[20] Most of this "flipping" is a part of channel orientation during the first five minutes of a program.[21]

Fast-forward zipping occurs in blocks of commercials, called *pods*. Most people zip indiscriminately, without regard to actual message content. The zipping rate is lowest for the first commercial in the first pod, and highest for commercials in the last pod.[22] The best strategy to counter zipping is to place very attention-getting material in the first few seconds of a commercial, but the high rate of block-zipping prevents anyone from seeing the first few seconds of anything but the first commercial.

Fortunately for broadcasters, traditional network viewers stay tuned an average of 27 minutes a show. Fox viewers keep watching for 18.5 minutes and cable viewers change channels after just 9.5 minutes. Some commercials emphasize brand identification to combat zipping.[23] Another strategy is to vary commercial lengths and the number of spots per pod to make it harder for viewers to estimate how long a commercial pod will last.

Even without gadgetry, many viewers learn to tune out commercials mentally, which may explain why some sponsors attempt to force their message with annoying or other provocative techniques. Otherwise, the viewer may tune out the commercial, or even leave the room to raid the refrigerator or to visit the bathroom. One study that looked at two types of commercial avoidance reported that commercials tend to stimulate physical avoidance, while programming content tends to promote mechanical avoidance behaviors. The researchers found that viewers physically avoid commercials five times more than they ignore programs.[24]

Oddly, reported attitudes about commercials do not reflect avoidance behaviors. A comparison of identical public opinion surveys done in the 1960s and again in the 1990s showed that 40 percent of the earlier respondents thought commercials "ordinarily in poor taste and annoying." Only 20 percent in the later sample thought commercials were offensive.[25] Perhaps commercials are getting better, or maybe viewers have slightly higher opinions of commercials because they are getting better at avoiding them.

TARGET AUDIENCES

Many advertisers are not interested in the entire broadcast audience. Depending on the product or service being offered, a particular target audience is selected, usually based on demographic factors like age and sex. Over the years, broadcasters have focused on what was considered the *ideal demographics;* young housewives were the holy grail of advertising. Advertisers assume that women aged thirty-four to forty-four buy the bulk of packaged goods.

Adult men are usually a difficult demographic group to reach, but some products and services are directed to them. Sports programming is the easiest way to reach male viewers, but the cost of televised events is very high. Part of the difficulty in targeting men is that most programming is aimed at women. As a result, men watch less television, which makes it harder to catch their attention.

Children are a special target of broadcasters because they are natural consumers. It is easier to persuade youngsters, and many social critics worry that commercials exploit young children and unduly create conflict between them and their caregivers. As we discussed in Chapter 5, the Children's Television Act of 1990 required the FCC to limit advertising to 12 minutes per hour during the week and to 10.5 minutes on weekends. Congress has further prohibited "host-based" commercials that feature characters who participate in the program content of the show in which the commercials are scheduled.

THE END OF MASS MEDIA?

Don Schultz of Northwestern University has theorized that modern marketing techniques could trigger big changes in the way television advertising is bought and sold. Until now, most advertisers bought exposure to general segments of the population without regard to their specific preferences for a product or service. Because there was no way of easily keeping track of customers, companies focused on those who were likely to buy. But with computerized databases, virtually all businesses today are tracking their customers. They use databases to advertise directly to those who actually spend regularly.

What is the implication for broadcasters? Schultz notes that radio and television stations are not building lists of their users to correspond with the customer databases of advertisers. Direct-mail advertisers, newspapers, and magazines know exactly who sees their printed advertisements. Schultz anticipates the day when advertisers will tell broadcasters, "We don't want to pay for the whole audience. We just want the ones who are already our best customers. Here's a list of our customers. Match it with your viewers and we'll pay you for reaching them."

Schultz argues that television advertising works by creating or enhancing brand or product images, by reinforcing previous product purchase choices, and by adding perceptual value for the product or service.[26] It does not work at getting customers to switch brands or stores, at getting immediate sales response, or at targeting specific groups. Schultz proposes that television broadcasters focus more specifically on customer retention. In order to help advertisers, broadcasters must create strategic alliances with direct marketers and learn exactly who are the viewers of a particular channel. The best customer is the one an advertiser already has, and television advertising can be vital to customer retention.

So far, however, broadcasters have not been too receptive to Schultz's predictions. Just as ratings services continue to segment the viewers in the same old way, broadcasters continue to attract viewers according to group membership rather than actual buying preferences. In order to understand how the system got to be the way it is, we will provide a brief history of the ratings business.

BROADCAST AUDIENCE MEASUREMENT

Measurement of broadcast audiences evolved from program ratings for radio networks in the 1930s.[27] Nielsen Media Research emerged in the 1950s as the dominant force in television measurement; it employed an *audimeter* attached to the television sets of 1,200 homes across the United States. The audimeter passively recorded data about channel selection. Because meters are installed in randomly selected homes, the measurement is statistically generalizable to all homes with televisions sets.

The original audimeter only recorded the program viewing of a single television set. The audience composition was still self-reported for each home. By the 1980s, Nielsen and its competitors AGB and Arbitron began using more sophisticated devices that recorded the age and sex of viewers by making audience members log onto an interactive system that required them periodically to press buttons on a handheld *peoplemeter.*

By the 1990s the national audience sample had grown to 5,000 homes in order to facilitate measurement of increasingly smaller audiences of each network or channel. Nielsen pays its sample households $50 to install the meter and offers inexpensive gifts from a catalog for continued participation. Viewing is measured from minute to minute by the meter, and is quite accurate as long as the viewers correctly operate the buttons. One problem is that younger children often do not press the buttons on the peoplemeter.

In 1994 Nielsen became the sole source for audience measurement of television viewing when Arbitron returned to being a radio-only service. In the late 1990s, Nielsen introduced innovations such as the AP Meter, which combines the active features of the peoplemeter with the passive system of the audimeter.

The national ratings are published in three different forms: overnights, pocketpieces, and MNA reports. As the name suggests, *overnights* are reports released each morning based on the previous night's prime-time programming as measured in very large cities like New York, Los Angeles, and Chicago. *Pocketpieces* are published every two weeks and contain information based on the entire national sample. Because some smaller markets do not have equal representation among the various networks, the *Multi-Network Area (MNA)* report gathers viewing information from the seventy largest television markets.

At the local level, ratings data is collected in a different manner. Using a combination of meters and self-report diaries, Nielsen measures all television stations four times per year (November, February, May, and July) during one-month periods known as *sweeps.* The results for each market are published in a ratings book that shows the audience size and demographic composition by time period, by program title, and by groups of people.

In all but the top thirty-five markets in which meters are used, Nielsen distributes diaries to a random sample of viewers. Audience members log their viewing in their diaries on a continuing basis over the week. Some participants occasionally neglect their chore and then mentally reconstruct several days of viewing just before the book is scheduled to be mailed back to Nielsen. For their trouble, diary keepers receive a token payment.

In the large metered cities, Nielsen must find homes in which the residents are willing to use the peoplemeter handheld devices to record their television viewing. In the past, Nielsen had disappointing cooperation rates, with only half of the homes approached to accept the peoplemeter actually agreeing to participate. Responding to criticism and threats of competition, Nielsen improved its data collection system and cooperation rates in the second half of the 1990s.

The cost for audience measurement is borne by the stations, each paying between $10,000 and $1 million annually for the service. Advertising agencies are the primary users of the data, but because they do not directly benefit from the measurement process their cost for ratings information is minimal.

Several limitations constrain the ratings system, in addition to the operational problems indicated earlier. The size of a given sample for a particular market is often too small to measure accurately increasingly smaller amounts of viewing. Years ago, when there were only three networks and few competitors, the size of the sample was adequate for simple measurement. Today, the cost of increasing the number of viewers in a sample has made audience measurement an expensive necessity for networks and television stations.

Another problem is achieving ethnic and demographic representativeness within a sample. Despite the questionable practice of weighting the sample to favor underrepresented groups, the ratings companies continue to struggle with *skewed* samples. Completely unrepresented are groups that are not allowed to participate in the viewing sample: people in hotels, offices, hospitals, dormitories, military barracks, and other non-home settings. Out-of-home viewing represents 4 percent of all viewing. Because college dorm viewers are eliminated, measurement of late-night viewing is skewed toward shows like *Nightline* and away from *Late Night with David Letterman.*

Activities by the stations themselves can also bias the measurement of television viewing. When a local news program features a viewer contest during a *ratings period,* the size of the audience can be inflated. This practice, called *hypoing,* is discouraged by Nielsen, but is still a problem.

RATINGS TERMINOLOGY

The measurement of audiences is often referred to as "the ratings," but the actual meaning of a rating point is more complex. A program *rating* refers to the total number of homes (or sometimes, people) tuned to a particular television channel during a given time period, expressed as a percentage of the entire universe of television homes, regardless of whether all those homes are using their television sets at a given time. It is an estimate that can be readily converted into the number of homes.

For example, there were 98 million television homes by Nielsen's estimate in 1997. A rating of 1.0 thus represents 1 percent of all the homes, or 980,000 homes. Each rating point is worth nearly one million homes. Advertisers, of course, are very interested in how many homes are exposed to their messages. If a commercial runs in a program with a rating of 20.0, then roughly 20 million (19.6 million in 1997) homes may have watched the advertisement, if the viewers were paying close attention. The cost-per-thousand homes reached (CPM) is calculated by dividing the cost of the commercial by the number of homes reached in units of 1,000. For example, if a program reached 20 million homes and the commercial cost $400,000 to air, the cost per thousand would be calculated as follows:

$$\frac{\$400,000 \text{ COST OF COMMERCIAL}}{20,000 \text{ UNITS OF 1,000 HOMES}} = \$20 \text{ COST PER THOUSAND}^{(\text{CPM})}$$

If the same advertiser buys five commercials in different programs, each with a 20 rating, the gross ratings points (GRPs) equal 100. Advertising agencies often express the goal of a campaign as reaching several hundred ratings points to garner sufficient exposures to be persuasively effective. Not many television shows attract 20 percent of the potential audience in a single instance, so many more than five commercials are needed to reach 100 ratings points.

Although prime-time programs before 1980 routinely attracted 20 ratings, the cutoff for deeming a show successful has slid considerably with the onslaught of competing cable channels and home video options. In the mid-1990s, the three major networks sought a 12 rating as the minimum prime-time rating, and Fox struggled to stay in the double digits. To give some perspective to the audience size of a 12 rating, remember that popular game shows that precede prime time (e.g., *Wheel of Fortune*) often attract an 11 rating in a given market.

Ratings are different for the cable industry. Instead of creating a percentage based on the total universe of television homes, Nielsen calculates cable ratings against the total universe of cable-subscribing households. Broadcasters do not agree that the yardstick should change for its multichannel competitors, but the ratings services generally report the size of the audience according to the wishes of the ultimate customer for the ratings report.

The time period itself receives a rating, too. The numbers of rating points for all programs for a given point in time (including fractions thereof) are totaled into estimates of all viewing, called *homes using television (HUT)*. Each moment of the day has a HUT level that fluctuates as television sets are turned on and off. The individual program rating is always less than the HUT level. For example, one program with a 20 rating competes with another show with a 10 rating, another with a 7 rating, and a group of channels accounting for the remaining 2 rating points, for a grand HUT total of 39 rating points. Programs that run in prime time typically reach only 59 percent of all television homes because not all homes are using television in the evening hours. A HUT level of 59, however, is the peak of viewing during the typical day. By 11:30 P.M. Eastern/Pacific Time, the HUT level slips to 24, or about 24 percent of the potential homes.

Programming executives are less concerned with increasing the actual number of homes tuned to their shows than with maximizing the competitive advantage of one show against another, regardless of HUT level. Thus, a program shown at 4 A.M. may only attract a 3.0 rating, but if the HUT level is 6.0 in the wee hours of the morning, the program is reaching half, or 50 percent of the *available* homes. Despite the low rating, the show's producer is pleased because the program was strong enough to capture a huge share of the small universe of homes using television. The counterpart of a rating, then, is a *share,* which represents the total of homes tuned to a particular channel at a given time, as expressed as a percentage of only those homes using television (HUT). Shares are *always larger* than ratings, and when all program shares are summed for a time period, the total is 100. As explained earlier, when all ratings are summed, the total is the HUT level.

An easy way to distinguish rating, share, and HUT is to build a bisected triangle of the three concepts (R, S, H) with the R at the top:

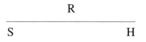

The R for rating is paramount because it is the pure percentage of homes so keenly sought by the all-important advertiser. In the preceding example, the triangle would be thus:

To calculate rating, cover the R with your finger, multiply S times H, and then divide by 100 to make the result a percentage. To calculate share, cover the S, divide R by H, and multiply by 100. To calculate HUT, cover the H, divide R by H, and multiply by 100.

Another way of measuring a channel's popularity is to count the number of different homes that tune in at least once in a single week's time. The measurement of this cumulative, unduplicated audience is called a *cume,* and is predominantly used in the radio industry. Cume ratings are also used widely in noncommercial television broadcasting in which shows run more than once in a given week, often to tiny audiences. When the total number of unduplicated viewers is added into a single cume rating, the programmer can more easily gauge the success of a repeated program. Cumes are occasionally used by commercial television broadcasters to track the appeal of their entire channel from sign-on to sign-off seven days per week.

Nielsen has divided up the entire country into distinct television markets, each known as a *Designated Market Area (DMA).* Each DMA is based on the number of television homes located in those counties that fall under the dominant influence of the local stations. In some cases, a county located between two major cities will alternate its inclusion in one of the two markets. Nielsen has 211 different markets listed in rank order by size. Some of these markets have hyphenated names (e.g., Flint–Saginaw–Bay City) to reflect the combination of different cities. Each name stands for the city of license for a different network affiliate or the cities that comprise a combined metropolitan area.

Each DMA is part of a larger Nielsen Survey Index (NSI) Area that contains the fringe counties of adjacent DMAs. The smallest geographic area used by Nielsen is a subset of some large DMA, and is called a Metro area. The Metro is most often used to designate the viewers that comprise the core of the DMA.

The entire system of DMAs, ratings, shares, HUTs, and cumes has been in place for over a half century without much innovation or change. Innovation has been thwarted by Nielsen's monopolistic hold on television audience measurement. Broadcasters would like to start a competing system, and at least one group owner made plans for a new ratings service in the late 1990s.

Another factor in the slow rate of change is the general satisfaction tacitly expressed by buyers and sellers, despite their intermittent complaints. Both groups know that the measurement system is flawed, but neither wants to disrupt the system to fix it. For example, the aging audience needs a better differentiation among plus-fifty viewing groups. Yet, the advertisers, their agencies, and the networks cling to demographic categories that represent increasingly smaller groups of viewers.[28] Even though the baby-boom generation continues to represent real buying power, the ratings companies lump older viewers into one big category.

Before leaving the subject of ratings, it is important to note that *error* is a necessary and often ignored component of audience measurement. Depending on the size of its various samples, Nielsen calculates a *standard error* for its ratings that should be, but almost never is, taken into account with the measurement of audiences. For example, the standard error for a given sample may affect the result by plus or minus 3 ratings points. In the case of two competing local news programs, a slim lead by one could just as easily have been a slim victory by the other. Nevertheless, virtually all television stations accept the numbers as gospel and make crucial decisions based on the ratings estimates, as if there were no error.

Another type of error is measurement error, which results from weaknesses of the data collection method or from imprecise diary-keeping, some of the same deficiencies we outlined earlier. It is wise to remember the slogan created by Arbitron and printed on the back of its ratings reports: "Remember, ratings are only estimates."

PROGRAM TESTING

As discussed in Chapter 6, the broadcast industry also conducts audience measurement on programming before a show makes it on the air. Concepts and program pilots are tested on groups of viewers using both quantitative and qualitative measurement. For example, a sample of viewers in a particular city may see a proposed program idea on a leased cable channel, followed by a survey of their opinions. A qualitative approach might entail a researcher intercepting shoppers at a mall and asking them to watch a television program. A subsequent focus group discussion would attempt to determine the participants' likes and dislikes.

The success of a program often depends on the popularity and appeal of the performers in the cast, measured by *TvQ scores.* TvQ scores gauge two aspects of potential performers: how recognizable or famous they are (familiarity) and how positively or negatively appealing they are (likability). Performers with high TvQ scores (e.g., Bill Cosby) are able to enhance a show's popularity almost regardless of other factors. When a comedian becomes popular through stand-up performances, for example, the network uses TvQ research to determine if that performer would be successful on a regularly scheduled program. Roseanne and Tim Allen had instant ratings success largely because their intense popularity as comedians preceded their appearance on a sitcom. Thus, both stars had strong TvQ scores when they started their series. Of course, their future scores would depend on their network series work.

Broadcast networks also conduct episode testing to determine if a particular idea for a current series will be acceptable to the audience. For example, networks might test the introduction of a new character into a story line, a new setting, or a new plot twist.

Even the promotional announcements *(promos)* that the network produces to run between shows are tested. Before committing millions of dollars to a brand-image theme for a promotional campaign, broadcasters conduct promo testing. This practice was modeled on the strategies advertisers employ for their commercials before placing them on the air.

CONCLUSION

The broadcast industry is very interested in audience measurement for two reasons. First, it needs to attract huge audiences, so the networks conduct research to improve their chances that a large number of viewers will enjoy their programming (spot-carriers). Second, the broadcast industry needs advertising revenue to pay the bills, so the stations and the networks purchase viewing data from Nielsen to prove that the spot-carriers were watched by the right demographic group in sufficient numbers to justify the price charged for commercials.

The commodity that is sold, the viewers' attention, is tentative at best. Advertisers have always known that the audience sometimes leaves the room or sometimes lets its attention waiver. Thus, the ratings process flourishes because of two questionable, but shared assumptions: that audience measurement is reliable and that viewers are attentive.

However, we must acknowledge the awesome power of television advertising to influence purchasing decisions, despite the vagaries of attention and measurement. In addition, advertiser-supported broadcasting has served the viewer quite well, offering attractive programming at no direct cost.

NOTES

[1]Raymond L. Carroll and Donald M. Davis, *Electronic Media Programming: Strategies and Decision Making,* (New York: McGraw-Hill, 1993), pp. 277–278.

[2]*USA Today,* April 1, 1996.

[3]Blayne Cutler, "Where Does the Free Time Go?" *American Demographics,* November 1990, pp. 36–39.

[4]Jim Spring, "Exercising the Brain," *American Demographics,* October 1993, pp. 56–59.

[5]Jim Spring, "Seven Days of Play," *American Demographics,* March 1993, pp. 50–53.

[6]John P. Robinson, "Quitting Time," *American Demographics,* May 1991, pp. 34–36.

[7]John P. Robinson, "I Love My TV," *American Demographics,* September 1990, pp. 24–27.

[8]Sydney W. Head, Christopher H. Sterling, and Lemuel B. Scholfield, *Broadcasting in America: A Survey of Electronic Media,* (Boston: Houghton Mifflin, 1994).

[9]V. Carter Broach, Jr., Thomas, J. Page, Jr., and R. Dale Wilson, "Television Programming and Its Influence on Viewers' Perceptions of Commercials: The Role of Program Arousal and Pleasantness," *Journal of Advertising,* 24(4), 1995, pp. 45–54.

[10]Kenneth R. Lord and Robert E. Burnkrant, "Attention Versus Distraction: The Interactive Effect of Program Involvement and Attentional Devices on Commercial Processing," *Journal of Advertising,* 22(1), 1993, pp. 47–60.

[11]Dean M. Krugman, Glen T. Cameron, and Candace McKearney White, "Visual Attention to Programming and Commercials: The Use of In-Home Observations," *Journal of Advertising,* 24(1), 1995, pp. 1–12.

[12]Krugman, Cameron, and White, op. cit., p. 10.

[13]Ron Lawrence, "The Battle for Attention," *Marketing & Media Decisions,* 24(2), 1989, pp. 80–84.

[14]Avery M. Abernethy, "Television Exposure: Programs vs. Advertising," *Current Issues & Research in Advertising,* 13, 1991, pp. 61–78.

[15]James R. Walker and Robert V. Bellamy, Jr., "Gratifications of Grazing: An Exploratory Study of Remote Control Use," *Journalism Quarterly,* 63, 1991, pp. 422–431.

[16]David Lachenbruch, "Commercial-Killing VCR," *Electronics Now,* April 1995, p. 89.

[17]Andrew Marton, "Ad Makers Zap Back," *Channels,* September 1989, pp. 30–31.

[18]Marcia Mogelonsky, "Coping with Channel Surfers," *American Demographics,* December 1995, pp. 13–15.

[19]Ashok Pahwa, "Boom Generation More Receptive to Quality TV Ads," *Marketing News,* September, 1990, pp. 8, 17.

[20]Fred S. Zufryden James H. Pedrick, and Avu Sankaralingam, "Zapping and Its Impact on Brand Purchase Behavior," *Journal of Advertising Research,* 33(1), 1993, pp. 58–66.

[21]Betsy Frank, "And Now a Word From Our. . . ZAP," *Marketing and Media Decisions,* July, 1984, pp. 162–166.

[22]John J. Cronin and Nancy E. Menelly, "Discrimination vs. Avoidance: 'Zipping' of Television Commercials," *Journal of Advertising,* 21(2), 1992, pp. 1–7.

[23]Patricia A. Stout and Benedicta L. Burda, "Zipped Commercials: Are They Effective?" *Journal of Advertising,* 18(4), 1989, pp. 23–32.

[24]Sandra E. Moriarty and Shu-Ling Everett, "Commercial Breaks: A Viewing Behavior Study," *Journalism Quarterly,* 71(2), 1989, pp. 346–355.

[25]Dave Vedehra, "Viewers Report Fewer Negative Responses to Commercials," *Advertising Age,* March 4, 1994, p. 20.

[26]Don E. Schultz, "Is Television Advertising Obsolete?" A presentation made to the NAB Management Development Seminar for Television Executives, Northwestern University, July 1992.

[27]This portion of the chapter is indebted to three sources: Douglas A. Ferguson, Timothy P. Meyer, and Susan T. Eastman, "Program and Audience Research," in *Broadcast/Cable Programming: Strategies and Practices* (5th ed.), eds. Susan T. Eastman and Douglas A. Ferguson, (Belmont, CA: Wadsworth, 1997), pp. 32–65; James Webster and Lawrence W. Lichty, *Ratings Analysis: Theory and Practice*, (Hillsdale, N.J.: Erlbaum, 1991); and Roger D. Wimmer and Joseph R. Dominick, *Mass Media Research: An Introduction* (4th ed.), (Belmont, CA: Wadsworth, 1994).

[28]Vicki Thomas and David B. Wolfe, "Why Won't Television Grow Up?" *American Demographics,* May 1995, pp. 24–29.

8

Public Television: The Struggle for an Alternative

BY *JOHN F. LONG*
California State University, Chico

INTRODUCTION

Public television emerges from values quite different from those that support the commercial broadcasting system discussed in the preceding chapters. The industry did not grow from the assumptions of the marketplace, with its imperative to enhance the corporate bottom line. Rather, it was grounded in cultural ideals, an educational mission, and the spirit of social debate. Programming decisions for public television were not made to achieve high audience ratings. Instead, program directors developed their schedules by identifying specialized audiences not readily served by commercial broadcasting. The lofty goals of public television, combined with unstable monetary support and political pressure, produced a volatile history and provide the substance for continued controversy.

While some criticize public television for its liberal bias, others contend that it is too sensitive to pressures from government and corporate supporters rendering its programming safe and bland. Recent critics portray the industry as an entitlement for the tastes of cultural elites, while supporters contend it remains a necessary alternative to commercial television's mass appeal programming.

The severity of criticism leveled at public broadcasting has varied with prevailing social and political conditions. For periods of its history, public television has

135

received substantial external support, even while experiencing severe internal strife. At other points, it has been soundly condemned even by those who acknowledge that it brings valuable programming to the airwaves. As an industry, it is sometimes innovative and dynamic, and at other times has been reactionary and static. Public television's fluid structure has been shaped by limited resources and forceful personalities.

We will examine the evolution of public television from the beginning of educational radio, which provided the noncommercial structure for the medium. We will describe the Ford Foundation's significant contribution and the development of the *Corporation for Public Broadcasting (CPB)*. We will discuss the chartering of the *Public Broadcasting Service (PBS)* and document the power struggles among PBS, CPB, and congress. Next, we will place in perspective the programming dilemmas created by the Nixon administration's partisan politics, which threatened funding for public television. Further, we will review the litany of conservative attacks during the 1980s and the structural changes in public broadcasting as it faced new economic realities. Finally, we will consider the trend toward privatization of public television and the effects of recent technological advances on the industry.

EARLY EDUCATIONAL BROADCASTING

Like commercial television, public television evolved from radio. Unlike commercial broadcasting, *noncommercial broadcasting* developed from many disparate entities, each with its own agenda and each providing both unique input and expertise. This loosely structured alliance, as opposed to commercial broadcasting's strong centralization of power, remained a trademark for public broadcasting throughout its development.

The inspiration for educational broadcasting came from Midwestern land grant colleges. With sparse populations located substantial distances from university centers, radio became the means to provide rural populations with academic programs. These "schools of the air" operated autonomously from the mid-1920s through the 1930s with varied success.[1]

In the 1920s, then Secretary of Commerce Herbert Hoover assembled a series of radio conferences that would set the tone for the future of broadcasting. Conferees who represented educational institutions recognized that they shared concerns and organized the *Association of College and University Broadcasting Stations (ACUBS)*. Later, this organization petitioned governors to support legislation reserving some channels for noncommercial or educational use. However, the Federal Radio Commission (FRC), formed in 1927 to regulate radio, and commercial users showed little sympathy for these channel requests.[2]

In an effort to expand its membership base and power, the ACUBS reorganized in 1934 to become the *National Association of Educational Broadcasters (NAEB)*.[3] This opened the association to other noncommercial entities, including those leasing time from commercial outlets. However, NAEB could do little program-sharing at the national level, relegating most programming to local production, which was expensive and often second rate. Clearly, some form of network was necessary if educational broadcasting was to prosper.

Although the creation of the NAEB provided a stronger national organization for educational radio, the issue of the medium's continued existence remained in the forefront of debate. The *National Committee on Education by Radio (NCER)* was formed as a lobby group for the traditional educational establishment.[4] In 1935, the NCER's policies provoked the Federal Communications Commission, which had replaced the old Federal Radio Commission, to act on the requirements of the Communication Act of 1934 that some radio frequencies be assigned to education. In deference to the NCER, the FCC in 1935 established the *Federal Radio Education Committee (FREC)* to integrate educators into the larger framework of U.S. broadcasting. Driven by NAEB interests, FREC's recommendations compelled the FCC in 1938 to reserve five channels for educational radio.[5]

As the new medium of FM radio emerged in the 1930s and 1940s, the NAEB pressed for FM channel reservations. The FCC responded by holding hearings that included testimony from NAEB, U.S. Office of Education, and NEA sources. In 1945, the FCC rewarded the NAEB's efforts, reserving twenty channels on the FM band specifically for noncommercial use. In addition, the commission mandated the construction of a nationwide allocation table, securing noncommercial radio frequencies in most U.S. markets. These decisions set important precedents that would shape the future of noncommercial television.[6]

EMERGENCE OF EDUCATIONAL TELEVISION

By the 1948 freeze on television frequencies (see Chapter 2), the NAEB rank and file considered themselves justifiably victorious. NAEB membership was growing and the organization had acquired a federally mandated reserve of FM radio frequencies to allow continued growth. But as the battle for television channels began, internal conflict over turf and tactics was leading to fragmentation in the NAEB's ranks. Nonetheless, someone would have to spearhead educational broadcasting's expansion into television, or the medium would quickly and forever be lost to commercial venture.

One NAEB faction proposed a model of spectral allocation for television that was similar to the allocation for FM radio. Ten adjacent channels would be sought in the UHF spectrum. Another NAEB faction, including FCC Commissioner Hennock, the NEA, and the U.S. Office of Education, took a more aggressive stance in demanding portions of both the UHF and VHF spectrum. Still other factions within educational broadcasting questioned the viability of "noncommercial" television. Some station personnel felt that some commercialism would help support the overall educational mission of a station. Then, the critical debate over the future of educational television was joined by two other educational television support organizations: the *Ford Foundation* and the *Joint Committee on Educational Television (JCET)*.[7]

THE FORD FOUNDATION

Established in 1936, the *Ford Foundation* had nothing to do with early educational broadcasting, but its charter was broad enough to include broadcasting, and it eventually granted hundreds of millions of dollars to educational broadcasting. Without funding from this philanthropic organization, educational television would not have been capable of protecting its interests or fostering its own growth.

The Ford Foundation was instrumental in providing an initial structure for the educational television industry. The Foundation promoted a model of decentralized control for its various projects, and identified school instruction and adult education as primary issues of concern. In 1951, the Ford Foundation established two corresponding organizations to fund independently: in-school and adult education projects. This decision was based on the belief that educational television could serve the larger audience and the altruistic goal of improving social conditions on a "global scale."[8]

Immediately, the Ford Foundation charted a course of action to weave educational programming into U.S. television. Its goals included reserving channels for education, constructing stations, and creating a national center for exchange of ideas and programs. The plan called for soliciting monetary support from agencies already seeking these goals and for creating agencies that would be charged with carrying out these tasks.[9]

JOINT COMMITTEE ON EDUCATIONAL TELEVISION

The Joint Committee on Educational Television (JCET) held its first meeting in 1950. It included all parties with a stake in educational television: NEA, NAEB, the U.S. Office of Education, and the National Association of State Universities. The result was a unified position, and JCET's proposal to the FCC regarding channel reservation and the noncommercial status of educational television stations. The JCET was so successful in its petitioning efforts that it became a permanent body in 1951. Its paid staff vigorously assisted educational stations in their organizational efforts and legal affairs and actively represented the interests of educational television before the FCC.

The influence of JCET was especially critical in 1951 when the FCC proposed an initial channel reservation for educational television. Commissioner Frieda Hennock argued that the proposed allocations for educational television were too limited and the JCET had provided firm evidence that more channels would be required to meet the nation's needs. The impact of JCET was realized with the issuance of the Sixth Report and Order, which reserved spectrum space for 242 educational television stations distributed across the nation. The document also embraced the ideal of the Ford Foundation that national education, not merely audience size, should be the measure of educational television's success.[10]

POST-FREEZE GROWTH AND DEVELOPMENT

The FCC had made clear to the educational community that these reserved frequency allotments could not remain dormant. The commission wanted evidence of use, or the channels might be reassigned to the commercial sector.[11] With the philanthropic cooperation of the Ford Foundation, and the support of interest groups such as NAEB and JCET, the FCC remained satisfied with the growth of this new industry.

During the 1948–1952 freeze on new television station construction, the Ford Foundation realized that educational broadcasting would best proliferate if there were a concentration of resources, particularly money for quality programming. In December 1952, key educators and business executives met to form the *Educational Television and Radio Center (ETRC)*. It functioned under the watchful eye of the *Fund for Adult Education (FAE)* with the express purpose of facilitating the sharing of productions among educational television stations. Moreover, it existed to promote creative activities both for scripting and station interconnection. Notably, it was not to engage in the production of any broadcast programs.

Under the direction of Harry Newburn, ETRC fulfilled its goals of networking by providing seven hours of weekly programming to thirty stations. By 1958, Newburn had been replaced by John F. White, a dynamic visionary and administrator. White expanded the scope and direction of ETRC, first by relocating the organization to New York City and then by renaming the organization the *National Educational Television and Radio Center (NETRC)*. During White's tenure, the quality of programming soared, competing with that of commercial television.[12]

Although NETRC accomplished much under the direction of White in the early 1960s, it had one major shortcoming. The Ford Foundation remained the only major supporter of educational television. In spite of rigorous fund-raising efforts within a well-conceived department of program development, adequate funds from outside sources could not always be found.

EDUCATIONAL TELEVISION FACILITIES ACT OF 1962

FCC Chairman Newton Minow's speech to the 1961 National Association of Broadcasters (NAB) condemning television as a "vast wasteland" combined with the fear of Soviet advances in education prompted the involvement of the federal government in educational television.[13] The *Educational Television Facilities Act of 1962* provided public television groups with matching funds to construct and equip noncommercial stations. In addition, the All Channels Receivers Act of the same year required all television sets to receive both VHF and UHF signals. As viewers bought new UHF-equipped receivers, the potential audience for the many UHF educational allotments made in 1952 increased. As a result of these two pieces of legislation, applications for noncommercial television licenses surged.

By 1963, the educational television industry was starting to take shape. Federal grants helped support facilities, and the Ford Foundation would continue *National Educational Television (NET)* programming support. But a professional production component seemed to be lacking. Filling this void became the responsibility of NAEB. In late 1963, NAEB formed the *Educational Television Stations* division *(ETS)* to address this problem. In addition, NAEB developed a program-sharing service for member stations.

CARNEGIE COMMISSION ON EDUCATIONAL TELEVISION

By the mid-1960s the Ford Foundation, headed by former Kennedy National Security Adviser, McGeorge Bundy, provided over $100 million to fund station activities. Emerging from its own NET, this organization was instrumental in establishing WNET in New York City. NET hired Fred Friendly, formerly of CBS News, to assist in laying the groundwork for a national network with programming designed to foster intellectual curiosity and critical thought.[14]

To survive, educational television funding, outside of the Ford Foundation, had to be secured. In late 1964, the First National Conference on the Long-Range Financing of Educational Television Stations was held, calling for a presidential commission to review this matter. In response, President Lyndon Johnson, in June 1965, announced the *Carnegie Commission on Educational Television (CCET).* Fourteen months later, the Carnegie Commission published its report, *Public Television: A Program for Action.*[15]

The Carnegie Commission report was instrumental in redirecting noncommercial broadcasting. It called for a television system that would be pervasive and securely financed. The CCET chose the word *public* as opposed to *educational* television to eliminate the perception that the system would be only "instructional" in philosophy. Public television would be an alternative to a commercial system tied to the need for high ratings. To implement this new system, the Commission recommended that congress create a Corporation for Public Television that would be a federally chartered, nonprofit, corporation.[16] The Commission also urged, unsuccessfully, a long-term federal funding effort, suggesting that funds be gathered from a 5 percent excise tax on television sets.[17]

CORPORATION FOR PUBLIC BROADCASTING

Following most of the recommendations from the Carnegie document, congress passed the *Public Broadcasting Act of 1967.* Although the Carnegie Commission had focused on television, congress also included public radio in the new legislation. The Act formed the *Corporation for Public Broadcasting (CPB),* a private corporation with a fifteen-member board selected from educational, cultural, and civic institutions, and the arts. Each year the board would elect a chairman and appoint a president. CPB was appropriated $9 million in federal funds for 1969.

CPB was charged with the aggressive development of a nationwide public broadcasting system by contracting for high-quality programming and live interconnection of stations, forming a true national network. In addition, CPB was expected to insulate public television from political pressure, serving as a bridge between government funding and program selection.[18]

PUBLIC BROADCASTING SERVICE

The 1967 Act provided that CPB would dispense federal funds for station operation, fund-raising, and program development, but could not own or operate stations or interconnections. For this reason, CPB created the *Public Broadcasting Service (PBS)* in 1969 to initiate a national network. Often termed a fourth network by industry observers, its visionaries were cautious in giving PBS any national agenda-setting power. Carnegie had strongly recommended that programming decisions come from local and regional groups. Public television's decentralized approach contrasted sharply with that of commercial television, which delegated the majority of programming decisions to strong national networks. It was this sense of local autonomy with a national presence that distinguished public television.

The incorporation of PBS was not an easy choice for CPB. The decision was influenced by other organizations that precipitated the creation of PBS. PBS was formed through joint agreement among CPB, local stations represented by NET, and ETS. Both CPB and, covertly, the Ford Foundation, reasoned that NET, the existing network, would be a poor choice for the new network because it was already the main producer of programming. Combining both interconnection and production under the same roof would concentrate too much power.[19] Moreover, station representatives felt that NET's programming was unresponsive to its membership and too controversial, especially given the election of a more conservative Republican administration in 1968. CPB also maintained that NET was already in a stronger position than itself, and could usurp control over station operations. As a result, PBS was formed, but with a myriad of questions as to its role. PBS was not exactly a CPB subsidiary, nor was it an organization acting at the behest of stations. It would be three years before its role was clarified.[20]

During its first year of operation, PBS was limited to station coordination activities and legal oversight of program content. Programming was supported by large *block grants* to major production centers such as KQED in San Francisco and NET. These production centers were responsible for programming decisions. However, CPB and PBS had become involved in selecting and prioritizing programming by late 1970. PBS developed guidelines, or "Standards and Practices," regarding controversial subject matter and attempted to invoke control by prebroadcast screenings. Production centers and station collectives saw this CPB–PBS coalition as a threat to the decentralized public television proposed by the Carnegie Commission.

During PBS's second season of operation, conflict over content control and other internal dissension mounted. The CPB–PBS relation was further strained when liberals criticized the CPB for submitting to government pressure, while conservatives criticized its inability to take control of programming decisions.[21] Finally, Arthur Singer, involved in organizing the Carnegie Commission, complained that public broadcasting had become far too centralized, with little autonomy at the local level.[22]

To make matters worse, a divisive struggle was developing between the Office of Telecommunication Policy (OTP) and the CPB. Clay Whitehead, chair of OTP, representing the Nixon administration, wanted more local control as a condition of any long-range funding. Whitehead also complained that PBS reporter Sander Vanocur (formerly of CBS and a friend of the Kennedys) was biased against President Nixon. CPB president John Macy explained that CPB only provided funds for production centers, and could not control policy. As a result, the OTP withdrew any tentative plans it had for long-range financing.

Whitehead again made his presence felt in an historic address to the NAEB convention in October 1971. He recommended that congress appropriate funds directly to stations to preserve their autonomy. He also claimed that news and public affairs programming was biased, and that there would be no long-term financing until public broadcasting became what the Nixon administration wanted.[23]

Under pressure from commercial broadcasters, who were experiencing increased competition from PBS, Nixon vetoed a two-year funding bill for CPB on June 30, 1972. The climate was right for such a move as it would serve to placate commercial interests during an election year and simultaneously send a message of contempt for liberal programming left over from Johnson's "Great Society."[24]

After the veto, PBS and NAEB sharply criticized the Nixon administration. CPB nearly disintegrated. John Macy resigned and the board reorganized with Republican leadership. Henry Loomis, formerly deputy director of the United States Information Agency (USIA), took over Macy's position as CPB president. Former Congressman Thomas Curtis (R–Missouri) became chair. With this change in CPB's political orientation, Nixon signed a compromise funding bill.

In one week's time CPB announced plans to make all program decisions. The new policy direction forced PBS into a hostile posture toward CPB. CPB had, seemingly, usurped PBS power, forcing television stations to seek alternative funding.

CPB contradicted its own mandate by centralizing decisions as opposed to encouraging a decentralized system.[25]

Prior to the breakdown of CPB–PBS relations, Ralph Rogers, a Texas industrialist and chairman of the board of KERA–TV in Dallas, anticipated the need for long-range funding. In concert with the Ford Foundation, and the ETS of NAEB, he entered into stewardship of the National Coordinating Committee of Governing Board Chairmen.[26] He wanted the organization to find support for federal funds and share fund-raising ideas at the local level. More importantly, he would devise an organizational scheme that would place PBS in a strong bargaining position and ally it with local stations and communities.

In March 1973, the existing PBS structure was scrapped and replaced by a merger of three existing organizations, namely ETS of NAEB, the National Coordinating Committee of Governing Board Chairmen, and the original PBS. The new structure established an elected board of governors made up of laypeople from the boards of local television stations and a PBS board of managers comprised of and elected by television station managers.[27] This alliance quelled criticism by CPB that PBS control was out of the hands of the stations, thus providing a unified front in continued negotiation.

By May 1973, a CPB–PBS "Partnership Agreement" had been achieved. Motivated in part to secure a $130 million two-year funding bill passed by the Senate weeks earlier, this was, in reality, only a working truce. The agreement gave CPB the right to decide which PBS programs it would fund, and it also established a committee to resolve issues of programming balance and objectivity. Finally, it included agreements to review partnerships at specified intervals. PBS had not been made institutionally free, nor did the constituents necessarily abide by the 1973 provisions. With federal funds hanging in the balance, PBS and CPB managed to exhibit a facade of cooperation. Short-term federal funding had once more been allocated to public broadcasting.

LONG-RANGE FINANCING FOR PUBLIC TELEVISION

The primary issue still unresolved was that of long-term funding. Without this support, there would be no insulation from the political arena, a warning strongly conveyed in the original Carnegie report. A Task Force on Long-Range Financing had been organized in spring of 1972 under the direction of Joseph D. Hughes, a CPB board member. This committee studied a substantial array of funding modes, such as a tax on advertising revenue, excise taxes on telephone use, and even a receiver license fee like the one used to support the British Broadcasting Corporation (BBC). The Task Force on Long-Range Financing estimated that public broadcasting would need $475 million to operate annually. Should federal support reach the rate of 30 to 50 percent, it would require about $200 million.[28]

In September 1973, the CPB submitted the task force report. The committee recommended that funding levels be for no less than five years, that matching funds for nonfederal support should be made by the CPB, and that congress make funds available for broadcasting facilities.

At this juncture, the Nixon administration was reeling from Watergate and needed to change its image. Clay Whitehead, still director of OTP, revised the committee's findings to include a smaller ratio of matching funds, and none for facilities development. By early 1974, the bill was sent to President Nixon for his perusal. The President rejected Whitehead's recommendation and refused to support the administration's own funding bill. According to Whitehead, Nixon was retaliating for PBS's decision to carry gavel-to-gavel coverage of the Watergate hearings, and its proclamation that it would do the same for any impeachment proceedings.[29] Thus, a more stable funding base for public television was lost due to an act of presidential vengeance.

Whitehead appealed the president's decision through White House Chief of Staff Alexander Haig. Even though Haig supported it, President Nixon rejected the funding bill a second time. In a desperate attempt, Whitehead leaked the story to the *New York Times,* which published an account of Nixon's rejecting the OTP funding bill. The *Wall Street Journal,* a former administration supporter, printed editorial criticisms of the president, while extolling the virtues of public television.[30]

The leak to the *Times* had the intended effect. On July 11, the White House announced approval of the five-year funding measure. Whitehead, realizing he had to resign, stayed on until he could get the administration's support on record by testifying before the Senate Communications Subcommittee. With the draft legislation on Capitol Hill, CPB was put on notice by congress that there was an early September deadline for allocation of FY 1976 and beyond. In August, Senator Pastore introduced legislation and began hearings on the Public Broadcasting Act of 1974. Congress, the FCC, and station representatives all testified in support of the legislation.[31]

With President Nixon's resignation, President Ford submitted a CPB funding bill to congress for an initial $70 million, increasing to $100 million by 1981. After a year-and-a-half of debate and endless compromises, the Public Broadcasting Financing Act of 1975 was signed into law on December 31, 1975. Although higher funding levels were achieved through lobbying efforts, only a three-year deal was made. As in years past, CPB would be forced to solicit congress annually for funding. Thus, the automatic entitlement, which public broadcasting wanted, would not materialize.

STATION PROGRAM COOPERATIVE

In 1972, Hartford Gunn, former PBS President, proposed a "market plan" that later would become the *Station Program Cooperative (SPC).* This new funding strategy was instrumental in bringing to public television quality programs, including *Sesame Street, Nova, American Playhouse, The MacNeil/Lehrer News Hour,* and *Great Performances.* The Station Program Cooperative allowed public television stations to participate in the funding of programs they chose to broadcast. In effect, the SPC rejuvenated public broadcasting's commitment to localism. The SPC increased the decentralization of program decision-making, reducing criticism that PBS controlled the national schedule. Stations utilized *Community Service Grants* to purchase programming from PBS. This gave PBS a prominent national role, but programming decisions were strongly influenced by local licensees.

A second round of SPC initiatives met with CPB resistance. SPC announced plans to enter program development unilaterally, without PBS consent, by funding pilot programs that focused on minority issues. Meanwhile, CPB had announced plans to phase out direct funding to SPC and support local stations with *Community Service Grants,* thus spelling certain death for SPC. CPB recanted, due largely to press criticism, and approved a second year at a $5 million level, if the stations would contribute $8 million.[32]

In 1976, Larry Grossman replaced Hartford Gunn at PBS and its relationship with CPB changed slightly. Grossman publicly acknowledged the apparent duplications between CPB and PBS, calling for a joint programming operation. Flexing its muscle, CPB lessened support for SPC's third year to $3 million for 1977 and offered no support beyond that funding year.

CARNEGIE II

In June, 1977 the Carnegie Corporation announced it was about to create another commission to study the past ten years of public broadcasting, and to contemplate the system's future. This Carnegie Commission on the Future of Public Broadcasting (known as *Carnegie II*) studied public radio and television for a year-and-a-half and published its recommendations in the 1979 book, *A Public Trust.*[33]

This report was highly critical of the way CPB had operated, especially its inability to provide leadership and insulation from political sources. It recommended enhanced federal funding and a significant change in the CPB. In effect, the CPB would be eliminated and replaced by a Presidentially appointed nine-member Public Telecommunications Trust (PTT), responsible for research, planning, and evaluation. Programming would be the responsibility of a semi-autonomous Program Service Department within PTT. Carnegie felt this new structure would provide adequate insulation from political influence.

By the time of Carnegie II, public television was a far different industry than it had been after the first Carnegie report. The key groups in public broadcasting (the Federal Government, private foundations, and reformers) shared a mutual mistrust. Despite Carnegie II's optimistic message, there was no grassroots organization, or major political coalition committed to public broadcasting.[34] In fact, congressional proposals for Communications Act revisions in 1978 and 1979 included reduced federal support for public broadcasting.

In conjunction with the Carnegie Report, two pieces of legislation were moved through Congress. In October 1978, the Public Telecommunications Act of 1978 was ratified, providing funding for 1981–1983. It is significant that the term *telecommunications* was used because it indicated that public broadcasting would be seen in the context of other technologies such as cable television, direct broadcast satellite (DBS), and multipoint distribution systems (MDS). Part of this act directed funds to new independent producers outside the established PBS "family." The post-Carnegie II era found new leadership at PBS with former FCC Chair, Newton Minow, assuming control. Because of PBS's complacency at the local level, four major regional networks developed, forming the Inter-Regional Council (IRC).[35]

CORPORATE UNDERWRITING

For the general public, the most controversial issue surrounding public television is that of government financing. However, other more subtle controversies emerged when funds were secured from commercial firms in the form of corporate underwriting. After 1975, when the government began to offer matching funds, this type of support became especially important. Corporate underwriting supported both national production centers and local stations through their Community Service Grants.

This alliance with the commercial sector has its roots in the early 1970s. The Nixon veto triggered a funding crisis for public television that was partially forestalled by another crisis: an explosive increase in oil prices. The oil companies were gathering windfall profits, which presented a severe public relations problem. To improve their image, the major oil companies increased support for "cultural" programming, while avoiding "public affairs" or "in-depth news" programming.[36] Although the FCC permitted only brief identifying announcements at the beginning and end of each program segment, critics began to refer to PBS as the new "Petroleum Broadcasting System." In response, one major underwriter, Mobil Oil, argued that its contributions to PBS were public-spirited and that it would be more economically sound to buy time on commercial television.[37]

In 1981, the Reagan administration came to Washington arguing that CPB again be abolished and funds for "liberal elitist" broadcasting be terminated. Overall, federal funds were cut by 25 percent with congress expecting the public to fill the funding gap. New FCC regulations allowed PBS to experiment with new forms of sponsor acknowledgment, so long as it was not inserted into program content. In addition, congress briefly rescinded the Communications Act's ban on advertising for public stations. It provided the *Temporary Commission on Alternative Financing for Public Telecommunications (TCAF)* to study the ramifications of commercial support. For fifteen months, ten public television stations advertised on a conditional basis. Legislation stipulated that the advertisements could not exceed two minutes, interrupt programs, or promote political or religious viewpoints. The experiment revealed no negative influences on viewing patterns, subscriber support, or other forms of systematic contribution. Moreover, there was no effect on programming or apparent control of programming by commercial supporters.[38] In spite of these findings, the 1983 TCAF report recommended that public television not become commercial.

In 1984, the Senate Communications Subcommittee continued debate on commercialism, which resulted in an FCC authorization for *enhanced underwriting*. These "almost commercials" could not interfere with programs, but could be marketed in thirty-second segments for two-and-one-half minutes between programs. The charge of "creeping commercialism" was supported by a proliferation of entertainment-based programming introduced to placate commercial sponsors.

Corporate underwriting clearly provides benefits to the sponsors. Herbert Schmertz, marketing director of Mobil Oil, explained that his company's support of *Masterpiece Theatre* allowed its viewers to feel "enriched and ennobled." He went on to point out that surveys suggested Mobil had become "the thinking man's gasoline."[39] Other corporate sponsors must have had similar audience experiences; between 1982 and 1991 seventeen major corporations provided at least $5 million to support public television programming. Among these were Aetna Life & Casualty, Ford Motor Company, IBM, Pepsi–Cola, and AT&T.[40] There was no clear pattern to the services or products offered by these companies; only the compelling desire for positive image, association, and visibility.

Sponsors also produce programs outside of public TV production centers. For instance, they offer conservative talk shows such as *One on One* (Pepsi–Cola), and *The McLaughlin Group* (GE) to local stations, usually at no cost. Financial shows such as *Wall Street Week* (Prudential–Bach, the Travelers) and *Nightly Business Report* (Digital Equipment Corporation) appear regularly on local stations. These programs are attractive to many stations because of their low cost to stations. These costs are subsidized by corporations that wish to have certain social and economic perspectives made public.[41]

Public television aggressively sought corporate sponsors after the Reagan federal funding cuts of the mid-1980s. As a result, market pressures played a major role in program development and production. In effect, programming was being designed to deliver upscale audiences under this new model of enhanced underwriting. But to deliver these audiences, programs had to appeal to those upscale audiences. Hence, diverse programming designed to serve special communities of viewers became noticeably absent. In its place, stations offered programming that maximized member support, a crucial element in the survival scenario. Viewers with high disposable incomes were targeted, precisely the same audiences sought by the commercial sector. The unfortunate criticism of public television for being "elitist" and laden with "snob appeal" is an artifact of this underfunding at the federal level. The narrow tailoring of programs to affluent audiences reflects a necessary survival strategy.

POLITICAL FUNDING ISSUES

Although the Reagan administration recommended abolishing CPB and cut funding 25 percent in 1981, public broadcasters were once again saved by the private sector. A gift of $750 million over fifteen years from Walter Annenberg, then the publisher of *TV Guide,* allowed CPB to expand its scope. These *Annenberg Foundation* funds were used to develop high-quality telecourses for college credit and general education. The money was also dedicated to other high-quality productions without corporate influence. However, even with this generous donation, increased membership drives, enhanced underwriting, and local government subsidy, it was clear that public television, to secure its position, would still have to rely on long-term federal funds.[42]

After the high-water funding mark of $172 million in federal funds in 1982, support for CPB fell to $137 million the following year. Charges of liberalism and elitism were used to justify these cuts. PBS aired *Vietnam: A Television History,* a 13-part documentary series, that presented the North Vietnamese in a favorable light. The conservative watchdog group, Accuracy in Media (AIM), even prepared a rebuttal. Under some pressure from the White House, PBS aired the program. More friction resulted from the 1986 broadcast of *The Africans.* This nine-part series had a clear anti-Western bias, supporting some of the activities of Libyan President Qaddafi. Inspired by the Reagan administration, Richard Brookhiser, CPB board member and editor of the conservative magazine, the *National Review,* suggested that CPB perform a scientific study to ascertain the leftward bias of PBS programming. However, PBS unanimously rejected the idea.[43]

In 1986, after two 1984 presidential vetoes, a three-year authorization bill for public broadcasting was signed. Appropriations were only for two years, until 1989. In 1988, a new authorization was passed through 1992, with appropriations, especially for facilities, falling well short of expectations. The passage of the Public Telecommunications Act of 1988 and the nonhostile Bush administration produced at least an acceptable environment for public broadcasting. A much-needed satellite replacement program (1991–1993) was included in the bill and supported by the president.

In spite of bipartisan congressional support, CPB, and public broadcasting in general, was not free to plan its future. Even though federal authorizations were increasing, often the appropriations were not fully funded. Each year, funding battles had to be fought, subjecting public broadcasters to the political agenda of the moment and giving them little reason to make long-range plans.

INDEPENDENT TELEVISION SERVICE

In 1988, Congress changed the structure of public television by creating the *Independent Television Service (ITVS).*[44] Previously, most programming funded by CPB was produced at one of the major production centers such as WGBH in Boston or KQED in San Francisco. During hearings before the 1987–1988 Subcommittee on Telecommunications and Finance, independent producers without direct ties to PBS or public stations argued they were not receiving funding to produce programs for PBS. The producers argued that federal funding must be reserved for programs that were outside the immediate programming priorities of stations, subscribers, and underwriters. To foster diversity and creativity, congress created the Independent Television Service to be administered by CPB.[45]

Legislation creating ITVS, with its $6 million three-year annual budget, also mandated funds for a consortium of minority producers. This required CPB to focus its resources on unserved audiences. The debate surrounding ITVS focused on redefining what public television is and how it should serve the public. The independents viewed this congressional action as a victory for minority voices and those who wanted to challenge the status quo. They would move public television away from the commercial market and into a new direction of public service.[46]

This new approach was politically timely. Supporters and professionals in public television were still reeling from Reagan administration attacks on content. Many in PBS felt that programming was becoming stale and apolitical. ITVS might provide a rich forum for discussion on important contemporary issues and, once more, democratize public television.

However, ITVS, with its propensity for innovative programs, was not without its critics. Conservatives blasted the controversial *Tongues Untied* for its portrayal of the gay community. Others, in particular the PBS old guard, criticized the quality of ITVS's productions, especially during its first two years. In spite of its initial rocky reception, ITVS productions have been honored by a host of organizations. An Academy Award nomination for Best Documentary *(For Better or For Worse)* and the American Library Association's Carnegie Medal of Excellence for Children's Video *(The Pool Party)* are only two of seventy-five notable ITVS awards. It has produced high-quality children's programming and highly acclaimed series targeted to minority audiences. ITVS continued to produce under CPB supervision through the 1995 season, with an annual budget of approximately $6 million.

STRUCTURAL CHANGES IN PBS

In the late 1980s, the Station Program Cooperative (SPC) was criticized by many producers, especially those outside of the major production loop. The major fault, critics claimed, was SPC's unwillingness to take risks. It had received a reputation for killing programs and not introducing new ones.

In 1990, in response to a federal task force report on the financial status of public television, CPB authorized PBS to replace SPC with a new model that stressed centralized executive authority. When PBS Executive Vice President Jennifer Lawson became public television's "programming czar," supervising a $100 million fund, public television began to reverse its course. The reason for the change was what many considered an East/West Coast bias in PBS's National Program Services.[47]

These regional biases were an artifact of the production structure. The major production sites, WGBH, WNET, and WETA, are located in Boston, New York, and Washington, D.C., respectively. From 1990–1993 these stations provided 73 percent of all programs to PBS's National Program Services.[48] It was Lawson's directive, with considerable political pressure from U.S. Senators Bob Dole and Jesse Helms, to diversify program sources extensively by gaining national programming through local station production resources. The new Chief Programming Executive, Lawson, called for substantial research in implementing this plan and for abandoning the SPC voting model that favored larger stations.

The timing of this transition proved optimal. WNET's production capability had been waning, leading to shutdowns of local production and loss of *The McNeil/ Lehrer News Hour.* WGBH was moving from production to multimedia, and WETA was seeking partnership agreements.[49] Other large community production centers, such as KQED (San Francisco), KCET (Los Angeles), and WQED (Pittsburgh), were cutting back because of decreases in local funding. The setting was perfect for a systematic reorganization.

POLITICAL VULNERABILITY

By late 1991, congressional conservatives introduced legislation to abolish CPB, and a Senate group led by Senate Minority Leader Bob Dole delayed three-year reauthorization for PBS. This action created substantial uproar at PBS; many stations publicly condemned the actions of the officials that supported these cuts. Dole argued that this reaction was contrary to public interest and, perhaps, illegal under the Communications Act of 1934. In June 1992, with appeals for accountability and "balance," opponents of public television called for a freeze on federal spending, pending further investigation.

However, the 1992 Congress, with a Democratic majority, was not without public television supporters. Many supporters, led by vice presidential candidate Al Gore, expressed high praise, particularly for PBS's educational programming. With this partisan support, the freeze was defeated, and the Public Telecommunications Act of 1992 was passed, authorizing funds for FY's 1994–1996, at $310, $375, and $425 million, respectively.[50]

But conservatives were able to impose two important riders on this authorization. First, the bill required the banning of indecent broadcasts. Second, it required that CPB review programs regularly for diversity, quality, objectivity and balance in reports submitted annually to the president and congress. These riders again illustrate CPB's inability to insulate public television from political interference.

BALANCE AND OBJECTIVITY

Realizing that questions of program balance and objectivity, although hard to define, would permeate the next funding round, CPB and PBS took precautionary measures through the 1993–1994 programming seasons. CPB President Richard Carlson tried to increase PBS's diversity by increasing funding for a minority program consortium. Each of the five consortium members, representing racial minorities, would receive $5 million apiece from various CPB funds. As part of the 1992 mandate, CPB initiated the Open to the Public project to gather data on programming balance through toll-free numbers and the Internet. It sponsored public forums and seminars throughout the United States to gain feedback on program objectivity. In response to critics, PBS focused much of its effort on children's educational programming. Then new President of PBS, Ervin Duggan, claimed that recent research indicated that viewers perceived PBS as fair and objective. Moreover, a recent Roper poll found *The MacNeil/Lehrer News Hour* to be the most credible evening newscast.[51]

In June 1994 authorization for FY's 1997–1999 was closely scrutinized in congress. Once more, advance funding, so vital for political insulation, was the heart of these discussions. The performance scorecard, mandated by the 1992 hearings, was central to the discussion. The leaders of PBS, CPB, and other public broadcasting organizations vigorously defended their activities and provided compliance data.[52]

CONGRESSIONAL ELECTIONS OF 1994

The specter of a Republican victory in both houses of congress and its effect on public television was hotly discussed in the trade press prior to the 1994 elections.[53] Most hypothesized that then-Senate Minority Leader Bob Dole, Rep. Richard Armey (R–Texas), and prospective House Speaker Newt Gingrich (R–Georgia) would lead a charge against continued support.

As predicted, by December 1994, new Speaker of the House Newt Gingrich had called for a "zeroing-out" of federal funding for CPB.[54] Working with new Senate Commerce Committee Chairman Larry Pressler (R–South Dakota), Gingrich called for privatization not only of CPB, but of the National Endowment for the Humanities, and the National Endowment for the Arts, arguing that their liberal "political twist" led to an imbalance in program standards. The new Republican congress was the most ominous threat to public television since Richard Nixon's vetoes of CPB funding.

The new congressional majority wasted no time. By January 4, 1995, a Republican committee introduced a bill to change the Communications Act of 1934 and repeal the statutory authority for CPB. PBS President Ervin Duggan denounced the move as an effort to kill noncommercial television rather than prioritize it. The rhetorical battle lines had formed, with the new congress accusing public broadcasting of being the mouthpiece of the liberal elite and an upper-class entitlement.

Supporters fought back at the grassroots level. Most at PBS realized that showcasing the network might be detrimental, and could even support Republican charges. Instead, they let individual stations tell their stories. WSKG highlighted its public service efforts on behalf of economic reform in Binghampton, New York. Kentucky Educational Television revealed that it was its commonwealth's only statewide emergency medium. WVMR in Dunmore, West Virginia noted that it provides the only local broadcast for its county. Such stories with strong human interest drew immediate press coverage. The approach strategically notified constituencies which, in turn, defused the agendas of their representatives.[55]

By late February, 1995, a professional campaign firm had established the Citizen's Committee for Public Broadcasting to coordinate local lobbying for full-funding measures. In early March, the group had organizers in twenty states, attempting to form coalitions with activists working in the arts and education.[56] Supported by consumers of public television, the organization hoped to make clear to politicians the risks of opposing funds for CPB, since this would likely be an issue in the 1996 elections.

In spite of an apparent groundswell of support for public television, the House Appropriations Committee initially approved CPB cuts of 15 percent, then of 30 percent for the next two years (1997–1998). Vice President Al Gore called the move an "all out attack" on the value of education and "part of a broad assault on programs that enrich the lives of our children."[57]

By late March of 1995, the House of Representatives had agreed on a plan rescinding by 15 percent FY 1996 appropriations to $265 million. For FY 1997, the House planned a 30 percent decrease to $221 million. Although the House rejected the far more radical Crane Amendment, calling for a 66 percent reduction in two years, House support for public television was still split along party lines. Republicans grounded their arguments in a gradual "glide path" to zero funding, allowing for development of alternative revenue streams. Democrats emotionally assailed the action as a vote against children and as an action against quality programming.[58]

However, once the House bill reached the Senate floor, the Senate Appropriations Committee had significantly reworked CPB cuts. The Committee froze funding at 1995 levels ($286 million) for the next two years. On April 6, the Senate unanimously approved the original Committee Report.[59] Although considerably more generous than the proposed House appropriations, the future funding of public television remained much in doubt because the Senate had suggested no allocations past 1997. Indeed, congress ordered the public broadcasting community to draft a plan for life after federal assistance.

COMPETING PLANS TO FUND PUBLIC BROADCASTING

By early May, 1995, two competing plans were submitted by two major proponents of the public broadcasting community. A joint plan constructed by four public broadcasting groups, *America's Public Television Stations (APTS), National Public Radio (NPR),* Public Broadcasting Service (PBS), and Public Radio International (PRI), recommended a three-part approach to make public broadcasters self-sufficient. At the heart of this plan was a Public Broadcasting Trust Fund that would provide, at least, a steady source of income without reliance on federal funding.

Financing this trust fund of approximately $4 billion became the most controversial part of the proposal. The trust fund would be financed through three major mechanisms. First, proceeds from the sale or lease of unused noncommercial spectrum space would go to the fund.[60] Second, a tax on the sale of commercial stations and part of a proposed spectrum fee for commercial broadcasters would add to the fund. In exchange for these contributions, the FCC would relieve commercial broadcasters of public interest obligations, including requirements for children's programming. Finally, a change in tax codes would allow for tax credits that encouraged private contributions to the trust fund.

While the Public Broadcasting Trust Fund plan was ambitious and comprehensive, it was not without its critics. The $4 billion trust fund was attacked as a remnant of President Johnson's Great Society. As expected, the strongest admonitions came from the National Association of Broadcasters. The NAB opposed the plan on the grounds that commercial broadcasters would be expected to assume the greatest financial responsibility for the support of public television.[61]

On the same day the Public Broadcasting Trust Fund plan reached the press, CPB President Richard Carlson took the CPB plan to the appropriation subcommittee. This set of recommendations, entitled *Common Sense for the Future,* was prepared by the New York-based investment bank firm, Lehman Brothers. Its strategy for achieving independence from federal funding was fundamentally different from the public broadcasting quartet's options. The crucial difference was CPB's claim that no combination of new revenue streams could fully replace current federal appropriation. Instead, the plan focused on cost-reduction measures. These included system-wide cost-reductions in the form of mergers and consolidations of licensees and joint operating agreements. In markets with multiple licensees, CPB would provide funding for only one television station, thus forcing consolidation of resources.

In short, the CPB analysis of new revenue sources led to one conclusion: Federal funding would need to be continued.

By design or not, these reports sent a host of disturbing messages to congress. The Lehman Brothers/CPB plan articulated a need to maintain federal funding. Otherwise, the noncommercial service, as it currently exists, would slowly dissipate. CPB's own data suggested that by 2000, with only a 40 percent reduction, sixty stations or 20 percent of the entire system would go dark.[62] With many of these stations serving the population of Republican constituencies, the political price was too high. The APTS/NPR/PBS/PRI report asserted with confidence that a Public Broadcasting Trust Fund would assure public television of solvency and meet the goals of the Carnegie II report. However, a large proportion of the trust fund would come from commercial broadcasters: a group with considerable influence over congress in an election year. The proposal for the Public Broadcasting Trust Fund languished.

NONPROFIT VERSUS NONCOMMERCIAL

With the proposed Public Broadcasting Trust Fund at an impasse and federal funding on an obvious decline, proponents of public television had to seek other revenue streams. Commercialism appeared to be the remaining alternative.

However, the Lehman Brothers/CPB report to Congress described the advertising approach as a money-loser because of the impact of taxes, lost donors, and production costs. Worse, it would create a situation in which stations in smaller markets, because of their smaller potential audience, could not provide services equal to larger market stations. Although advertising violates one of the core principles of public television, the prevailing political climate mandated consideration of a new set of commercial objectives.

One plan, drafted by a consortium of PBS affiliates, does not require all public stations to sell commercial time. Instead, it proposes that congress create a third class of licensee, the "community service" station. Commercials would not interrupt programs; they would only be run at the end of programs. To maintain this tax-free licensee status, these stations would have to reassign portions of their revenue to rural and small-market stations. This addresses some of the concerns articulated in the CPB report.

Creation of the "nonprofit" public television station is not without its critics. Steve Bass, general manager of WGBY in Springfield, argued that advertising would alter programming. To compete, public television would have to program for younger audiences, coveted by advertisers, not the older audience it now serves. In addition, *copyright fees* might explode. Because public television is noncommercial, national guilds provide rights at reduced costs. The entire cost structure for future and existing programs may increase dramatically if commercials become a reality.[63]

PBS-2

In early September 1995, the John and Mary Markle Foundation commissioned Larry Grossman, former PBS president, to conduct a feasibility study on an advertising-supported sister network for PBS. Grossman's model would provide for a national network, *PBS–2,* offering free programs to public television stations for six hours per week. PBS would sell the commercial time to support these programs and other programs that would have no commercial attachment. PBS stations would voluntarily participate and effectively become affiliates for this new service. The concept is similar to Britain's Channel 4, which is commercial but is chartered to serve diverse audiences. The study, examining revenue, legal, and political dimensions, was to be ready by early 1996.[64]

In the meantime, CPB commissioned a survey of various viewer groups concerning their reactions to increased commercialism. Surprisingly, all the surveyed groups favored an increase of commercial activity as a viable means to generate revenue. Most preferred alternative funding, such as videotape sales and other products. However, given a scenario of decreased federal funding, commercialism was considered an acceptable revenue source.[65]

FUNDING ISSUES, 1995–1996

In early summer of 1995, the initial fears that public television would be eliminated from federal funding had subsided, at least for the immediate future. But public broadcasting considered its recent struggles a stern warning. The industry must find alternatives to federal aid and recognize that funding levels will never reach past levels.

For years, station managers and PBS administrators have experienced decreasing federal funds for public television and have taken measures to replace the lost funding. A CPB report released in August 1996 indicated that 1995 operational revenues came from sources that were 82.4 percent nonfederal money. In addition 53 percent were from nontax-based sources. At this rate, many stations could absorb a "zeroing out" of federal funds in a few years, but doing so could affect the substance of public television. For example, federal funds provide developmental funds for program series. Many of these series are intended for underserved or rural audiences, not regular supporters. In addition, other federal agencies that contribute programming to PBS, such as the National Endowment for the Arts (NEA) and National Endowment for the Humanities (NEH), had suffered severe congressional cutbacks. Therefore, many industry observers argue that a bottom line of 15 percent federal funding represents a necessary cornerstone for public television.

CONCLUSION

Public television was rooted in the civic ideals of cultural and intellectual enlightenment. Early educational broadcasting organizations developed a structure for the delivery of noncommercial programming. The original Carnegie report affirmed the virtues of a system free from the requirement of delivering a large audience to advertisers. Public television was able to educate and inspire audiences and provide a forum for public debate. Despite its lofty goals, conflicts over internal control among public television groups have ignited with predictable regularity in this ever-evolving industry.

From its inception in 1967, noncommercial television was an experimental and an uncertain venture, especially in a capitalistic society. Its maiden voyage, launched during the "Great Society" period, met its first whirlpool of distress with the Nixon funding vetoes. During the Nixon years, public television's true role began to evolve. Continued support at the local level for children's programming and cultural affairs provided new missions for public television. However, CPB had to face the harsh reality that its funding would remain a political issue.

Each congress since 1968 has placed the future of public television in some jeopardy. The industry has been forced to change to appease the prevailing political forces. Still, through each of these episodes, public television has been able to redefine itself, uniquely serving audiences not served by commercial interests. This segment of the U.S. broadcasting industry has survived both because of, and in spite of, itself.

The activities of the 104th Congress have forced the public television community to evaluate its options. When all sources of federal subsidy are retracted the industry will have to change radically. Many allege that public television should survive in the prevailing policies of a free market economy. Others contend that the changes will lead to a demise of the last bastion of cultural dignity on the airwaves. The debate over funding seems never-ending. Given the recent history of public television, it seems ironic that at the creation of Public Broadcasting the Carnegie Commission would urge lawmakers to "free the Corporation from the highest degree from the annual governmental budgeting and appropriations procedures."

NOTES

[1]Paul Saettler, *A History of Instructional Technology* (New York: McGraw-Hill, 1968), p. 199.
[2]George H. Gibson, *Public Broadcasting, The Role of the Federal Government, 1912–76* (New York: Praeger Publishers, 1977), p. 6.
[3]Ibid., p. 29.

[4]Erik Barnouw, *A Tower in Babel, A History of Broadcasting in the United States, Volume I, to 1933* (New York: Oxford University Press, 1966), p. 261.

[5]Gibson, op. cit., pp. 33–35.

[6]Donald N. Wood and Donald G. Wylie, *Educational Telecommunications* (Belmont: Wadsworth Publishing, 1977), p. 31.

[7]Erik Barnouw, *The Golden Web, A History of Broadcasting in the United States, Volume II, 1933–1953* (New York: Oxford University Press, 1968), pp. 293–295.

[8]Gibson, op. cit., pp. 119–120.

[9]Ibid., p. 121.

[10]Barnouw, *The Golden Web*, p. 294.

[11]Paul A. Walker, "The Time to Act is Now," in Carrol V. Newsom (ed.), *A Television Policy for Education* (Washington, DC: American Council on Education, 1952), p. 31.

[12]Wood and Wylie, op. cit., p. 47.

[13]Erik Barnouw, *The Image Empire, A History of Broadcasting in the United States, Volume III, from 1953* (New York: Oxford University Press, 1970), pp. 196–198.

[14]Gibson, op. cit., p. 121.

[15]Ibid., p. 123.

[16]Carnegie Commission on Educational Television (New York: Bantam Books, 1967), p. 5.

[17]Ibid., p. 81.

[18]Gibson, op. cit., p. 133.

[19]Robert K. Avery and Robert Pepper, *The Politics of Interconnection: A History of Public Television at the National Level* (Washington, DC: NAEB, 1979).

[20]Ibid., p. 21.

[21]Ibid., p. 30.

[22]Gibson, op. cit., p. 174.

[23]Ibid., p. 175.

[24]Avery and Pepper, op. cit., p. 32.

[25]Ibid.

[26]Wood and Wylie, op. cit., p. 97.

[27]Ibid., p. 103.

[28]John Macy, Jr., *To Irrigate a Wasteland: The Struggle to Shape a Public Television System in the United States* (Berkeley: University of California Press, 1974), p. 110.

[29]David M. Stone, *Nixon and the Politics of Public Television* (New York: Garland Publishing, 1985), p. 309.

[30]Ibid., pp. 310–313.

[31]Avery and Pepper, op. cit., p. 52.

[32]Ibid., p. 35.

[33]Robert K. Avery and Robert Pepper, "An Institutional History of Public Broadcasting," *Journal of Communication* 30 (1980): 134.

[34]Willard D. Rowland, "Continuing Crisis in Public Broadcasting: A History of Disenfranchisement," *Journal of Broadcasting and Electronic Media* 30 (1986): 265.

[35]Avery and Pepper, "An Institutional History of Public Broadcasting," op. cit., p. 135.

[36]Barnouw, op. cit., p. 178.

[37]Wood and Wylie, *Educational Telecommunications*, p. 138.

[38]Sydney Head, Christopher Sterling & Lemuel Schofield, *Broadcasting in America: A Survey of Electronic Media* (Boston: Haughton Mifflin, 1994), p. 280.

[39]P. Aufderheide, "Public Television and the Public Sphere," *Critical Studies in Mass Communication* 8 (1991): 176.

[40]William Hoynes, *Public Television for Sale: Media, Market, and the Public Sphere* (Boulder: Westview Press, 1994), p. 100.

[41]Ibid., p. 105.

[42]Marilyn Lashley, *Public Television: Panacea, Pork Barrel, or Public Trust?* (New York: Greenwood Press, 1992), pp. 58–61.

[43]David Horowitz, *The Problem with Public TV,* Center for the Study of Popular Culture, 1991, p.6.

[44]Lashley, op. cit., p. 64.

[45]U.S. Congress, *House Subcommittee on Telecommunication and Finance on H.R. 4118,* 100th Cong., 2d. sess., 1988, pp. 525–527.

[46]Auferheide, op. cit., p. 180.

[47]Hoynes, op. cit., pp. 95–96.

[48]L. Friedland, "Public Television as Public Sphere: The Case of the Wisconsin Collaborative Project," *Journal of Broadcasting and Electronic Media* 39 (1995): 158.

[49]Ibid.

[50]Hoynes, op. cit., p. 169.

[51]U.S. Congress, Senate, *Subcommittee Hearings on Communications on S.2120,* 103rd Cong., 2nd. sess., 1994, p. 21.

[52]Ibid., pp. 10–13.

[53]"What If Congress Tips toward the G.O.P.?," *Current,* October 31, 1994, p. 15.

[54]"What to Kill First? CPB Is Nominated to Save Tax Money and 'Privatize the Left,'" *Current,* December 12, 1994, p. 1.

[55]Ibid., p. 15.

[56]"Now, a Flurry of Options for the Future," *Current,* March 6, 1995, p. 1.

[57]"Gore Assails 'All Out Attack' on Enrichment for Kids," *Current,* March 6, 1995, p. 14.

[58]"First CPB Cuts of Newt Era Pass House," *Current,* March 20, 1995, p. 7.

[59]"Will 'Glide Path' Reach Beyond 1997?" *Current,* April 17, 1995, p. 1.

[60]"Funding Scramble Is 'Nature' of Public TV," *Broadcasting and Cable,* January 31, 1994, p. 22.

[61]"Conferences Okay Smaller Cuts for '96–'97," *Current,* May 15, 1995, p. 7.

[62]"Effects of CPB Recission to Public Television Stations," *America's Public Television Stations,* March 1995.

[63]"Pubcasters Pull Together a Plan for Congress," *Current,* May 1, 1995, p. 13.

[64]"Commercial Sister Network Would Subsidize Public TV," *Current,* October 9, 1995, p. 6.

[65]W. Charlton, "Perceptions of Commercial Activities in Public Broadcasting," [http://www.cpb.org/library/ researchnotes/commercial.study.html], February 1996.

9

The Impact of Television

In ordinary conversation, facts and opinions are frequently ascribed to an anonymous source. "*They* say that it's going to rain tomorrow." "*They* say it's very expensive to travel in Europe these days." "*They* say the Taurus is the best-selling car in America." This attribution to an all-knowing, if vague, source is both comforting and convenient. After all, if there is an error, it's *their* fault, not the speaker's. In addition, communication researchers have long known that, over time, people often forget the source, disassociating it from the message. Thus, messages from a less credible source, such as advertising, may become more credible because the listener remembers the message but not its source. *They* becomes a credible source because we don't know who it is. And, unlike outlaw Lyle Gorch in Sam Peckinpah's revisionist western *The Wild Bunch,* we seldom stop to ask: Who in the hell is *they?*

For citizens of the United States in the last half of the twentieth century, *they* is often television. Television is named as the primary source of news for 72 percent of the population, and its lead over the second most important source, newspapers, has steadily increased since 1959 (*America's Watching,* 1994).[1] Television is also considered the most credible news medium by a more than two-to-one margin over its nearest rival, newspapers. On a typical Sunday evening in February during the peak of prime time (9 P.M.), about 65 percent of all U.S. homes are using television.[2] As we noted in Chapter 7, the television set is on more than seven hours a day in the average U.S. household. Although it is sometimes combined with other activities, watching television consumes more time than any other activity except for work and sleep. Indeed, as the hours spent working and sleeping decrease during retirement years, television viewing increases. The average man over fifty-five watches 5.5

hours per day; the average woman over fifty-five views 6.3 hours.[3] Who the hell is *they? They* is our most pervasive medium, one with which we spend a significant portion of our days and most of our evenings.

In this chapter, we will examine some of the effects attributed to television. Television programming has been carefully measured in hundreds of studies and social scientists have documented the effects of the medium using a variety of methods, including laboratory experiments, field experiments, survey research, and qualitative–observational research. We will begin with a brief review of the evolution of effects research. Next, we will investigate some of the major concerns addressed by researchers, including the representation of minorities in television content, television's role in socializing the young, the impact of television violence, the relationship between television viewing and academic performance, and how the medium has changed politics.

A BRIEF HISTORY OF TELEVISION EFFECTS RESEARCH

As we noted in Chapter 2, television's evolution from mechanical experiment to FCC-approved system was widely reported over a period of three decades. Thus, by the time of its emergence as a mass medium in the 1950s, both critics and academic researchers were concerned with its potential impact. Popular magazines of the period saw television as a "window to the world," but critics of the new medium were not silent. T. S. Eliot saw the potential for isolation in "a medium of entertainment which permits millions of people to listen to the same joke at the same time, and yet remain lonesome."[4] Caustic comedian Groucho Marx quipped, "I find television very educational. Every time someone switches it on I go into another room and read a good book."[5] However, film director Orson Welles summed up the viewer's love–hate relationship with the new medium: "I hate television. I hate it as much as peanuts. But I can't stop eating peanuts."[6]

Although critics could be merciless, their criticism was a reaction to the stunning success of television in the 1950s. At the start of the decade, one in ten U.S. homes had television. By the end of the decade, nearly nine of ten would be tuning in.[7] The widespread interest in the new medium stimulated research both within the television industry and among psychologists and sociologists at universities. Systematic studies of the content of television began in the early 1950s,[8] and by the end of the decade social scientists had made several serious inquiries into the impact of the emerging medium.

The Bureau of Applied Social Research Studies

In the 1930s, the radio industry commissioned several studies of radio audiences, including a detailed examination of the panic that followed Orson Welles's *War of the Worlds,* broadcast on Halloween, 1938. A particularly strong professional relationship developed between CBS and the scholars of the Bureau of Applied Social Research at Columbia University. Paul Lazarsfeld and his Columbia colleagues worked with Frank Stanton, later President of CBS, to evaluate the role of radio in the lives of listeners.[9] Lazarfeld's radio work inspired a generation of studies when the new medium of television emerged. Major research projects on television surveyed audience attitudes in 1960, 1970, and 1980. A particularly influential volume growing out of this tradition was *The Effects of Mass Communication* by Joseph Klapper, then a consultant to CBS.[10]

Klapper's review of some of this first generation of research on the effects of the mass media, and television in particular, produced conclusions that were very soothing to a television industry already under attack by critics of its violent programming. Research indicated that media rarely stimulated users to convert to other points of view because of mediating factors, including *selective exposure, perception,* and *retention*—that is, the tendency for individuals to select, perceive, and retain messages consistent with their current attitudes. Also, research revealed that media effects are mitigated by the influence of primary groups, such as parents and peers, on the development of attitudes. Instead of viewing the media as major shapers of public opinion and behavior, Klapper suggested their primary effect was to reinforce current attitudes.[11] For example, steadfast Republicans were rarely converted into supporters of a Democratic candidate because they rarely encountered or retained a campaign message from that candidate, and when they did, they tended to distort the message. In addition, they tended to be surrounded by other Republicans who would not support their new point of view. However, this GOP supporter was likely to receive many partisan messages, from the media and individuals, that would reinforce and strengthen his or her convictions. In a similar way, more aggressive individuals might be drawn to more violent programming, but television violence should have little impact on individuals not predisposed to aggressive behavior. Thus, what became known as the *limited effects tradition* relieved television executives of the burden of negative message effects. Entertainment programming would, at most, only reinforce attitudes and behavior. Ironically, at the same time, evidence had mounted quickly that television advertising was particularly effective at changing consumer behavior.[12] The medium would seem to have limited impact on deeply held political values, but could introduce consumers to new products and services most effectively.

The Columbia tradition did not end with Klapper's review. In 1963 in *The People Look at Television,* Gary Steiner moved from questions of effects to attitudes about television.[13] Using CBS-funded survey research data, collected in 1960, Steiner found that the medium had become an accepted member of the household. Viewers were, in general, satisfied with what they saw: more than two-thirds saw television as the most entertaining medium and about half viewed it as a medium that "seems to get better all of the time."[14] The medium was viewed positively by 60 percent of the respondents and negatively by only 23 percent.[15] It seemed that initial inquiries into the use of and attitudes toward television were full of good news for the emerging industry.

The Columbia tradition of inquiry continued in the 1970s and 1980s with two volumes by Robert T. Bower, *Television and the Public* and *The Changing Television Audience in America*.[16] Using samples directly comparable to Steiner's, Bower documented a decline in the public's positive feelings for television, but not in the time they spent with the medium. In 1970, television was still considered the most entertaining medium by 72 percent of respondents, but only 38 percent thought that it seemed to be getting better all of the time.[17] The number of "superfans," those who agreed that television is wonderful, had dropped from approximately 28 percent in Steiner's 1960 study to 19 percent in Bower's 1970 report.[18] As documented in Bower's second volume, this trend toward more negative public attitudes regarding the medium continued in a 1980 survey. Comparing figures from Steiner's and his own research, Bower found viewers with the most favorable attitude scores had declined from 33 percent in 1960 to 24 percent in 1970 to 19 percent in 1980.[19] This erosion of public enthusiasm was reflected in a more critical view of television by a new generation of academic researchers. Although the hours spent viewing had increased steadily from the 1960s to the 1980s, the medium came under increasing scrutiny from scholars whose research in many instances was supported by research grants from the federal government.

Government-Sponsored Research

Although congressional hearings on television violence were held on several occasions between 1952 and 1967, the first major government-sponsored research into the issue of violence arose from the turmoil of the 1960s. The assassinations of John F. Kennedy, Robert Kennedy, and Martin Luther King, Jr. are perhaps the most memorable events in a decade framed by violence. The murder of civil rights workers, major riots in Watts, Detroit, Washington and many other cities, the Vietnam War protests, and the television mayhem in Chicago during the 1968 Democratic convention raised public awareness and government concern about domestic violence. In response to a decade of unrest, covered by the then established medium of television, the National Commission on the Causes and Prevention of Violence issued *Violence and the Media,* a 600-plus-page volume, as part of its fifteen-volume series of reports.[20] *Violence and the Media* provided a groundbreaking examination of the levels of violence on television. George Gerbner of the Annenberg School of Communication supervised a study of the content of entertainment programming during prime time and Saturday mornings in 1967 and 1968, initiating a series of studies that continues today. Arguing that the repetition of violent messages over time would lead to violent behavior, Gerbner found that over 80 percent of network programs contained violence, with over half of the major characters encountered committing violent acts.[21] Television violence was not equally practiced by all characters. The most violent characters were more likely to be unmarried, young or middle-aged, nonwhite or foreign, and strangers. In addition to these studies of violent content, researchers used surveys to examine the levels and types of violence accepted by the public, their actual experience with violent behavior, and their attitudes about television violence. Nearly two-thirds of the respondents disapproved of the kind of violence shown on television, although 53 percent of the teens sampled approved of it. *Violence and the Media* was a substantial inquiry into the potential impact of television, but it would not be the last.

A second major investigation of the medium was sponsored by the Surgeon General of the United States, starting in 1969. This effort was multifaceted, yielding five volumes reporting the results of twenty-three studies and the summary report *Television and Growing Up.*[22] In addition to a second Gerbner-led content analysis of the 1969 television season that confirmed his earlier findings, television professionals were interviewed on the reason for violent content; experimental studies of aggression were conducted; the use of television by adolescents and others was examined; and, most significantly, the relationship between viewing violence and aggressiveness was assessed. Despite considerable network influence on the Committee charged with drawing conclusions from these studies, the summary volume reported a connection between viewing television violence and aggressive behavior. In particular, the Committee concluded that findings from laboratory experiments and survey research documented

> *a preliminary and tentative indication of a causal relation between viewing violence on television and aggressive behavior; an indication that any such causal operation operates only on some children (who are predisposed to be aggressive); and an indication that it operates only in some environmental contexts.*[23]

Thus, this second round of government-sponsored research had connected the high levels of violence on television documented in *content analyses* and aggressive, if not violent behavior, by some children. As a result of the Surgeon General's report, the nation, having observed a decade of violence and civil unrest on television, now heard the medium implicated in the creation of that violence.

Although the issue of televised violence and its effects remained prominent in discussions of the medium, federal research funds made it possible for scholars to examine a broader range of questions during the 1970s. This new activity culminated with the 1982 publication of *Television and Behavior: Ten Years of Scientific Progress and Implications for the Eighties.*[24] The emphasis shifted from television's impact on behavior to its impact on knowledge. The underlying thread that connected the studies reported in this volume was television's role as the nation's master teacher for a variety of subjects. Health care and health-related behaviors received special attention in content analyses, revealing that television networks spent considerable time peddling nonprescription medications during commercials, but little time promoting healthy lifestyles. Programming abounded with images of snacking and drinking, but characters rarely became obese or drunk. Risky driving was common, but drivers and passengers rarely used seat belts.

In addition to health issues, the second Surgeon General's examination looked at family and interpersonal relations, gender, race and ethnicity, the elderly, children's responses to advertising, and the impact of television on religion, respect for laws and norms, public security, and politics. For most topics, quantities of particular content were relatively easy to document, but impact was harder to assess. The effects of television were often seen as gradual and long-term and not likely to surface in short-term studies. Thus, the most lasting result of these far-ranging inquiries is the shifting of research attention from television's role in violent and antisocial behavior to the impact of television on our perception of reality. In short, how television becomes the *they* of "they say."

University Research

In addition to the efforts of the Bureau of Applied Social Research and the federal government, television has been studied by hundreds of researchers at universities all over the world. Academic interest in the medium has grown steadily in the five decades since its emergence after World War II. Scholars from psychology, sociology, political science, communication, journalism and mass communication, and other disciplines have all made significant contributions to our understanding of the impact of the medium. Surveys of public attitudes toward television, examinations of its content, and *laboratory* and *field experiments* examining the medium are regularly published in academic journals such as the *Journal of Communication,* the *Journal of Broadcasting & Electronic Media, Journalism Quarterly,* and *Communication Research.* Some scholars of television are supported by government, philanthropic, or industry grants, but the vast majority rely on research support from their universities to pursue their studies.

Because many different thinkers are involved, the goals of academic research are varied and its direction ever-changing. Research trends seldom follow a straight path in a clear direction. Much of the research is comprised of *snapshot studies* that examine a particular aspect of the medium at only one point in time. Programmatic research that repeatedly studies the same phenomenon over a period of years is especially rare. Studies are not often repeated or replicated, so conclusions are frequently tentative. Limited resources also mean that the samples studied, be they people or program content, are smaller than would be optimal. Nonetheless, as both government and private funding of television research has decreased, university-sponsored research has become the major source of new information about television's effects.

THE EFFECTS OF TELEVISION

Examining the vast body of research on the impact of television necessarily restricts us to identifying broad themes. Literally thousands of empirical studies have been conducted on the various effects produced by watching television. As early as 1978, one definitive summary found over 2,500 pieces of scientific literature on television and human behavior.[25] In sorting through this maze, we will limit our examination to six topics of clear importance to the larger society that have received substantial examination: the content of television, television and socialization, the impact of televised violence, television and learning, television and politics, and the significance of the gratifications we seek from the medium in predicting its effects.

OUR THEORETICAL APPROACH

Although we have argued throughout this book that broadcast television is still the most influential medium for the general population, we do not believe that its influence is boundless. Despite its omnipresence and the amount of time devoted to it, television is only one medium of information and entertainment, and the media represent only one major source in a complex communication mosaic.[26] Although broadcast television news reaches the largest number of people, print media such as books, newspapers, and magazines are still the most important source of new and detailed information. Indeed, television news editors often draw their story ideas from the daily newspaper. The motion picture industry is still a major worldwide entertainment medium, and feature films provide thousands of hours of programming to stations and networks. Consumers increasingly find entertainment options in videotapes, compact discs, cable networks, video games, and 900 telephone numbers. On-line information services and the World Wide Web have become home libraries in a significant minority of U.S. households. Finally, even in an increasingly urbanized and fragmented culture, family and friends and social institutions, including schools and churches, are still the most important socializing agents. For most people, families and friends and religious institutions are the primary source of values and beliefs, while formal education still provides most baseline knowledge. Television may be our most pervasive medium, but it is hardly the only source of influence on culture.

As we examine the impact of television, we must acknowledge the larger communication context of the medium. Television can and does have a major impact for several reasons. First, television has the widest exposure of any mass medium. More people are exposed to the same information and at the same moment than with any other medium. Second, television has both sight and sound. Of the established media, it is the one closest to direct experience. Third, television can be immediate. Events can be experienced in real time and with unplanned consequences that heighten the dramatic impact. The outcome, be it a baseball game, a rescue effort, or O. J. Simpson's flight from law enforcement officers, is often unknown.

The wide exposure, visual–audio channels, and the immediacy of television are likely to be most influential on subjects seldom sought or available from other sources. As media researcher Wilbur Schramm argued, any communication will have its most immediate impact when it falls on new ground.

When we introduce one drop of communication into a person where millions of drops have already fallen and left their residue, we can hardly expect to reshape the personality fundamentally by that one drop. . . . [However,] if we are communicating in an area where ideas and values are not yet determined—if our drop of communication falls where not many have fallen before—then we may be able to see a change as a result of our communication.[27]

Thus, television has its greatest influence when it deals with subjects that are frequently ignored or deemphasized by other socializing agents. Schools and parents may teach facts of reproduction, but they typically have little to say about sexuality, a topic tirelessly explored and exploited in daytime talk shows, soaps, and prime-time dramas. Most people rarely experience violence, but millions view it every night on television. New products, politicians, social causes, or superstars become known through the nearly universal glass tube. Like mortar on a brick wall, television fills in the gap between what others want us to know and what we believe we need to know.

Although television can have its most dramatic impact on subjects when an individual has little access to information, the medium also can have gradual effects over time. Schramm has compared the gradual effects of communication to the water dripping from a cave that builds a stalagmite.

The stalagmite builds up from the calcareous residue of the water dripping on it from the cave roof. Each drop leaves only a tiny residue, and it is very seldom that we can detect the residue of any single drop, or that any single drop will make a fundamental change in the shape or appearance of the stalagmite. Yet, together, all these drops do build the stalagmite, and over the years it changes considerably in size and somewhat in shape.[28]

Short-term exposure may have limited influence on deeply held beliefs and values, but over a period of months and years even these pillars of personality may change.

Television's full impact proceeds in a similar way. For example, deep-seated attitudes about the essential fairness and responsibility of the federal government, shaped during the Great Depression and World War II, have changed in the decades after Vietnam and Watergate. The repeated exposés of governmental misdeeds, aggressively pursued by a more competitive and suspicious generation of television journalists, have reinforced the cynicism of some and gradually increased the skepticism of others. In a similar way, great social causes such as the civil rights and women's movements, experienced by most through television, have reshaped centuries old attitudes about racial and gender stereotypes. These changes occur so slowly that it is easy to forget that the bigotry of today was once the received wisdom of the past, or painful to imagine that the more enlightened attitudes of the present may only be a passing fad. Such gradual but profound effects of television and other media have been postulated and tested by a variety of scholars under theories such as *cultivation,* which see television content as shaping our perception of reality for some topics, and *agenda-setting,* which suggests that the medium orders our priorities for issues of public concern.

THE CONTENT OF TELEVISION

Most theories of television effects, both academic and popular, start with the assumption that the content of the medium is important. Thus, an accurate, impartial assessment of that content is vital to the understanding of the medium. Although most television critics rely on isolated examples in evaluating television programs, governmental agencies, media activists, and scholars have long employed systematic *content analysis* to measure what's on the tube. This technique requires the researcher to specify a unit of television content (a program, a scene, a line of dialog, a speaking character) and a universe of that unit of content (prime-time network television, children's programming, network television newscasts). Once these are specified, an appropriate sample of these units is drawn from the universe and the content of this sample is systematically analyzed by trained coders. Typically, the observations of the coders are compared, for at least part of the sample, to ensure that measurement is accurate with limited personal bias. If the researcher's method and practice are sound, other coders, similarly trained, should produce similar measurements. Most content analyses produce counts of the number and percentage of particular types of content in the sample (e.g., the number of women in a sample of speaking characters during prime-time programming and that number expressed as a percentage of speaking characters).

Using these methods, researchers have published hundreds of studies of the content of broadcast television programs, examining many types of content. Content analyses have often been commissioned by minority groups and professional associations (trade groups, labor unions) that wish to document the negative representation of their group on television. Other pressure groups use content analyses to document the high levels of what they believe is inappropriate behavior (typically sex and violence). Central to all such studies is the stated or implied belief that television teaches us about our world and that knowledge affects what we believe and how we behave. Thus, a false or misleading representation of a group or organization, or an overemphasis on negative behaviors, should be corrected. For most groups, television should reflect the world the way it is, or perhaps the way it should be. If the medium is a window to the world, it should be an undistorted one.

We will next focus on categories of content that have been of long-standing interest to researchers, and that have produced relatively stable findings over time. These include the demography of television characters and presence of certain verbal and physical behaviors.

The Demography of Television Characters

A frequent goal of content analyses has been to reveal the proportion of series characters that occupy different gender, ethnic, age, and occupational categories. These head counts typically tally the number of different characters with speaking parts in a program episode, typing them as major or minor characters. Although head counts tell us little about what a character does or says, they do provide insights into the population characteristics of broadcast television.

One of the more enduring findings is the great proportion of male characters in broadcast television. For several decades, male characters outnumbered female characters by 3 to 1. Recently that ratio has been decreasing slightly, but even two decades after the women's movement, television programming is more about men than women. Ironically, this imbalance continues even though women represent the greater portion of the viewing audience and are highly desired by many advertisers.

There are several explanations for this imbalance. Despite some progress, the broadcast television industry is still predominately run by males in upper and middle management. Symptomatic of this gender inequity is the fact that, until the mid-1990s, none of the three largest and oldest networks (ABC, CBS, NBC) had a female head of programming. Although women are represented on programming staffs, the final decisions are almost always in the hands of males, who may be likely to favor male characters. Despite the much-publicized influence of Roseanne *(Roseanne)* and Diane English *(Designing Women, Murphy Brown)*, the same gender differences are common among series producers. In short, an industry dominated by males is likely to favor male characters. Second, some research supports the conventional industry wisdom that females will watch male characters, but males will not watch female characters. Because males are more likely to select programs during prime viewing periods, networks may lean toward more male protagonists in an attempt to maximize ratings. Finally, television characters may simply be reflecting the entrenched gender differences in society. If males occupy a larger percentage of the positions of power, public influence, and out-of-home activities, it is not surprising that women are underrepresented on most television programs (other than domestic comedies) located in these settings.

Progress in equal head count representations has been greater for one ethnic group, African Americans, but limited for most others. In television's first decade, African Americans rarely appeared in entertainment television, and when they did it was as domestic servants *(Beulah)* or as derisive caricatures *(Amos 'n' Andy)*. However, progress in civil rights was reflected on network television with the introduction of African American protagonists in two 1960s series (Diahann Carroll in *Julia* and Bill Cosby in *I Spy*). Since then most content analyses have shown a representation of African Americans on broadcast television that is roughly proportional to the group's 12.6 percent representation in the U.S. population.[29] However, African Americans have been increasingly ghettoized in series in which most of the characters are African American. Resonating with an *Amos 'n' Andy* broadcast heritage, African American characters are seen most frequently in comedies, and less often in action–adventure programs or dramas.[30] Representations in television news have been dominated by racially centered or crime stories.

These characteristics of African American representation on network television may be symptomatic of racial biases in our society. African Americans may be more acceptable to the still predominately white audience of broadcast television when they appear in nonthreatening comic roles. Dramas are more lifelike and their white audiences may be less willing to empathize with minority experiences. However, the ghettoizing of African American characters may simply reflect the fact that the majority of these characters appear in family comedies, and most families, both on television and in reality, are racially uniform. In television news, the overrepresentation of African Americans in crime stories may reflect the group's actual disproportional representation as both victim and perpetrator of violent crime. In any event, content analyses of broadcast television show a proportional, but not necessarily a realistic, representation of African Americans.

Content analyses have shown that three other major minorities are greatly underrepresented on television. Hispanics constitute about 10 percent of the population, Asians and Pacific Islanders about 3.5 percent, and Native American–Eskimo–Aleut populations 0.9 percent.[31] Yet these groups are seldom represented on television. A recent review of studies of minorities concluded that Hispanic characters were rare and other minorities were "most conspicuous by their absence."[32] The lack of significant numbers of these groups in the television industry may be the reason, once again, for their underrepresentation on television, but the growth of specialized, non-English language stations and networks may also have reduced pressures on the television industry for greater representation of these groups in English-language programming.

Content analyses over several decades have shown that television is a medium dominated by young and middle-aged adults. Males tend to be older than females. The very old and the very young are rarely seen on television. Older children and adolescents are seen in substantial numbers, but are still underrepresented compared to their numbers in the population. The most overrepresented group as characters are 18–49-year-olds. The preponderance of this age group is not surprising given its importance to many television advertisers. Viewers are most likely to watch programs populated with characters similar to themselves. Thus, 18–49-year-old television characters do a good job of delivering 18–49-year-old consumers to advertisers.

Verbal and Physical Behaviors

Although not as common as head counts, content analyses have also examined complex behaviors, focusing on what characters say and do as well as what demographic groups they represent. For example, in *Life on Television,* Bradley Greenberg and his colleagues examined not just the number of males and females in prime-time programming, but the kinds of behaviors exhibited by each.[33] Males exhibited more verbal control than females. They were more likely to give orders to other males and have those orders followed. Males were more likely than females to need physical assistance, but females were more likely to need emotional assistance. Females were more likely to request aid and get it. Males were more likely to make plans than females. Finally, among common behaviors, men were more frequently seen driving a motor vehicle, using firearms, engaging in athletics, drinking/smoking, and making business phone calls. Women were more likely to perform indoor housework, prepare food, and entertain others (e.g., singing). Findings such as these suggest that television tends to present genders in stereotypic roles: Men are more verbally dominant and more likely to be engaged in physical activity outside the home, while women are more likely to express need and perform traditional household duties.

Although they have a long history, content analyses continue to be a major form of new research on television. Their continued prominence reflects the belief of many scholars, most media watchdogs, and much of the general public that what is seen on television affects how we behave and how we view the world. Meanwhile, other scholars have developed theories and pursued research on just how these cognitive effects of television evolve.

TELEVISION AND SOCIALIZATION

Media critics and commentators have described television as one of the great *socializing agents* in modern society, as influential as parents, peers, schools, and churches in the education of the young. Children watch television an average of 3.7 hours per day, with younger children watching more than older ones.[34] And it is this youngest age group that is most active in accruing knowledge about the world. Because television is accessible to children as young as two years old, most children become viewers long before they become readers. Most children remain intensely interested in television throughout childhood; their viewing levels only begin to decline during their teens when peer influence becomes greater.

But television socializes more than the young. Although it has been challenged on both theoretical and methodological grounds,[35] cultivation theory and research have persuaded some scholars to view television as a major influence on how we develop our perceptions of reality. According to cultivation theory, television provides images of the world in both nonfictional and fictional programming that, over a period of time, become the version of reality accepted by most members of the culture.[36] For instance, heavy television viewers are more likely than light viewers to perceive the world as more violent, crime-infested and populated by police officers than government statistics show. The strong tendency for commercial broadcasters to imitate successful programming and the limited number of successful program types results in a homogenized world of television. As we have seen in our discussion of content analysis, this television reality is distorted in many ways, and this distortion can have unanticipated consequences.

For example, the high levels of violence on television documented in content analyses are especially significant, not because they promote violence, but because they may promote actions consistent with the perception that the world is a violent place. If viewers believe the world is violent, they are likely to behave in ways consistent with that reality by buying handguns for protection, by supporting increased police power, or simply by avoiding contact with strangers. Similarly, if men are seen much more frequently and in more dominant roles on television, gender stereotypes of male activity and female passivity are taught to the young and reinforced in the old. In this model, the content of specific programs is not very important, but the content of the medium is paramount. Thus, television becomes a socializer of both the young and the old.

Although challenged by other researchers, subsequent cultivation research has found that television has a mainstreaming effect.[37] Heavy viewers of television are more likely than light viewers to hold political and social views that are less extreme and more conventional. The effect of television is to homogenize culture for most and to marginalize groups, values, and ideas that are not frequently seen on the medium. Although television is not the only socializer in modern societies, it is the most pervasive: It reaches virtually every home and is attended to, in differing amounts, by nearly every citizen.

THE IMPACT OF TELEVISED VIOLENCE

Broadcast television in the United States uses violent content to sustain audience interest in much of its programming. Content analyses of the medium have recorded 7.5 acts of violence per hour of programming.[38] Saturday morning children's programming is even more violent than prime-time programming, with nearly 18 acts of violence in a typical hour.[39] Although levels of violence have varied over the years, it has been consistently excessive and has often triggered public concern.

In every decade since the emergence of television in the 1950s, the United States Congress has held at least one major investigation of televised violence.[40] As noted earlier, the National Commission on the Causes and Prevention of Violence (1969) and the United States Surgeon General (1971, 1982) commissioned research on the issue of television violence. This concern was expressed most recently by congress in the Telecommunications Act of 1996 that requires manufacturers to install, in all television sets manufactured in the United States, a *V-Chip,* capable of screening out violent programming.[41] As we have already reported, cultivation researchers have argued and to some extent documented a relationship between exposure to television and its violent content and distorted perceptions of reality.

The concern over what televised violence does or does not do to the behavior of children and adults has generated two prominent and contradictory theories to explain the medium's effect. The *catharsis theory* states that televised violence does not stimulate increased levels of aggressive behavior, but may actually decrease that behavior. Conversely, social cognitive or modeling theory, says that, under the right circumstances, televised violence will increase levels of aggressive behavior.

Cathartic theory traces its origins to Greek philosophy of the 4th century B.C. Aristotle saw a relationship between the emotional experience of an audience and the need to reduce emotional tension.

A tragedy, then, is the imitation of an action that is serious and also, as having magnitude, complete in itself . . . with incidents arousing pity and fear, wherewith to accomplish its catharsis of such emotions.[42]

Applied to televised violence, catharsis theory predicts that viewers will purge some of the aggressive feelings that are generated by ordinary conflicts and frustrations through vicarious participation in the violent fantasies that abound on television. Televised violence functions as a form of tension reduction, allowing viewers to release harmlessly the angers that they feel, just as they might in daytime fantasies or nighttime dreams. For example, employees may become very angry at their supervisors, but they know that physical or verbal aggression directed at their superiors would have devastating consequences. However, these angry feelings must not be allowed to increase in intensity. By watching violent television programming, they may be able to transfer those emotions to villains vanquished by the hero of the moment.

Despite the elegance and reassurance that this theory offers, there is only marginal empirical support for it.[43] Only a few studies have demonstrated a positive cathartic effect from televised violence, while the preponderance of studies have shown that watching television violence increases aggressive behavior.

Perhaps the most widely accepted explanation of the relationship between viewing television violence and increased aggressive behavior is provided by *social cognitive or modeling theory.*[44] Developed by psychologist Albert Bandura, the theory holds that much of what we learn comes from observing others. Humans continually monitor the behavior of others and the consequences of these activities. Although other means of learning, such as direct instruction, are certainly important, they cannot account for all of the behaviors that we learn and later practice. The theory states that we are more likely to reproduce the behaviors we observe if we accept the source of behavior as a role model, if we see the behavior being rewarded or reinforced, and if we find ourselves in a situation similar to the one in which the original behavior was observed.

Applied to our most pervasive medium, social cognitive theory suggests that televised violence will increase levels of aggressive behavior for three reasons. First, incidents of violent behavior are plentiful on television and easily accessible to virtually the entire population. Children, the age group most likely to model behavior, receive particularly heavy doses of violence in programming directed at them. Second, much of the violent behavior depicted on television is rewarded. Violence is frequently used to subdue villainy, and its use is approved of in this context. Nonviolent solutions are often not presented as realistic possibilities. Also, the full effects of violent behavior are often not presented. In many instances, villains die quickly and with little pain, while heroes receive minor injuries or no injuries at all. In addition, violence is, for many viewers, exciting and enhances the viewing experience. Finally, for some viewers, the use of the aggressive behaviors observed on television may be rewarded, at least temporarily. For example, in gang-infested areas, violence may be part of the rites of passage and the major means to gaining respect and status.

Beginning in the 1960s, Bandura and his associates examined the impact of televised violence on children. In a famous series of experiments, they found that children were more likely to engage in aggressive play during a period scheduled after they viewed a film of an adult role model engaging in aggressive behavior, including punching and kicking an inflated "Bobo" doll.[45] Bandura and his colleagues also found that the aggressive behaviors could be reduced if they were punished when first performed, or if an adult observer was present during the play period. Thus, the impact of televised violence was not universal and could be limited by adult intervention.

Research supports social cognitive theory and its extension to observational learning from television. In controlled laboratory experiments, viewing violence has been shown to cause an increase in the instances of aggressive play. However, it has been much more difficult to document the consequences of that aggressive play (e.g., increases in violent crimes, domestic violence, or physical coercion), although a few researchers have attempted this difficult task in long-term studies that show a relationship between early exposure to heavy levels of televised violence and later violent criminal activity. Critics of this research admit that children may see and imitate some of the aggressive acts on television, but argue that sanctions against violence are strong in most families, schools, and organizations. Violence may be rewarded in the fantasy world of television, but it is usually punished elsewhere. In addition, the television industry and others argue that violent behavior is much more likely to be the result of "real world" factors (poverty, lack of parental control or even abuse, peer group socialization) than the viewing of televised violence that was never intended to be taken seriously. Although there has been no resolution of this debate, social modeling theory does show that televised violence can promote short-term increases in aggressive behavior.

In addition, the consequences of television violence are not limited to increases in aggressive behavior. As we noted earlier, cultivation theorists believe that violence in the world of television changes viewers' perceptions about the levels of violence in the real world. In addition, other researchers have found that violence on television changes how we react to violence. Heavy measures of violent programming seem to desensitize viewers, reducing the intensity of their emotional reactions to violence. Just as heroin addicts must increase the dosage of heroin they take to get the same effect of the drug, viewers must see increasing levels of violence to remain interested. Even a casual review of television programming since the advent of the medium reveals an increase in the graphic representations of violence. Violent theatrical motion pictures that later play in edited form on broadcast television seem especially subject to more intense violent content. But conventional television programming, especially news programming, seems to have upped the violence ante as well.

The result of these increasing doses of violence may be an increasing resignation to the violence in our society. An earlier generation of sociologists labeled the development of this kind of public resignation the *narcotizing dysfunction* of the mass media. As we become less concerned about the violence we see on television, we start to see it as an accepted part of life. Or, when we do worry about violence, we conclude that the only means of dealing with it is for law enforcement agencies or private citizens to respond with more violence. Ultimately, the greatest impact of violence on television may be its power to change how we think about the world around us and the people who inhabit it.

The issue of violence on television is not likely to go away. Given that the only purpose of most television programming, including the most violent, is to hold an audience's attention for an advertiser's commercial, it is unlikely that programmers will willingly reduce violent content without government pressure. Broadcasters have long argued against any limitations on violent content because these limits would violate the First Amendment right of free expression. However, the government has always maintained the right to require some restrictions that affect program content (indecency rules, emergency broadcast system participation, programming that serves the public interest) as a part of the price the industry must pay to use the public's electromagnetic spectrum (see Chapter 4). Other than viewers with a taste for action, the only groups that appear to benefit from violent programming is the television industry, an industry already granted the use of a scarce public resource.

TELEVISION AND ACADEMIC PERFORMANCE

Parents and educators are frequently concerned about the negative effects of popular entertainment on learning. In the 1940s English teachers criticized the "creative" grammar and pronunciations used by St. Louis Cardinals baseball announcer Dizzy Dean. As television assumed popular entertainment dominance in U.S. households in the 1950s, it also assumed the role as distracter of the young. Children were quickly drawn to the new medium and spent thousands of hours in front of it. The educational value of much of this early programming was limited. In fact, much of the early programming aimed at children included motion picture cartoons *(Bugs Bunny)* and short features *(The Three Stooges)* that were originally intended for adult motion picture audiences.

Initially, there was little evidence to support the contention that watching television was related to lower academic performance.[46] The first generation of children to grow up with television performed as well on standardized tests of academic achievement as their old "radio age" siblings. However, beginning in the mid-1960s test scores began to decline steadily. Although many explanations have been offered for this decline (changes in family structure, the lowering of standards by schools, inadequate funding of public education, particularly in poorer school districts, etc.), educators and parents decried the increasing amounts of time young people spent viewing entertainment television, videotapes, and video games at the expense of print media (newspapers, magazines, books).

High levels of television viewing could be related to lower academic performance for at least three reasons. First, time spent watching television is time that cannot be spent doing homework, reading textbooks, or studying. Second, television viewing does not substantially improve the reading skills needed for many kinds of academic work. In fact, television may become an alternative route to information that serves as a weak substitute for print media, instilling emotional rather than rational responses. Finally, entertainment television provides few role models that seem to derive their status from academic achievement. Even successful professionals (physicians, lawyers, scientists) are seldom shown engaged in study, and the years of academic preparation necessary to prepare for these professions are seldom portrayed.

Some studies have examined the relationship between academic performance and television viewing,[47] and they have found a slight negative relationship: As time spent viewing television increases, academic performance decreases. This relationship seems to hold up even when other factors that might affect academic performance are taken into consideration. Although the relationship is modest, parents who want their children to excel in school are advised to limit the amount of time their offspring spend in front of the tube.

THE IMPACT OF TELEVISION ON POLITICS

As early as 1952, when only a quarter of U.S. households had television, observers began to see the influence of television on politics. Early television advertising advocate Roster Reeves conceived a campaign for General Dwight Eisenhower that included a series of successful short commercials in which actors posing as "citizens" asked the general for his very brief answers to questions about the key campaign issues. Although Eisenhower reportedly grumbled "that an old soldier should come to this,"[48] television commercials were already seen as an effective means of reaching undecided or uninterested voters. Because commercials were implanted in programs, they were more difficult to ignore than partisan print advertisements or program-length political messages. Critics attacked the condensing of political rhetoric into sixty-second capsules, but television spot advertising would become increasingly popular with candidates at all levels of government.

However, longer political talks could also be very effective, especially with party partisans. Republican vice presidential candidate Richard Nixon used a thirty-minute NBC broadcast on the evening of September 23, 1952 to convince party regulars, and especially presidential candidate Eisenhower, that he was innocent of misusing campaign funds. Nixon vowed that, except for the family dog "Checkers" (a gift from a devoted supporter), he had never used funds for personal expenses, not to purchase the family Oldsmobile or buy his wife something nicer than her "Republican cloth coat." Nixon's "Checkers" speech served notice that candidates could use the medium to stimulate a public response that would influence party leaders.

Since that first presidential election of the television age, the medium has become our most important means of political communication. Politicians running for major federal and state offices use television as their primary means of reaching many voters through paid advertising, typically in the form of fifteen- or thirty-second spots, and by careful exploitation of television news as a form of *free media*. Stump speeches are crafted for two audiences: the partisans at hand and the more abundant viewers of network and local station news. Politicians know they must deliver the essence of their message in intense, colorful, dramatic, and hopefully entertaining ten- to twenty-second sound bites. These equivalents of audio–visual bumper stickers will be integrated into ninety-second news stories that will be the only contact most voters will have with these speeches. Just as speeches must be crafted for television news, each party's political convention must be staged for television. In the age of television, political conventions have evolved from centers of major party decision-making (selecting a presidential candidate and a party platform) to the longest period of free publicity for the party.

But television has influenced more than just stump speeches and conventions. Political debates must be carefully orchestrated so that a candidate will appear to win or at least not lose a debate. The timing of and rules for each debate are hotly contested by each candidate to produce the most favorable conditions possible. Speech writers develop answers to all anticipated questions, and candidates rehearse their responses. Once the debate is over, party professionals work as "spin doctors" to persuade reporters of the superiority of their candidate's ideas and performance. The focus of much of the debate coverage as well as much of the general campaign coverage is on who will win and why. As a result, most candidates must achieve goals in debates and primaries that are established by media consensus. Thus, the true winner of the 1992 New Hampshire Democratic primary was not Paul Tsongas, the candidate who received the most votes, but Bill Clinton, the candidate who most exceeded media expectations.

The Cost of Elections

If money is the "mother's milk" of politics, as the late Speaker of the House Tip O'Neill was fond of saying, then television is the infant with the biggest appetite. Many media consultants recommend that U.S. Senate candidates spend at least 75 percent of their funds on television in a close race and about half of their funds on television in less spirited contests. In the hotly contested 1990 Senate race in North Carolina, Republican incumbent Jesse Helms spent over $5 million on broadcast advertising (99.5 percent of his advertising budget), while his Democratic challenger, Harvey Gantt, spent nearly $4.4 million (94.2 percent of his advertising budget).[49] In their 1996 rematch, Helms upped the total campaign ante to $6.7 and Gantt to $7 million. These figures are particularly amazing considering that the salary of a

U.S. Senator is only $133,600 a year.[50] In 1952, both presidential candidates spent approximately $1.6 million; by 1972 the figure was $24.6 million, and by 1984 it was $154 million.[51] By the 1996 presidential campaign, both major political parties were working to find loopholes in federally imposed spending limits so they could spend more for television advertising.[52]

With costs so high, only the very wealthy, or those who can effectively raise money from wealthy individuals, corporations, or other groups, can afford to run for major office. Like an arms race, candidates must try to match the television muscle of their opponents by buying more advertising during prime voter viewing times. Indeed, the candidate's ability to raise money is a major consideration in how seriously the media, including television, treat her or his candidacy. The results of these expensive campaigns, driven to such extremes by the price of television advertising, are a source of political cynicism among the electorate. Voters openly wonder what favors will be granted to those who made the greatest contributions to the massive war chests needed for televised campaigns.

Agenda-Setting

Television has certainly made political campaigning more expensive, but it is also true that "money was the mother's milk of politics" long before the emergence of the medium. Television's influence on the issues addressed by candidates has been examined in many studies. In 1972, researchers Maxwell McCombs and Donald Shaw demonstrated the power of the news media to establish a hierarchy of issues during a campaign.[53] Their comparison between respondent rankings of issues during the 1968 presidential campaign and the amount of coverage of each issue by the national and local news media available in Chapel Hill, North Carolina produced an extremely high correlation. The issues that had received the greatest coverage by the press were the issues of greatest importance to the voters. The issues receiving the least coverage were the least important.

Later research identified some factors that increase or decrease the intensity of this *agenda-setting* effect. Agenda-setting by the media is stronger for issues that do not intrude on our lives, and weaker for obtrusive issues that are part of our direct experience.[54] For example, a voter that has been laid off is likely to rank unemployment (in this case, an obtrusive issue) as an important issue in a campaign, regardless of its press coverage. Similarly, agenda-setting is greater when voters have a high need for orientation on the issues and less when voters already have substantial background. Despite these qualifications, most research has found support for the agenda-setting effect. It seems that political scientist Bernard Cohen was right when he noted that "the press may not be successful much of the time in telling people what to think, but it is stunningly successful in telling its readers what to think about."[55]

Agenda-setting research has established an important role for television during elections. Because television news is both the most frequently used and trusted source of information, it has an important impact on the issues discussed during a campaign. Our positions on these issues may vary greatly, but television plays a key role in our assessment of on what issues we should have a position. Thus, political consultants labor diligently to keep issues that work well for their candidates before the media and, thereby, before the public.

Negative Political Advertising

Politics in the United States has always had a rough-and-tumble quality. In 1840, supporters of Willian Henry Harrison dubbed his opponent President Martin Van Buren "Little Van."[56] In 1884, Republicans, referring to Grover Cleveland's illegitimate child, taunted him with cries of "Ma, ma, where's my pa?" while Democratic supporters replied "Gone to the White House, ha, ha, ha!"[57] In the 1930s, Republicans savagely attacked Franklin Roosevelt's "New Deal,"[58] sometimes changing his middle name from *Delano* to *Damnation*. Nevertheless, the heavy reliance on negative advertising in many recent televised campaigns has raised the issue of the role of negative political advertising in the democratic process.

Researchers have assessed the costs and benefits of "going negative." On the benefits side, negative ads are more likely to be remembered than more positive ads and can be very effective, particularly if they are sponsored by a source other than the candidate.[59] On the costs side, negative ads can produce a backlash against the originator of the ad, particularly if they are countered quickly by the candidate attacked in the negative ad. Negative ads are also seen as a sign of desperation, especially when they are used by candidates who are far behind in the polls. Thus, proponents of negative advertising can point to numerous instances of success, but critics of the ads can find plenty of examples of failure as well.

Some critics have attacked the preponderance of negative ads in U.S. politics. Negative ads focus on the limitations of one candidate, but do not necessarily show what the attacking candidate has to offer. They focus the campaign on the issues and activities that can be easily attacked, ignoring far more important topics that deserve full debate. For example, attack ads often concentrate on personal indiscretions that may have little bearing on how effectively an individual will govern. Finally, negative advertising fans the flames of political cynicism, leading to voter apathy expressed in declining voter turnout. Voters as a percentage of the voting age population declined over 22 percent from a peak of 63 percent in the 1960 presidential election to a low of 49 in 1996.[60] Voting in off-year elections declined 37 percent from a peak of 45.4 percent in 1962 to 33.1 percent in 1990.[61]

Television and Political Cynicism

Some researchers have found this tendency toward cynicism, expressed as a waning belief in the political system, to be directly related to our dependence on television. In the mid-1970s, political scientist Michael Robinson first noticed the condition he called *videomalaise*.[62] Several researchers have demonstrated a modest difference in political efficacy, the belief in the value of the political process, between citizens who depend on television and those who depend on newspapers for their political information.[63] Television-dependent citizens tend to be more distrustful of politicians and the government and to believe that voting makes no difference. Robinson argued that this distrust came from images of turmoil graphically presented on television during the decade. However, later studies also substantiated the connection between television dependency and political cynicism.[64] Recently, the most significant third-party presidential candidate since before the Civil War, Ross Perot, captured 19 percent of the popular vote in 1992. His success has been traced by some to the rise of an angry electorate: an electorate increasingly dependent on television for political information.

WHO IS MOST LIKELY TO BE AFFECTED?

The Uses and Gratifications Approach

While most of the research on the impact of television has tried to find connections between television viewing and some, usually negative, effect, many researchers have argued that effects are more likely if the viewer is actively using the medium. The *uses and gratifications* tradition of television/media research has sought to identify the reasons why viewers use the medium as much as they do. They identify the gratifications derived from viewing the medium, particular types of programming, or in a few instances, particular programs. Uses and gratifications researchers argue that we can better understand what television does to us if we first understand what we do with television.

Although there are variations of this construct, the uses and gratifications approach starts with the assumption that the viewer has psychological or social needs that can be gratified by both the use of a mass medium, like television, or through other nonmediated means.[65] These needs lead to expectations of gratification that will be obtained from exposure to television. The expectation of gratification encourages exposure to a medium (television) or particular messages (a television program or channel). The gratification is obtained, in varying degrees, or not at all. Successful gratification should lead to repeated use of the medium or message, and eventually to its habitual use. In addition to the expected consequences of the medium, the gratification sought, exposure to the medium can produce unexpected effects. Thus, viewers may turn to a police drama as a means of escape from their daily concerns or simply to be entertained. They are likely to receive these intended gratifications. However, they may also be persuaded by commercials that sell a particular product or they may become temporarily more aggressive as the result of the violent content contained in the police drama.

This approach, which spawned a large body of research starting in the 1970s, has identified general gratifications obtained from television, including an information or surveillance gratification, a personal identity gratification, and a cognitive gratification. Research has linked these particular gratifications to expected effects with varying degrees of success. Other researchers have explored the gratifications obtained from particular television programs, programming sources, such as cable and VCRs, and even remote controls.

At the heart of the uses and gratifications approach is the notion that viewers will be more affected by media and messages from which they seek strong gratification than those that hold little promise of reward. The degree of viewer involvement with the medium or the program content is critical in determining when television will produce significant effects and when it will be more or less benign. The more actively the audience is involved in program viewing, the more likely television effects will follow. Thus, the uses and gratifications approach has focused television effects research on the relationship between viewer and medium, a relationship that can vary greatly depending on the viewer, the viewing situation, and the particular medium or programming examined.

Dependency Theory

Closely aligned with the uses and gratifications approach is the *dependency theory,* proposed by sociologists Melvin DeFleur and Sandra Ball–Rockeach.[66] As with uses and gratifications theory, DeFleur and Ball–Rockeach argue that media effects will increase as the involvement with or "dependency" on media increases. This dependency can operate at both the individual and societal level. Individual viewers can come to depend on a particular medium to fulfill important functions and, as their dependency increases, the impact of that medium grows. In a similar way, a society can be more readily transformed by media when its dependency is greatest.

At times of great societal stress and turmoil, the media assume special importance. During the 1960s, as anti-Vietnam protests, an emerging youth culture, blossoming social movements, and violence rocked the nation, public reliance on the news media in general and television news in particular grew dramatically. The rapid changes in society stimulated widespread reliance on the mass media. As the pace of change subsided in later decades, the impact of television and other media declined, promoting more of the reinforcement effect noted by an earlier generation of "limited effects" theorists. Thus, the effects of television are augmented by both individual and societal dependencies, and these dependencies are influenced by the needs of both the individual and society.

CONCLUSION

The impact of television has been studied for over four decades. Much of this research has examined the possible negative effects of the medium, including the perpetuation of negative images of minorities, the propagation of a false "television" reality studied by cultivation theorists, the promotion of aggressive and antisocial behavior, a decline in academic achievement among the young, and dubious changes to the political campaign process. Although results have not always been consistent, considerable evidence supports many of the negative effects ascribed to the medium. Television has become the major source of entertainment and information for most people in the United States, but at some cost to society.

However, it is important to place these costs of television in a larger context. Broadcast television does entertain and inform nearly two-thirds of the U.S. population each evening with little direct cost. Viewers do pay, but only when they buy advertised products and services. Television is our most popular entertainment medium and our most trusted source of news. The extent of our reliance on the medium can occasionally surprise even its severest critic. For example, one-quarter of those surveyed by *TV Guide* in 1991 claimed they would not permanently give up watching television for the sum of $1,000,000.

The mosaic model of communication that we endorse reminds us that television should be viewed as only one part of a larger communication context. The larger context includes other mass media, as well as family, peers, and social institutions as major forces in the development of the young. Thus, it appears that television content is most likely to have significant effects when other forces of socialization are absent or silent. In addition, most effects of the medium are likely to develop over time with repeated exposure, rather than quickly as the result of one program or televised event. The uses and gratifications approach and dependency theory suggest that the impact of the medium is likely to be influenced by our involvement with and reliance on it. However, for most people in the United States, television is a constant, pervasive presence. It is in nearly every home and it is turned on seven hours each day. At least, that's what *they* say.

NOTES

[1]*America's Watching: Public Attitudes Toward Television,* (New York: Roper Starch, 1994), pp. 17–18.

[2]"Night-by-Night Nielsen Prime-Time Household Ratings," *Electronic Media,* February 19, 1996, p. 30.

[3]Raymond L. Carroll and Donald M. Davis, *Electronic Media Programming: Strategies and Decision Making,* (New York: McGraw-Hill, 1993).

[4]Robert Andrews, *The Concise Columbia Dictionary of Quotations,* (New York: Columbia University Press, 1993), p. 899.

[5]Ibid.

[6]Ibid., p. 900.

[7]*Nielsen 1992–93 Report on Television,* (New York: Nielsen Media Research), p. 4.

[8]Dallas W. Smythe, *Three Years of New York Television,* (Urbana IL: National Association of Educational Broadcasters, 1956).

[9]Paul F. Lazarsfeld and Frank N. Stanton, *Radio Research 1942–43,* (New York: Essential Books, 1944).

[10]Joseph T. Klapper, *The Effects of Mass Communication,* (New York: The Free Press, 1960).

[11]Ibid., p. 15.

[12]Erik Barnouw, *The Sponsor: Notes on a Modern Potentate,* (New York: Oxford University Press, 1978), p. 46.

[13]Gary A. Steiner, *The People Look at Television: The Study of Audience Attitudes,* (New York: Knopf, 1963).

[14]Ibid., p. 31.

[15]Ibid., p. 38.

[16]Robert T. Bower, *Television and the Public,* (New York: Holt, Rinehart, and Winston, 1973).

[17]Ibid., p. 14.

[18]Ibid., p. 25.

[19]Robert T. Bower, *The Changing Television Audience in America,* (New York: Columbia University Press, 1985), p. 22.

[20]Robert Baker and Sandra Ball, eds., *Violence and the Media,* (Washington, DC: Government Printing Office, 1969).

[21]Ibid., p. 327.

[22]*Television and Growing Up: The Impact of Televised Violence,* (Washington, DC: Government Printing Office, 1971).

[23]Ibid., p. 11.

[24]*Television and Behavior: Ten Years of Scientific Progress and Implications for the Eighties,* (Washington, DC: Government Printing Office, 1982).

[25]Comstock et al., *Television and Human Behavior,* (New York: Columbia University Press, 1978), p. xiii.

[26]Samuel L. Becker, "Visual Stimuli and the Construction of Meaning," in Bikkar, S. Randhawa, and William E. Coffman, eds., *Visual Learning, Thinking and Communication* (New York: Academic Press, 1978), p. 44.

[27]Wilbur Schramm, "Procedures and Effects of Mass Communication," in N.B. Henry, ed., *Mass Media and Education II: 53rd Yearbook of the National Society for the Study of Education* (Chicago: University of Chicago Press, 1954), p. 125.

[28]Ibid.

[29]*Statistical Abstract of the United States,* 115th ed., (Washington, DC: Government Printing Office, 1995), p. 14.

[30]Bradley S. Greenberg and Jeffrey E. Brand, "Minorities and the Mass Media: 1970s to 1990s," in Jennings Bryant and Dolf Zillmann, eds., *Media Effects: Advances in Theory and Research* (Hillsdale, NJ: Erlbaum, 1994), p. 278.

[31]*Statistical Abstract of the United States,* op. cit., pp. 14 & 18.

[32]George Gerbner, June, 1993, "Women and Minorities on Television" (a report to the Screen Actors Guild and the American Federation of Radio and Television Artists, Annenberg School, University of Pennsylvania, Philadelphia), p. 4.

[33]Bradley S. Greenberg, *Life on Television: Content Analyses of U.S. Television Drama,* (Norwood, NJ: Ablex), pp. 47–95.

[34]Carroll and Davis, op. cit.

[35]For example, see Paul Hirsch, "On Not Learning from One's Own Mistakes: A Reanalysis of Gerbner et al.'s Findings on Cultivation Analysis: Part II," *Communication Research,* 8 (1981): 3–37 for methodological criticism, and W. James Potter, "Cultivation Theory and Research: A Conceptual Critique," *Human Communication Research,* 19 (1993): 564–601, for a theoretical critique.

[36]George Gerbner and Larry Gross, "Living with Television: The Violence Profile," *Journal of Communication*, 26(2) (1976): 173–199.

[37]Gerbner et al., "Growing Up with Television: The Cultivation Perspective," in Jennings Bryant and Dolf Zillmann, eds., *Media Effects: Advances in Theory and Research*, (Hillsdale, NJ: Erlbaum, 1994), pp. 27–28.

[38]Barrie Gunter, "The Question of Media Violence," in Jennings Bryant and Dolf Zillmann, eds., *Media Effects: Advances in Theory and Research*, (Hillsdale, NJ: Erlbaum, 1994), p. 192.

[39]Ibid.

[40]Willard D. Rowland, Jr., *The Politics of TV Violence*, (Beverly Hills, CA: Sage, 1983).

[41]Doug Halonen, "Historic Rewrite Finally Passes," *Electronic Media*, February 5, 1996, p. 54.

[42]*The Works of Aristotle*, Vol. II, (Chicago: Encyclopedia Britannica, 1952), p. 684.

[43]Gunter, op. cit., p. 167.

[44]Albert Bandura, "Social Cognitive Theory of Mass Communication," in Jennings Bryant and Dolf Zillmann, eds., *Media Effects: Advances in Theory and Research*, (Hillsdale, NJ: Erlbaum, 1994), pp. 61–90.

[45]Bandura et al., "Imitation of film-mediated aggressive models," *Journal of Abnormal and Social Psychology*, 66(1) (1963): 3–11.

[46]Schramm et al., *Television in the Lives of Our Children*, (Stanford, CA: Stanford University Press, 1961), pp. 152–153

[47]W. James Potter, "Does Television Viewing Hinder Academic Achievement among Adolescents?" *Human Communication Research*, 14 (1987): 27.

[48]L. Sandy Maisel and Charles Bassett, *Political Parties and Elections in the United States: An Encyclopedia*, (New York: Garland, 1991), 1101.

[49]Sara Fritz and Dwight Morris, *Handbook of Campaign Spending*, (Washington, DC: Congressional Quarterly, 1992), p. 53.

[50]Ibid., p. 55, and "The 10 Biggest Campaign Bankrolls," *Time*, November 18, 1996, p. 41.

[51]Sig Mickelson, *From Whistle Stop to Sound Bite: Four Decades of Politics and Television*, (New York: Praeger, 1989), p. 155.

[52]Ruth Marcus, "Loophole Lets Dems Stretch Scarce Cash for TV Ads," *Chicago Sun-Times*, July 1, 1996, p. 16.

[53]Maxwell McCombs and Donald L. Shaw, "The Agenda-Setting Function of the Mass Media," *Public Opinion Quarterly*, 36 (1972): 176–187.

[54]Maxwell McCombs, "News Influence on Our Pictures of the World," in Jennings Bryant and Dolf Zillmann, eds., *Media Effects: Advances in Theory and Research*, (Hillsdale, NJ: Erlbaum, 1994), pp. 7–9.

[55]Ibid., pp. 13–14.

[56]Keith Melder, *Hail to the Candidate: Presidential Campaigns from Banners to Broadcasts*, (Washington, DC: Smithsonian Institution, 1992), p. 48.

[57]Paul F. Boller, Jr., *Presidential Anecdotes*, (New York: Penguin Books, 1982), p. 179.

[58]Melder, op. cit., p. 50.

[59]Gina M. Garramone, "Effects of Negative Political Advertising: The Roles of Sponsor and Rebuttal," *Journal of Broadcasting & Electronic Media*, 29 (1985): 147–159.

[60]"Voter Turnout," *Time*, November 18, 1996, p. 41.

[61]*Statistical Abstract of the United States*, op. cit., p. 290.

[62]Michael J. Robinson, "Public Affairs Television and the Growth of Political Malaise: The Case of 'The Selling of the Pentagon,'" *American Political Science Review,* 70 (1976): 409–432.

[63]James R. Walker, "How Media Reliance Affects Political Efficacy in the South," *Journalism Quarterly,* 65 (1988): 746–747.

[64]Michael Pfau et al., *Influence of Individual Communication Media on Public Confidence in Democratic Institutions,* a paper presented at the International Communication Association Conference, May 1996.

[65]Palmgreen et al., "Uses and Gratifications Research: The Past Ten Years," in Rosengren et al., *Media Gratifications Research: Current Perspectives,* (Beverly Hills, CA: Sage, 1985), pp. 11–37.

[66]Melvin L. DeFleur and Sandra Ball–Rockeach, *Theories of Mass Communication,* 5th ed., (New York: Longman, 1989), pp. 297–327.

10

The Future of
Broadcast Television

PREDICTIONS

The preceding chapters have outlined the present condition of the television broadcasting industry in the United States, with a few indications of things to come. In this chapter, we examine the future more comprehensively.

The traditional sources of information on industry forecasting continue to release linear-based predictions for broadcast television. Revenues and expenses are expected to grow at a consistent rate, despite inevitable irregularities. For example, local broadcast advertising has been projected to mushroom to $25.6 billion by the year 2000, up from $18.9 billion in 1995, according to investment banking firm Veronis, Suhler, & Associates.[1]

Discontinuities are harder to predict. We focus in this chapter on the various forces that could bring fundamental change to the present system of television broadcasting. Several possible scenarios will be explored.

In order to understand what can change in the future, it is useful to look at what is *not* likely to change. Stability is reasonably certain in three important areas. First, the continuation of free markets and laissez-faire capitalism in the United States is an underlying assumption throughout this chapter. Second, one might expect that leisure time will continue to grow, albeit at a much slower pace. The implication for television broadcasting is that competition among a growing field of video providers will grow more fierce for the attention of audiences. Finally, there is presently no functional equivalent to broadcast television programming: It combines universal and instantaneous delivery of locally-originated sight, sound, and motion at no direct cost, in a way that no other medium can or is likely to do. To the extent that broadcast television can corner the universal delivery market, it can expect to survive forever. To summarize, broadcast television offers:

- Instantaneous delivery
- Universal access by viewers
- Full-motion color video and high-fidelity sound
- No direct cost
- Capacity for local programming

The current status of the broadcast industry relies on present marketing conditions. In the past, it has been costly for the consumer to move from wireless to wired delivery of television programming because a second wire, or ancillary dish antenna, had to be added to each home. But eventually the one-wire world will unfold. Nearly every home already has a twisted-pair phone connection, and that link to the major telephone corporations will eventually evolve into an optical fiber cable with the bandwidth to provide all varieties of video service along with telephone.

Furthermore, universal delivery may not be the virtue that many broadcasters believe it to be. The most important viewers in an advertiser-supported universe are those with money, because many products are targeted to the affluent. This audience is also the one that can afford cable, DSS, and other video services.

The saving grace for broadcasters is that advertisers want universal access to audiences in order to protect brand equity for their clients. Successful brands used by every household (e.g., bathroom tissue) must appeal to all 100 million television households, not just the 66 million with cable. The top advertising rates are earned by the top-ranked programs.

The mass audience may be the goal of the advertiser, but the individual homes that comprise the television universe may have other plans. Portions of the television audience may become demassified, with individuals constructing their own unique video environments from pay-per-view menus of options rather than from predetermined schedules of programs.[2] Although we lack compelling evidence that a significant portion of viewers is interested in interacting with television, new technologies at least give them a chance to try out new vistas. This will become more apparent by 2007, the year that the new all-digital television standard is fully deployed.

Broadcast and multichannel television is a spectator-oriented medium. A key question for the future is how computers will stimulate the desire for participation rather than merely watching. For instance, will viewers be content with channel-surfing as a means of program selection, or will they want menu-driven programming that provides a nonsequential selection process? With newer technologies and eventual diffusion of such innovations, broadcast television could appear antiquated. Consumers sometimes adopt innovations once a critical mass is reached. For example, reluctant buyers of answering machines and VCRs simply got tired of explaining why they did not own such devices. Clearly, computers will become the next home appliance in the future.

By September 1996, 14.7 million homes were hooked to the Internet (compared to 6.2 million a year earlier), with 20 million adults logging on weekly.[3] The computer interconnection is so powerful that some predict 10 million users will eventually transmit television signals on the Internet.[4] Such "webcasting" could further dilute the mainstream broadcast programming options. Already "cybernetworks" are showing broadcast-type soap operas on the Internet, each hoping to become a mainstream television network.[5]

Beginning in late 1998, the government plans to stimulate the industry by offering each broadcast television station a new channel to use for delivering high-definition (digital) television.[6] Broadcasters will have to invest heavily in new transmission equipment to remain competitive with digital wide-screen images promised by cable operators and direct satellite programmers. Although everyone agrees that digital TV is coming and coming fast, it is not clear what that will mean to the average viewer or the industry. Whether the technology will be used to improve the quality of images or to multiply the number of programs offered is far from certain.[7] For example, as we mentioned in Chapter 3, television stations may decide to divide their single digital channel into multiple channels under the old, low-definition standard rather than one high-definition channel.

Technology is just one force to be considered. This chapter also looks at several other forces shaping the future of the broadcast industry. These include internationalization of media, consolidation of the television industry, convergence of television and computer industries, and expansion of television reality into the larger culture.

INTERNATIONALIZATION

Television networks and the producers who supply them have traditionally been U.S. corporations. The motion picture industry is based in Hollywood and the original three networks sprang from New York City. Foreign-based media evolved at about the same time, but U.S. companies largely dominated world production of filmed entertainment.

Until recently, the most-watched television programs in many countries were dubbed versions of U.S. programs, but the privatization of foreign media has prompted countries to produce their own programs. Still, there is an increasing number of countries to which programming can be sold, and even those countries that have increased domestic production continue to buy U.S. programs. However, new partnerships will be formed to meet the worldwide appetite for sports programming.[8] Already, broadcast networks like NBC, and cable networks like the Discovery Channel, are trying to create global brand names for their programming products.

One likely scenario is that a small handful of global companies will swallow up the dozen or more major players in Europe, Asia, and South America. America has its Ted Turner, Australia spawned Rupert Murdoch, Italy/France/Spain has Silvio Berlusconi, and Germany has Leo Kirch. Together these media titans and their conglomerates strike strategic alliances. For example, Kirch is programming its new digital TV service in Germany with millions of dollars worth of Hollywood material, including a ten-year deal with Disney for exclusive pay-TV rights to existing and future live-action films.[9]

Economics are a key consideration in joint ventures and strategic alliances among global media interests. Although conditions may change in the next century, the 1990s were characterized by improvements in advertising revenues and more money lent from world banks as a result of improvements in the global economy. As other countries privatize their media, there are more opportunities for U.S. companies to defray the costs of mergers with their unmatched capacity to produce high-quality entertainment and information.[10] NBC, for example, has expanded into worldwide markets to take advantage of its vast news organization. NBC plans to dominate the global distribution of news through its ownership of the NBC Super Channel in Europe, CNBC in Europe and Asia, NBC Asia, and the worldwide MS–NBC network.

CONSOLIDATION OF THE TELEVISION INDUSTRY

The fact that this book covers the broadcast industry as a separate topic is somewhat at odds with the convergence of media that were once only competitors. But, as we explained in Chapter 1, there are benefits to broadcast television's unique strengths. Before multichannel television was first popularized by cable operators and then by direct satellite providers, the practice of putting programs "on the air" was the dominant method for reaching mass audiences. Broadcast television connected homes to a nearly continuous stream of programming through antennae on set-tops and rooftops.

Cable television originally operated at the fringe of the television industry, in opposition to broadcast television but greatly dependent on it. Television networks lobbied the FCC to impede the growth of cable channels, except in their capacity to extend the reach of over-the-air programs. Over time, however, broadcasters realized the inevitability of a multichannel world and began to diversify into cable. Broadcast networks bought into cable networks when they saw that channels would arise from new arrangements with production studios. NBC begot CNBC and MS–NBC, and ABC became a part-owner of ESPN. Fox started its own all-news channel in 1996 to compete with CNN and MS–NBC. CBS withdrew from cable after a disastrous attempt to launch a cultural channel in the early 1980s, but ventured back in the late 1990s with its Eye on CBS channel.

By 1997, the threat of direct broadcast satellites (DBS), also called digital satellite service, sufficiently threatened both broadcasters and cable operators that the two former enemies began to rethink their competition. Some projections forecast 20 million DBS subscribers by the year 2000. Interestingly, some 30 percent of the new DBS subscribers still have cable service, making each a "multiprovider household" (MPH). Such early adopters of DBS are the cream of the cable subscribers, who are far more likely to subscribe to pay-per-month or pay-per-view services. The threat of DBS to conventional broadcast service is particularly sharp when cast against the original projections of 5 million subscribers by the year 2000, yet it is clear that the broadcast networks have less to fear than their local broadcast affiliates. Nothing, beyond affiliation contracts, prevents the major networks from distributing their popular programs and embedded commercials via direct satellite. For them the big question is whether they can compete alongside a cornucopia of choices.

If affiliates become second-class providers of video programming, many broadcasters worry about their futures. Even within the ranks of network broadcasters, some programmers have called for less cutthroat, head-to-head competition among broadcast networks in order to maximize the programming strengths of individual networks. To the extent that networks can optimize their offerings, affiliates and networks alike will continue to prosper, as long as their program suppliers continue to bring the best shows to the networks first, before shopping them to multichannel providers like cable and DBS. This is a real concern for the networks. As newer forms of program distribution evolve, the broadcast television networks may lose their first-refusal status for the best new shows.

The movie studios have branched into broadcast and cable, either by buying networks (as Disney did with Capital Cities/ABC) or founding them (as Fox, Paramount, and Warner Brothers did). The same companies that make the shows also distribute the programs, publish the books and music, and own the cable systems. The three largest conglomerates are Time Warner/Turner, Disney/ABC, and Viacom/Paramount, accounting for 58 percent of the 1994 revenues generated by the top ten media companies.[11]

The largest broadcast merger in 1995 was the Disney/ABC alliance. The new production division combined Walt Disney Pictures, Touchstone Pictures, and ABC Productions. On the distribution side, Disney/ABC boasted eleven owned-and-operated (O & O) television stations and 228 broadcast affiliates. In the multichannel content arena, the merger brought ABC Television into the fold with the Disney Channel and part-ownership of the ESPN, Lifetime, and A&E channels. All told, the deal represented $4.6 billion in cash flow and affected 85,000 employees.

The number of broadcast owners is shrinking as government ownership limits loosen. Westinghouse bought CBS in 1995 and quickly expanded to an array of fifteen owned-and-operated stations, reaching 33 percent of all homes in the United States.

Group owners of television stations are also busy buying up each other. In 1995, three mergers alone accounted for nearly $1.2 billion. More ownership consolidation is expected to follow the loosening of restrictions under the 1996 Telecommunications Act. Broadcasters were elated that the new regulations would not charge them for additional digital spectrum, as some in congress had threatened.[12]

There are three types of mergers: those who want in (e.g., Westinghouse buys CBS), those who want more control (e.g., Disney buys ABC to guarantee distribution for its programs), and those who want to diversify (e.g., newspaper giant Gannett buys television giant Multimedia).[13] Regardless of the reasons for media acquisition, the result is a broader scope for the media giants.

For example, the 1996 merger of Time Warner and Turner Communications resulted in the world's largest media empire, for the time being. The $7.6 billion merger (substantially less than the $19 billion Disney paid to buy ABC, but larger in scope) brought together a staggering array of entities:

Film/TV Programming:	Warner Brothers Television, Warner Brothers Filmed Entertainment, Castle Rock Entertainment, New Line Cinema, Turner Pictures Worldwide, Hanna-Barbera Entertainment, Savoy Pictures (3 percent)
Cable/Satellite TV Channels:	HBO, Cinemax, CNN, Headline News, Cartoon Network, TBS, Turner Classic Movies, TNT, Court TV (55 percent), Comedy Central (50 percent), E! Entertainment (49 percent), Sega Channel (33 percent), Black Entertainment Television (15 percent), SportSouth Network (44 percent)
Broadcast Television Network:	The WB
Cable/Telecommunications:	Time Warner Cable (11.7 million U.S. homes)
Music:	Warner Brothers Records, Atlantic Group, Elektra
Publishing:	Time Inc., Book-of-the-Month Club, Time Life, Warner Books, Sunset Books, Little, Brown & Co., Oxmoor House, and Leisure Arts
Sports:	Atlanta Braves, Atlanta Hawks, World Championship Wrestling
Theme Parks:	Six Flags Theme Parks (49 percent)

In order to understand the future of media mergers, it is useful to consider why they take place in the first place. The media industry has three main characteristics: high fixed costs of production and distribution, high risk of consumer rejection, and static revenues.[14] As explained in Chapter 3, only very large companies have the economies of scope and scale to reduce risk and spread costs. Only giant media empires can absorb the high costs of production and can afford to wait for the high returns.[15] Consequently, it is not so much a question of whether broadcasters can afford to merge with new media and others in the vertical chain, but whether they can afford not to. External forces, primarily government restrictions, may limit the number of mergers in the future, but no evidence of a slowdown is apparent today.

THE INFORMATION SUPERHIGHWAY: WILL BROADCAST TELEVISION SURVIVE OR THRIVE?

In the midst of conglomerization of various media, the very stability of television as a medium is under threat from new technologies. The World Wide Web as a means of easy access to the Internet did not exist until 1993. Now, every product and nearly every television program and network is linked to a steady stream of on-line information. A rapidly growing number of television stations are putting their call letters between a "www." and a ".com" on the Internet.

In 1996, Philips introduced a product that takes on-line interactivity out of the computer room and into the living room. WebTV combines Internet access with conventional television, using an interface designed by Microsoft. Despite an initial gradual start for WebTV, Microsoft purchased the new venture from Philips in 1997 for $425 million. Microsoft's strategic ventures and alliances with major media corporations (like the MS–NBC channel with the NBC television network) point to a future where computers will influence viewing behavior.

For example, one component of viewing behavior is channel flipping. The audience has become sophisticated over time in the use of remote control devices to "channel-surf" during commercial breaks, sometimes creating an unplanned video environment. With the advent of TV-based computer-surfing, viewers are no longer limited to a predetermined number of television channels to view. The audience can surf the networks and surf the web simultaneously. The World Wide Web has already embraced the television networks and syndicated broadcast/cable programming, and vice versa.

The cable television industry seems uniquely poised to take advantage of technological advancements. For example, Cable Television Laboratories established an agreement in 1996 to standardize new digital set-top boxes and digital cable modems. Menu-driven television programming via cable networks or the computer Internet is not that far away.

On the other hand, innovations from the cable industry are often more promise than fruition. In the late 1970s Warner spent millions on an interactive television system known as Qube and learned that the audience was not interested. Maybe the idea was ahead of its time, however, and future viewers, especially those who grew up with home computers and Sega games, will want their television fare served up from menus rather than cafeteria-style.

The Telecommunications Act of 1996 established a context that enabled fundamental changes in the delivery of video programming. For example, the telephone companies and the cable "multiple system operators" (MSO) have begun to offer interactive programming via a "full service network" (FSN). At least in small markets, entrepreneurs can begin providing telephone and video services on one wire.[16] Neither the broadcasters nor the newer forms of distribution have much expertise in offering interactive programming, but both sides have the financial resources to make strategic alliances with companies like Microsoft and other multimedia providers. John Pavlik notes that the new Telecommunications Act exempts DBS from rate and tax regulation. He further speculates that DBS providers like Rupert Murdoch will attempt to offer local television stations via satellite.[17] It is hard to imagine, however, that the full complement of 1,200 local stations would be available.

The key unanswered question surrounding the possible demise of broadcast television is whether viewers are willing to pay for programming that was once free. Even if the viewers are willing, will their finite leisure time justify the incremental expense of pay television?

Baldwin, McVoy, and Steinfield argue that different tiers of nonbroadcast service (*video-on-demand, à la carte* channel packages, broadcast basic) allow consumers to direct their entertainment resources toward the most desirable programs.[18] Just as motion pictures have exhibition "windows" that begin in theaters and end with television syndication, television programs may eventually begin with premium distribution and later appear on "free" broadcast television. To the extent that broadcasters are owned by movie studios, this trend may be controlled, but viewers will nevertheless have more options to see better programs first by paying a fee.

This so-called "consumer underinvestment in television"[19] may mean that there is an untapped demand for television programming that the conventional over-the-air networks will never fulfill. Forecasters have long predicted competition for the broadcast networks,[20] and it eventually materialized.

In the early 1990s, the future looked very dim for the broadcasters. Ken Auletta wrote a scathing indictment of the broadcast industry that led many to predict the networks' demise.[21] By the mid-1990s, as we have seen, the networks were again making record profits and controlling the television industry. The broadcasters themselves wrote books defending the future of their brand of television media.

Gene Jankowski and David Fuchs have argued that the old system is still firmly in place, and is unlikely to change significantly.[22] First, they maintain that the network–affiliate arrangement is presently the sole means of reaching nearly every television home at negligible cost to the viewer. As such, it will have no real competition for some time to come, implying that network hegemony is intact. This "nothing-will-change" assessment is a popular prediction among other media scholars as well. W. Russell Neuman and Clifford Stoll have also predicted a long, happy life for the *status quo* in their books on the future of the media.

Second, Jankowski and Fuchs have convincingly argued against technological determinism by exploring technology issues in the context of three requirements: distribution, programming, and funding. The latter two, the authors contend, are ignored in visions of broadcast television's future. Prognosticators envision new means of distribution without answering the thorny questions of who will pay, given finite consumer resources of money and time, and what mechanism will fill the additional hours of required programming.

Third, Jankowski and Fuchs have characterized the machinations of the cable industry and the telephone companies as protective of their own overpenetrated markets. In their opinion, both industries have run out of ways to make money from their core businesses and are looking to expand into other domains. The largest cable operator, TCI, saw its stock value plummet in the latter half of 1996 because analysts predicted little revenue growth potential in this largely saturated industry. The recent retreat from video services testing by some regional telephone companies may mean that wired competition is not nearly as imminent as once predicted, although Bell Atlantic continues to press forward. As we observe later in this chapter, the transition to a wired nation may take time.

Finally, the new communication technologies appear to be serving small-scale interests, nibbling at the margins of the network audience by presenting old reruns of programs produced by the networks or an ever-dwindling supply of theatrical releases from Hollywood. Jankowski and Fuchs characterized the predicted 500-channel menu as 490 niche services fighting each other over "ever smaller fragments."

It is too simplistic, however, to pit networks against cable at a time when the industries are converging. The future is instead evolving toward more partnerships among the various technologies and the major studios that supply the software. Television icon Ted Turner, for example, looks for partnerships with computer maven Bill Gates.

Those who claim that the future of broadcasting is secure focus too much attention on domestic broadcasting and not enough on the globalization of telecommunication. Broadcasters have begun to look beyond the continental borders for economic opportunities.

Apologists for the broadcast industry still harbor enmity for the cable industry. One oft-repeated argument is that cable has somehow stolen the networks' programs, even though the advertiser-supported system requires that the supplier give away the product to one customer (viewers) in order to maximize the market for the other customer (advertisers).

The most misleading idea espoused by pro-broadcast forces has been that audience circulation somehow connotes quality. When asked how he knew his network had high-quality shows, Bud Grant, former programming chief at CBS, once replied that the high audience ratings proved that the viewers liked what they were seeing.[23] The real truth, of course, is that the viewers, like voters, can only vote for the candidates who make it onto the ballot.

DEMOGRAPHIC TRENDS

A more diverse country will also influence media trends in the twenty-first century. The newer, urban-based television networks (The WB and UPN) have already begun to focus on more diverse programming, often appealing to ethnic viewers in large metropolitan areas. Although situation comedy on the older broadcast television networks has never been particularly adverse to ethnic families, the newer networks have been featuring an even heavier mix of nonwhite casts (see Chapter 7).

Television has always attempted to reflect the U.S. mainstream, so it is not a surprise that networks are adapting to the more diverse makeup of viewing groups. In the 1950s, shows like *Ozzie and Harriet* and *Leave It to Beaver* showed us an America that was mostly white and middle-class. Until the 1970s, the "typical" viewer was assumed to be Caucasian.

Demographers have noted some trends in population diversity in the latter part of the twentieth century, specifically between 1990 and 1995.[24] For example, white non-Hispanic persons make up nearly 74 percent of all Americans but account for just 38 percent of the population growth. Hispanic persons only make up 10 percent of the total population but account for 30 percent of the five-year growth. The African American population (12 percent) is growing more evenly with a 16 percent increase. At these rates, the ethnic composition of America is destined to change in the next twenty-five to fifty years. As far as television consumption is concerned, one can expect more viewing among nonwhite groups, which traditionally spend more time watching TV.

TELEVISION AS A CULTURAL FORCE

As television evolves into a stronger presence in U.S. homes through the decline of print-based media and the rise of an electronic marriage with the computer, the broadcast (and wired) version of TV in the new millennium is likely to exert an even stronger influence on U.S. culture. To the extent that television replaces other functional alternatives for leisure time, it is conceivable that television will become an integral part of daily life, especially as the telephone and fax machine become linked to computers, as computers are wedded to television sets, as cable television companies compete for local telephone service, and as telephone companies begin to offer video services.

An abundant supply of mediated communication may sound wonderful, but to what extent does the typical person want to be electronically linked to the rest of the world? Baldwin, McVoy, and Steinfield list several drawbacks of increased video services: information overload, irresponsible use of unedited content, increased commercialism to subsidize higher programming costs, social isolationism and alienation, less privacy, and loss of traditional communities.[25] They also discuss the many kinds of technological gaps between the economic haves and have-nots: information gaps, entertainment and sports gaps, social gaps, urban–rural gaps, and freedom of choice gaps.[26]

Some television broadcasters are adamant that academics and social critics have it all wrong about television's potential as a cultural force. According to them, given a choice, "the audience will opt for relaxation."[27] But is it desirable for viewers to become less and less interested in serious information, especially about political campaigns? By giving the viewers what they want, is broadcast television (and its multichannel conspirators) really serving the public interest?

A key question is how much diversity and choice the public can stand. Until now, the "electronic hearth" that broadcast television represents has served to unify the nation under a set of common experiences. For good or bad, network news programs have commanded the audience's attention, providing their interpretations of events and fads. Would that be possible in a world of limitless channel choices?

If culture is based on what is "in" or "out," what mass medium will communicate the "national norm," whatever it should become? If each viewer is watching a different program, what is the incentive for program producers to make a product good enough to appeal to a large audience?

In 1993, Cox Cable executive Ajit Dalvi predicted that the so-called 500-channel universe would become 250 channels for premium movies, 50 channels of pay-per-view events, and a 100-channel "grazing zone" similar to cable television, with another 200-channel "quality zone" providing an additional two channels for each grazing channel.[28] Will there be 100 channels, each with a 1 percent share of the viewing? Beyond the needs of advertisers to efficiently reach the masses, what will address the need for cultural institutions to reach the masses?

POSSIBLE SCENARIOS

Throughout this chapter, we have examined the various influences on the future of the broadcast television industry. Although it is difficult to predict the future, it is still useful to explore the more likely scenarios. Each of the following educated guesses centers on the ultimate victory of either distribution or content forces (or a mixed outcome). We will also discuss the implications for the broadcast television industry.

Distribution Wins

The first and most plausible scenario is that the telephone companies (telecos) will buy their way into every television home. This one-wire solution, as discussed earlier, is the natural outcome of a switchover from coaxial cable to fiber-optic wires. Like universal telephone service, the big telecommunications giants will be common carriers regulated by the government. Content providers will be separate corporations, with the usual program producers (e.g., movie studios, niche channels, full-service networks) at the top level.

Cable operators who had already installed their own fiber wires will be required to lease back their infrastructure to the phone companies, although the telecos will be anxious to purchase the systems outright. The situation is somewhat analogous to pole-attachment fees paid by cable operators to the telecos in earlier times. As it becomes more and more clear that cable will yield to the telecos, the likelihood of massive system buyouts by the phone companies will increase. Cable-multiple system operators will forge strategic alliances with the remaining broadcast companies who provide ancillary wireless communication to unwired homes (e.g., rural homes, houseboats, mobile vehicles, etc.).

In this scenario, broadcasters will still operate as network affiliates carrying local programs, but distribution will be primarily wired instead of exclusively over-the-air. Because legislators probably will require the phone company to provide free entertainment and information shows to those who cannot afford value-added premium programming, an advertiser-supported system of mass appeal network programming probably will survive. The main difference will be that fewer one-time-only events will be provided by the broadcast networks. But because the new-style networks will still have universal access to nearly all viewers, the most popular and successful shows will remain on ABC, CBS, NBC, Fox, UPN, The WB, and any other networks that survive the transition to wired communication. Even before its merger with ABC, Disney had made joint ventures with BellSouth, Ameritech, and SBC Communication to provide content to wired teleco ventures.

How long would it take for this change to occur? By conservative estimates, fiber-to-the-curb (FTTC) and fiber-to-the-home (FTTH) is many billions of dollars and several years away (circa 2030). By that time, direct satellite broadcasting could largely supplant over-the-air broadcasting with "through-the-air" broadcasting. The telephone companies will upgrade all homes except those in the most remote areas, which will have satellite receivers.

Wireless cable, using high-frequency direct-line frequencies originally reserved for educational purposes, will serve as a stopgap for multichannel distribution until all twisted-pair copper wiring is replaced. Moreover, existing coaxial cable systems will be purchased by telephone companies in many smaller locales to aid in the transition to fiber.

Although distribution is the focus, content will remain crucial nevertheless. Less reliance on schedule-based programming will not mean the total adoption of menu-based selection. Most viewers will still opt for relaxation and will continue to seek novelty. The important difference is that, with the advent of Internet-based programming, it is entirely possible to install a "something else" button on every remote control that would promise limitless random choices. Such a device could first run through dozens of mainstream channels, then hundreds of niche channels, and finally thousands of random web channels and pages. The something-else button could easily remember where it had been in the past twenty-four hours to avoid cycling through old options, offering endless choices of thousands and thousands of channels. Instead of singer Bruce Springsteen's refrain of "fifty-seven channels and nothing on," 57,000 channels and nothing on may be the cry in the twenty-first century.

Content Wins

Another possible scenario is that the many entertainment program producers will consolidate into a vertically-integrated distribution system, offering a choice of distribution systems to viewers at different windows of opportunity. In this case, the actual delivery of programs will remain a hodgepodge of terrestrial broadcasting, *digital satellite systems,* conventional cable, *fiber optics,* and *wireless cable.* Content, however, would be controlled by a very small handful of suppliers operating at a global level.

Big-budget productions would be delivered over high-definition digital transmission systems to pay-per-view audiences. Subsequent distribution would cycle through various à la carte windows and pay-per-month schedules. Instead of HBO producing programs for exclusive exhibition on pay channels, for example, premium channels would offer up television shows in the same way that theatrical movies are distributed in today's entertainment world, with all programs eventually available on "free" television channels.

Governments probably would likely regulate these producers' control of distribution channels, but content providers undoubtedly would be allowed ready access to, and part ownership of, the delivery systems. Home video and premium television would continue to offer independent producers reasonable access to audiences, but viewers would primarily watch programs made by the major conglomerates. As discussed earlier, no one but the giants can afford the high costs of production and withstand the momentous risk of predicting changing tastes in programming.

In this scenario, broadcasters would probably fare less well than in the previous distribution-wins model. For many years, television networks have used the unique advantage of their distribution system to maintain high advertising rates. With a system based on programs, the broadcast networks would have little advantage as mere packagers of shows. The motion picture studios would retain a great deal of influence over public tastes, especially when coupled with a news-gathering force (e.g., Disney/ABC). Broadcast networks without strong links to the production of entertainment probably would be forced to sell off their information-gathering expertise to the select number of entertainment program providers.

Nobody Wins

This scenario projects "more of the same," with the attendant ebb and flow of distribution technologies and program formats. Such a future seems unlikely, even though many people expect it to happen. They argue that the evolution of other media formats has not triggered discontinuous change. When film and radio evolved, the newspapers adapted and survived. When television appeared, film and radio adapted and survived. If past is prologue, then broadcast television will adapt and survive, too.

However, this scenario does not imply that there will be no change at all. We can reasonably expect that computers will get faster, moving images will get better, and virtual reality will be perfected. But, cataclysmic reordering is not on the horizon, or even just beyond the horizon. The nobody-wins scenario acknowledges that institutions, governments, and societies exert a powerful inertia.

We believe that this third scenario is the least likely one. Our crystal ball is no better than the readers', but we hope that this chapter and the preceding ones have illuminated the complexities that underlie broadcast economics, technology, regulation, and audience tastes. We do not believe that the future belongs principally to the television broadcasters, as others have argued.[29] If we had a million dollars to invest, it would likely be with a visionary telephone company. If "let-the-marketplace-decide" forces continue to hold sway, the future may belong to the one-wire world, not the over-the-air broadcaster.

NOTES

[1]Keith J. Kelly, "Bright Prospects Seen for Cable TV, New Media," *Advertising Age,* August 19, 1996, p. 8.

[2]William Bradley, "Behind the Megamedia Mergers," *San Francisco Chronicle,* August 6, 1996, Sec. A, p. 19.

[3]*Wall Street Journal,* October 21, 1996, Sec. B, p. 11.

[4]Ken C. Pohlmann, "Channel Envy," *Video,* September, 1996, pp. 23–25.

[5]Bruce Haring, "PCs as TVs : Dramas Kick Off Cyberspace Networks," *USA Today,* April 16, 1996, Sec D, p. 3.

[6]Chris McConnell, "FCC Enumerates TV's Future," *Broadcasting & Cable,* August 19, 1996, pp. 17–22.

[7]Joel Brinkley, *Defining Vision: The Battle for the Future of Television,* (New York: Harcourt Brace, 1997).

[8]Jim McConville, "Everybody Wants to Get into the Game," *Broadcasting & Cable,* April 8, 1996, pp. 50–51.

[9]Lisa Bannon, "Kirch of Germany Gets Pay-TV Rights to Disney Movies," *Wall Street Journal,* August 30, 1996, Sec A, p. 5–D.

[10]Joe Mandese, "Media World on Brink of M & A Frenzy," *Advertising Age,* July 25, 1994, pp. 1–2.

[11]Douglas A. Ferguson, "A Framework for Programming Strategies," in *Broadcast/Cable Programming,* Susan T. Eastman and Douglas A. Ferguson, eds., (Belmont, CA: Wadsworth, 1997).

[12]Bill Carter, "The Networks See Potential For Growth," *New York Times,* February 2, 1996, Sec D, p. 6.

[13]Douglas Gomery, "Mass Media Merger Mania," *American Journalism Review,* December, 1995, p. 46.

[14]"Meet the New Media Monsters," *The Economist,* March 11, 1989, pp. 65–66.

[15]Mandese, op. cit.

[16]Thomas F. Baldwin, D. Stephens McVoy, and Charles Steinfield, *Convergence: Integrating Media, Information & Communication,* (Thousand Oaks, CA: Sage, 1996).

[17]John V. Pavlik, "Competition: Key to the Communications Future?" *Television Quarterly,* 1996, 28:2, pp. 35–43.

[18]Baldwin et al., op. cit., pp. 137–143.

[19]Ibid., p. 8.

[20]Cited in Baldwin et al., op. cit., p. 9.

[21]Ken Auletta, *Three Blind Mice: How the Networks Lost Their Way,* (New York: Random House, 1991).

[22]Gene F. Jankowski and David C. Fuchs, *Television Today and Tomorrow,* (New York: Oxford, 1995).

[23]From a television program, "CBS Reports: Don't Touch That Dial," (New York: CBS News, 1982).

[24]Peter Francese, "America at Mid-Decade," *American Demographics,* February, 1995, pp. 23–31.

[25]Baldwin et al., op. cit., pp. 384–391.

[26]Ibid., pp. 392–395.

[27]Jankowski and Fuchs, op. cit., p. 163.

[28]Kate Maddox, "The Big Picture: Visions of a New TV Begin to Merge," *Electronic Media,* November 8, 1993, p. 23.

[29]Jankowski and Fuchs, op. cit.

Glossary

À La Carte   Programs chosen separately by viewers, as items on a menu. See *video-on-demand*.

Access time   Daypart preceding prime time, usually between 7 and 8 P.M. (EST).

Adjacencies   A commercial spot next to a program that can be sold locally, especially spots for station sale appearing within (or next to) network prime-time programs.

Adjacent channel interference   Interference between stations that occupy side-by-side broadcast channels on the electromagnetic spectrum.

Affiliate   A commercial radio or television station receiving more than ten hours per week of network programming, but not owned by the network.

Agenda-setting   The media's power to increase the importance of an issue in the public's mind by giving it more coverage.

America's Public Television Stations (APTS)   Lobby group working for excellence in public television, supported by most PBS member stations.

Annenberg Foundation   A major supplier of funds to public television, financed by Walter Annenberg, publisher of *TV Guide.*

Association of College and University Broadcasting Stations (ACUBS)   Organization that united early educational radio broadcasters.

Audience flow   The movement of audiences from one program or time period to another, either on the same station or from one station to another; includes turning sets on and off. Applied to positive flow encouraged by similarity between contiguous programs.

Audimeter   Nielsen's in-home television rating meter, used until 1987. See also *peoplemeter.*

Authoritarian approach   An approach to controlling broadcast television, based on the assumption of complete governmental control, in which television is seen as a tool of the state.

Avail   Short for a sales availability.

Availability   Commercial spot advertising position *(avail)* offered for sale by a station or a network.

Avoidance   Intentionally not watching commercials, through the use of remote control devices (RCDs) or leaving the room.

Barriers to entry   Economists' description of the difficulty a new business encounters in its attempt to compete in an existing market.

Barter   Licensing of syndicated programs in exchange for commercial time (inventory) to eliminate the exchange of cash.

Barter syndicated   The method of program distribution in which the syndicator retains and sells a portion of a syndicated program's advertising time. In cash-plus-barter deals, the syndicator also receives fees from the station licensing the program.

Baumols disease   Rapid cost inflation of television program costs over time because networks try to outspend one another as audience expectations escalate.

Beat(s)   The geographic areas or topic-related areas in which a reporter gathers news (for example, White House, state government, northern suburbs).

Bidding   Practice whereby stations simultaneously compete for the best selling price for a syndicated program, usually to the benefit of the seller.

Blacklisting   The boycotting of actors, writers, directors, and other individuals by television networks and stations because of their believed or real association with Communists, Communist organizations, or organizations sympathetic to Communism.

Block grants   Funds advanced to major PBS production centers by CPB.

Blocking   Placing several similar programs together to create a unit promoting audience flow.

Blunting   A strategy of scheduling a show with a format identical to that of a competing program in a time slot; the opposite of the counterprogramming strategy.

Bridging   Beginning a program a half hour earlier than competing programs to draw off their potential audiences and hold them past the start time of competing programs.

Camcorder   A portable video camera and videotape recorder in one unit.

Carnegie Commission on Educational Television (CCET)   A committee appointed by former President Lyndon Johnson to study the long-range future of educational television.

Carnegie II   A second study by the Carnegie Commission that was highly critical of public television's previous ten-year performance.

Carrier wave(s)   The radio wave that carries the modulated video or audio signal in broadcast transmission.

Cash-plus-barter   A syndication deal in which the station pays the distributor a fee for program rights and gives the syndicator one or two minutes per half hour for national advertising sale; the station retains the remaining advertising time.

Category killer Domination by one large company or distribution channel for a particular product or service, whereby smaller competitors can no longer effectively compete on price.

Catharsis theory A theory that suggests humans can relieve aggressive feelings by viewing violent television content.

Cathode ray tube The glass vacuum tube used to display images in electronic television.

Chain Broadcasting Rules FCC rules designed to reduce the growing power of radio networks over their affiliated stations in the early 1940s.

Channel A band of radio frequencies used to transmit a radio or television signal.

Checkerboarding Scheduling five stripped programs alternately, one each day in the same time period; that is, rotating two, three, or five different shows five days of the week in the same time period.

Chicago School of Television An innovative group of locally produced television programs originating in Chicago during the late 1940s and early 1950s.

Clearance Acceptance of a network program by affiliates for airing; the total number of clearances governs a network program's potential audience size.

Coaxial cables Broadband cables capable of carrying many television signals. Once used by broadcast television networks to link stations with the network and currently used by cable television as the principle means of distributing television signals to homes.

Co-channel interference Interference between stations that occupy the same broadcast channel.

Cognitions Conscious thoughts about a message received through an exposure.

Communications Act of 1934 The federal law, as amended, that regulates broadcasting in the United States; it established the Federal Communications Commission to regulate broadcasting in "the public interest, convenience, and necessity."

Community Antenna Television (CATV) The first form of cable television that focused primarily on providing better reception of broadcast stations to consumers.

Community Service Grants (CSGs) Local station funding by CPB allowing stations to purchase programming from PBS.

Compensation A broadcast network payment to an affiliate for carrying network commercials.

Compression Technical process for reducing the necessary bandwidth of a television signal so that 2, 4, or more signals can fit in the same width of frequencies.

Concepts Ideas for proposed television programs.

Conservation of resources Management of supply to exploit price (e.g., releasing programming into various exhibition windows to maximize revenue).

Content analysis(es) The systematic counting of some part of the content of television programs or other media messages.

Co-op   Shared costs for advertising.

Copyright fees   Payment for the right to use a literary, dramatic, musical, or artistic work owned by another person or organization.

Corporation for Public Broadcasting (CPB)   The federally chartered private organization formed in 1967 to fund and oversee noncommercial broadcasting.

Cost per point (CPP)   The amount an advertising agency will pay for each ratings point.

Cost per thousand (CPM)   How much it costs an advertiser to reach a thousand viewers, listeners, or subscribers.

Counterprogramming   Scheduling programs with contrasting appeal to target unserved or underserved demographic groups.

CPM   See *cost per thousand.*

Cultivation   A theory that argues that one of the most important effects of television is its ability to shape our perceptions of reality.

Cume   Cumulative rating; the total number of different households that tune to a station at different times, generally over a one-week period.

Daypart   Period of two or more hours, considered as strategic unit in program schedules (for example, prime time in television—8 to 11 P.M.).

Dayparting   Altering programming to fit with the audience's changing activities during different times of the day.

Deficit financing   Licensing television programs to the broadcast networks at an initial loss, counting on later profits from syndication rights to cover production costs; practiced by the major Hollywood studios.

Demand   Needs and wants of consumers.

Demographics Descriptive information on an audience, usually the vital statistics of age and sex.

Dependency theory   A theory of media effects that suggests the media's impact is proportional to a person's or a society's dependency on it.

Deregulation   The movement, starting in the late 1970s, to reduce or eliminate unnecessary government regulations.

Designated market area (DMA)   Nielsen's term for a local viewing area.

Digital satellite system (DSS)   Growing cable television rival that delivers cable networks, pay-per-view programming, and other audio–video services directly from satellite to a small receiving dish.

Direct wave   The wave radiation pattern that is used by broadcast television. Waves move in a line of sight pattern from the station's transmitter.

Double-running   Scheduling strategy whereby episodes of a program are shown twice per day.

Downlink   The receiving dish in a satellite transmission system.

Dual clients   Term for the idea that broadcasters have two customers: the audience and the advertisers.

DuMont Network   Early U.S. television network owned by a major television equipment manufacturer; it stopped operation in 1955.

Duopoly Rule FCC rule limiting ownership of stations with overlapping coverage areas.

Economies of scale Lower cost per unit realized by very large companies that produce many units.

Economies of scope Lower risk associated with a single product or service, as a result of a company's control of a wide range of related products and services.

Educational Broadcasting Facilities Act A 1962 law that provided funds for the construction of educational television facilities.

Educational Television and Radio Center (ETRC) An organization formed by the Ford Foundation to stimulate networking among educational TV stations.

Educational Television Stations (ETS) A production center created by NAEB in the early 1960s.

Enhanced underwriting Disguised advertising in public broadcasting whereby corporate logos and products of companies that provide funding are mentioned during broadcasts.

Exposure Opportunity to watch a television commercial.

Fairness Doctrine Former FCC regulation that required stations to offer a balanced perspective on controversial issues of public importance.

Federal Communications Commission (FCC) The independent regulatory agency created and charged by congress to regulate broadcast television and other forms of telecommunications in the United States.

Federal Radio Education Committee (FREC) FCC appointed group that advocated educational radio channel reservation.

Fiber-optic transmission A newer type of transmission cable that uses fiber optics and has much greater channel capacity. It is replacing coaxial cable in some local cable systems.

Fiber optics Very thin and pliable glass cylinders capable of carrying wide bands of frequencies.

Field experiment An experiment conducted in an existing location rather than in a laboratory setting.

Financial interest and network syndication rules FCC regulations prohibiting broadcast networks from owning an interest in the domestic syndication rights of most television and radio programs they carry; modified to increase the number of hours a network can produce for its own schedule in 1991; eliminated in 1995.

Fin-syn Industry shorthand for Financial Interest and Network Syndication Rules.

First-run syndication Distribution of programs produced for initial release on stations, as opposed to the broadcast networks. Compare *off-network syndication.*

Flowthrough See *audience flow.*

Footprint The geographic area covered by a signal transmitted from a communications satellite.

Ford Foundation   A philanthropic organization responsible for the early growth of public television.

Free media   The news and entertainment media when they are used by a political campaign to transmit the campaign's message(s).

Fringe   The television time periods adjacent to prime time from 4 to 7 P.M. and 11 P.M. to midnight or later (EST). Early fringe means the time preceding the early local newscast; late fringe starts after the end of late local news, usually at 11:30 P.M.

Fund for Adult Education (FAE)   A Ford Foundation fund dedicated to increasing the use of television for educating adults.

Futures   Projected episodes in a series that have not yet been produced; typically, network series programming intended for syndication that may be purchased while the series is still on the network for a negotiated price that accounts for the purchaser's risk.

Geostationary satellite   A satellite whose orbit is synchronous with Earth's orbit. From the point of view of a revolving Earth, the satellite appears to remain in a fixed location.

Graphics   Titles and other artwork used in programs, newscasts, promos, or commercial spots.

Gross rating points   In advertising and promotion, a system of calculating the size of the delivered or anticipated audience by summing the rating points for all airings of a spot.

Group owner   An individual or company having the license for more than two broadcast facilities.

Hammocking   Positioning a program between two successful programs; they support a new or less successful program by lending their audience to it.

Happy news   News format that features journalists who speak very informally between segments and stories, to appear more warm and friendly.

Hiatus   Temporary (or permanent) vacation for a television program, during which the show is improved or dropped.

High-concept   Description for programs that feature extremely unusual plot premises or characters (e.g., superpowers, ghosts, aliens, witches).

High-definition television (HDTV)   Various technical systems for distributing video with higher quality and a wider aspect ratio than standard television broadcasting; generally uses a greater bandwidth in the spectrum and has more scanning lines.

Households (or Homes) Using Television (HUTs)   Ratings industry term for the total number of sets turned on during an average quarter hour; that is, actual viewing audience to be divided among all television stations and cable services in a market.

Hypoing   Extended promotion of a program or airing of special programs to increase audience size during a ratings period.

Iconoscope   First electronic television pickup tube used to convert light energy into electrical energy.

Ideal demographics The theory that a particular age and sex group should be the target of prime-time network television programs.

Image dissector The first electron gun used to scan the photosensitive surface of an electronic television picture tube.

Indecency A category of restricted broadcast programming created by the FCC. The FCC has attempted to restrict indecent programming to late-night hours.

Independent A commercial television broadcast station not affiliated with one of the national networks (by one FCC definition, it carries fewer than fifteen hours of prime-time network programming per week).

Independent Television Service (ITVS) A congressionally mandated organization providing funds for programs not under the authority of PBS or its members.

Infomercial A long sales pitch disguised as a program, called a "program-length commercial," usually lasting from fifteen to thirty minutes or more, typically presented on TV stations in less popular time periods.

Inventory The amount of time a station has for sale (or the commercials, records, or programs that fill that time).

Involvement Use of attention-getting devices during television commercials to increase effectiveness.

Joint Committee on Educational Television (JCET) Consortium of stakeholders in public television in the early 1950s.

Kids' Clubs Promotional vehicle for animated children's television programs in which young viewers are invited to join and win prizes.

Kilohertz One thousand hertz (cycles per second). The hertz is the standard unit of measure for radio waves.

Laboratory experiment Research conducted in a setting designed for the completion of experiments.

Lead-In Program preceding others, usually intended to increase audience flow to the later programs. Called *lead-off* at start of prime time.

Lead-off See *lead-in.*

Least objectionable programming (LOP) The concept that viewers watch, not just programs that they like, but programs that are the least offensive among the available choices during a particular time period.

License transfer The shifting of a broadcast license by the FCC from one station owner to another.

Limited effects tradition Early media research that concluded that the media, including television, mostly reinforced people's existing attitudes.

Live televised drama The production of anthology dramatic programs in real time, using multiple television cameras. The major form of dramatic programming in the first decade of television.

Local avails Similar to station breaks, the number and positioning of available commercials for sale by the local station in local and syndicated programs.

Local marketing agreements (LMAs) Contracts for sharing the functions of programming, staffing, and commercials time sales largely entered into by economically weak stations, much like newspaper joint operating agreements within a market. Also known as *lease management agreements.*

Localism   FCC policy of encouraging local ownership of broadcasting and community-oriented programming.

Loss leaders   Products that make no profit, but that attract consumers to other profitable products (e.g., sale items in a grocery).

Low power television station (LPTV)   A class of broadcast television stations with limited transmitter strength (usually covering less than ten miles), generally assigned in areas where a full-power signal would interfere with another station using the same channel.

Made-for-TV   Movie feature produced especially for the broadcast television networks, usually fitting a two-hour format with breaks for commercials.

Magazine format   A television program composed of varied segments within a common framework, structurally resembling a printed magazine.

Major market   One of the 100 largest metropolitan areas in number of television households.

Master control   Location at a television station or network where centralized electronic switching equipment is housed. Programs and commercials are played back on video machines in the master control room.

Mechanical television   The first form of television that used a spinning disk to scan and reproduce an image; replaced by electronic television.

Megahertz   One million hertz (cycles per second). The hertz is the standard unit of measure for radio waves.

Microwave relay   The television–telecommunications transmission system that uses multiple microwave stations to receive, amplify, and retransmit a signal over land.

Miniseries   An intentionally short-lived television series, usually aired on consecutive nights. *Roots* was the first widely acclaimed miniseries.

Modulated or modulation   The imposing of a video or audio signal onto a carrier wave for broadcast transmission.

Multichannel multipoint distribution service (MMDS)   A form of pay television also called *wireless cable;* distributes up to thirty-three channels (without compression) in a market.

Multi-network area (MNA)   This report gathers viewing information from only the seventy largest television markets.

Narcotizing dysfunction   The tendency for media to overwhelm their audiences with too much information about too many issues, leading to audience apathy.

National Association of Broadcasters   The major trade association for broadcast stations in the United States.

National Association of Educational Broadcasters (NAEB)   Organization that brought together all segments of educational broadcasting and acted as a federal lobbying group.

National Cable Television Association   The major trade association for the cable television industry in the United States.

National Committee on Education by Radio (NCER) Lobbying group formed in the 1930s to help preserve channels for educational radio.

National Education Television (NET) An enhanced production and networking center that grew from NETRC in the early 1960s.

National Educational Television and Radio Center (NETRC) A New York City production center that grew from ETRC.

National Public Radio (NPR) An organization created by CPB to oversee production and program services for public radio stations.

National sales representative See *rep* (representative).

National Television Systems Committee (NTSC) Committee of primarily electronics industry representatives formed by the FCC in 1941 to establish technical standards for electronic television.

Network An interconnected chain of broadcast stations that receive programming simultaneously.

News hole Remaining time available in a news program for actual news content, after the time devoted to commercials and filler music are subtracted from the total length of the program.

Nipkow disc The first type of disc used by mechanical television systems to scan and reproduce images.

Nonclearance Written refusal to carry a particular network program by an affiliate.

Noncommercial broadcasting Term referring to public broadcasting.

Nonlinear editing Digital assembly of video programming through the use of computer storage devices.

Obscenity Offensive material that is not protected by the First Amendment to the U.S. Constitution.

Off-network syndication Selling programming that has appeared at least once on the national networks directly to stations or cable services.

Option periods The length of time buyers have to decide if they want to take a risk on a new program.

Overnights Ratings reports released each morning based on the previous night's prime-time programming as measured in very large cities like New York, Los Angeles, and Chicago.

Owned-and-operated station (O&O) Broadcasting station owned and operated by one of the major broadcast networks.

Participating sponsorships Opportunities for advertisers in which the programming vehicle is associated directly with the advertiser.

Paternal approach A governmental approach to controlling broadcast television based on the assumption of that an elite group should use funds collected by the government to secure programming. Television should be used to improve society as well as to provide entertainment and information.

Pay-per-view (PPV) Cable or subscription television programming that subscribers pay individually for, purchased per program viewed rather than monthly.

PBS-2 A proposed plan that would partly commercialize PBS stations, thus providing funds for quality programs.

Peoplemeter Electronic meter attached to TV sets measuring both tuning and audience demographics; requires viewers to push buttons to identify themselves.

Permissive approach A governmental approach to controlling broadcast television based on the assumption that viewers will be best served if programming decisions are made by private, usually profit-seeking, interests. The success of a particular program is best measured by the size of its audience.

Pilot A sample first program of a proposed television series.

Play A single showing of a program.

Pocketpiece An abbreviated version of weekly national ratings, available to network executives, covering prime-time broadcast and larger cable network programs.

Pods A grouping of commercials within the broadcast schedule.

Price Primarily determined by the interaction of two opposing forces, supply and demand, this is the cost associated with a product or service.

Prime-time access rule (PTAR) FCC rule forbidding network affiliates from carrying more than three hours of network programs and off-network reruns (with some exceptions) in the four hours starting at 7 P.M. EST.

Prior censorship The removal of material prior to its broadcast. The Communications Act of 1934 forbids the FCC to exercise prior censorship.

Producer In news, the person in charge of organizing the various tasks for a news story or news segment.

Profit The remaining amount of money when expenses are subtracted from revenues.

Profit margin A company's net income divided by revenue (total sales).

Promo A broadcast advertising spot announcing a new program or episode, or encouraging viewing of a station's or network's entire schedule.

Public Broadcasting Act of 1967 Congressional bill that incorporated most of the Carnegie Commission's recommendations concerning public broadcasting.

Public Broadcasting Service (PBS) An organization created by CPB to oversee program production and program services of public television stations.

Public interest, convenience, and/or necessity According to the Communications Act of 1934, the standard the FCC must use in judging the performance of a broadcast station during its licensing period.

Quiz show rigging (scandal) The fixing of big money network quiz programs by program producers in the later half of the 1950s. As a result of the scandal, congress investigated both the networks and quiz show producers.

Radio Act of 1927 The first law specifically regulating broadcasting; it served as the model for the Communications Act of 1934.

Rating   Audience measurement unit representing the percent of the potential total audience tuned to a specific program or station for program or time period.

Ratings period   Usually, four sequential weeks during which local television station ratings are collected, reported week by week, and averaged for the four weeks, called a *sweep*. Four sweeps are conducted annually in November, February, May, and July. In network television, the term may refer to only one week in a pocketpiece.

Reach   Cumulative audience or total circulation of a station or service.

Reality shows   Low-budget television series using edited tapes of real people (supplemented by on-camera interviews and reenactments).

Red Channels   Published listing of supposed Communists and Communist sympathizers in the broadcast industry.

Reps   See *station rep* (representative).

Rerun   Repeat showing of a program first aired earlier in the season or some previous season.

Resources   Scarce items that are allocated in an economic system.

Rest   Length of time a feature film or other program is withheld from cable or broadcast syndication (or local station airing) to avoid overexposure.

Revenue   Total sales for a broadcast station, primarily derived from advertising in the case of commercial broadcasting.

Scarcity   The relative absence or presence of a desired item, which influences its value.

Scatter plan   A short schedule of spots covering a variety of time slots over a few weeks.

Schedule (of spots)   A series of commercial messages spread out over a period of time.

Seamless programming   An audience-flow scheduling strategy that cuts all interrupting elements at the break between two programs in order to move viewers smoothly from one program into the next. It is difficult to achieve because most contracts with producers require the play of closing and opening credits, and the advertising time at breaks between programs is especially valuable.

Secondary affiliation   An affiliate, usually in a sparsely populated area, with more than one network affiliate, whose main affiliation is primary and whose other affiliate is secondary.

Section 315   The section of the Communications Act of 1934 that requires stations to offer candidates for political office equal opportunity in the use of their facilities.

Selective exposure, perception, and retention   The tendency for receivers of media messages, including television programming, to select, interpret and remember messages in ways that are consistent with their current attitudes.

Sellout rate   The percentage of advertising inventory sold.

Share   A measurement unit for comparing audiences; represents the percentage of total listening or viewing audience (with sets on) tuned to a given station; total shares in a designated area in a given time period equal 100 percent.

Simulcast   The broadcast of a program on both radio and television simultaneously.

Situation comedy (sitcom)   A humorous program (usually a half hour in length) in which characters react to new plots or altered situations.

Sixth Report and Order   The 1952 FCC order that ended the freeze on television station licenses.

Skewed   Uneven distribution of a group of people, usually slanted toward one age group (e.g., skewed young, skewed old). In the case of targeting potential viewers, skewed audience is desirable. In the case of audience research, skewed samples are undesirable because one age group is overrepresented.

Snapshot studies   Individual research studies completed at only one point in time and thus not allowing for comparison over time.

Social cognitive or modeling theory   A theory of learning by observation developed by psychologist Albert Bandura.

Socializing agents   Social forces that have an important role in teaching the young. Television is thought to be a major socializing agent.

Special   One-time entertainment or news program with special interest; usually applied to network programs that interrupt regular schedules.

Spectacular   Term used by early NBC Television President Pat Weaver to refer to extraordinary programming that would bring attention and acclaim to the medium.

Spectrum allocation   The assignment of parts of the electromagnetic spectrum by the government for certain uses. The FCC allocates portions of the spectrum for broadcast television.

Spin-off   New television program based on another existing (or previously popular) show.

Spot   A commercial advertisement usually of fifteen or thirty seconds in length, or a period of time in which an advertisement, a promo, or a public service announcement can be scheduled.

Stakeholder   An interested party or constituent in an organization (e.g., stockholders, employees, customers).

Standard error   Statistical term accounting for unavoidable measurement differences between any sample and the population from which it was drawn.

Station breaks   Commercial interruptions provided to local affiliates during network programs.

Station Program Cooperative (SPC)   Resource pooling by PBS member stations for higher quality productions.

Station rep (representative)   Firm acting as sales agent for client station's advertising time in the national market.

Stripping   Across-the-board scheduling; putting successive episodes of a program into the same time period every day, five days per week (for example, placing *Baywatch* every evening at 7 P.M.).

Stunting   Frequent adding of specials and shifting of programs in schedule to improve ratings.

Superstation   An independent television station that has its signal retransmitted by satellite to distant cable companies for redistribution to subscribers (for example, WGN from Chicago).

Supply   Goods and services produced and available for sale to consumers.

Sweeps   The periods each year when Nielsen gathers audience data for the entire country; the ratings base from a sweep determines the network and station rates for advertising time until the next sweep. For television, the four times are November, February, May, and July.

Switcher   An electronic/mechanical device for selecting and mixing video sources.

Syndicated exclusivity rule   Called *syndex,* an FCC rule (reinstated in 1989) requiring cable systems bringing in distant signals to block out syndicated programming (usually on superstations) for which a local broadcaster owns exclusive rights.

Syndication   The marketing of programs on a station-by-station basis (rather than through a network) to affiliates, independents, or cable systems for a specified number of plays; syndicators are companies that hold the rights to distribute programs nationally or internationally.

Tabloid news   Sensationalistic news resembling supermarket tabloid newspapers.

Targeting   Aiming programs (generally by selecting appropriate appeals) at a demographically or psychographically defined audience.

Telecommunications Act of 1996   The major revision to the Communications Act of 1934 that reduced regulatory barriers to entry to telecommunications industries.

Temporary Commission on Alternative Financing (TCAF)   A brief lifting of the commercial ban on public TV in a few select markets in the early 1980s.

Tent-poling   Placing a highly rated program between two series with lower ratings (often new programs); intended to prop up the ratings of the preceding and following programs.

Theatricals   Movies made especially for showing in motion picture theaters (as opposed to made-for-TV).

Traffic   Television station department that schedules programs, commercials, promos, and other elements into a daily log.

Tuning inertia   A theory that viewers tend to view the next program on a channel until they are motivated by an unacceptable program to switch channels.

TvQs   Program and personality popularity ratings, typically measuring familiarity and liking, characterized by viewer surveys asking respondents to tell if a program or personality is "one of their favorites."

Ultra High Frequency (UHF)   A portion of the electromagnetic spectrum assigned by the FCC for use by television in 1952; transmission characteristics are considered inferior to VHF signals.

United Paramount Network (UPN)   A recently developed national television network with limited, prime-time only programming, owned by BNC Communications.

Upfront   In broadcasting sales, the amount of money spent on commercial advertising spots prior to the beginning of a new television season. In production, the amount of money spent for a television series in anticipation of future sales to other forms of program exhibition, like syndication or foreign markets.

Uplink   A satellite dish that sends signals to a geostationary satellite.

Uses and gratifications   A media research tradition that emphasizes studies of the motivations for exposure to media content, including television programming.

V-Chip   A monitoring technology that will be incorporated into new television receivers allowing parents to screen out programs with violent content.

Vertical integration   An industry in which the owners of the means of production also own the means of distribution.

Very High Frequency (VHF)   First portion of the electromagnetic spectrum assigned by the FCC for use by commercial television, it has transmission characteristics that are superior to UHF.

Videographers   Employees who operate camcorders and other video equipment.

Videomalaise   Increasing political cynicism traced to a reliance on television news.

Video-on-demand   Systems that instantaneously deliver only those programs a consumer wants to see to the home. See *pay-per-view*.

WB network, The   A recently developed national television network with limited prime-time only programming, owned by Time Warner.

Window   Period of time within which a network or distributor has the rights to show a feature film or other program (generally after the first theatrical distribution).

Wireless cable   See *multichannel multipoint distribution service (MMDS)*.

World Wide Web   Component of the Internet that allows the posting of information, entertainment, and advertising in the form of homepages by individuals and organizations.

Zapping   Erasing commercials on home-taped videocassettes; sometimes used synonymously with flipping—changing channels by remote control to avoid commercials.

Zipping   Fast-forwarding through commercials on home-taped videocassettes.

Bibliography

Abernethy, Avery M. "Television Exposure: Programs vs. Advertising," *Current Issues & Research in Advertising,* 13, 1991, 61–78.

Adams, William J. and Eastman, Susan T. "Prime-Time Network Television Programming," in *Broadcast/Cable Programming: Strategies and Practices,* 5th ed. Susan T. Eastman and Douglas A. Ferguson, eds. Belmont, CA: Wadsworth, 1997.

Albarran, Alan B. *Media Economics: Understanding Markets, Industries and Concepts.* Ames, Iowa: IA: State University Press, 1996.

Alexander, Alison, Owers, James and Carveth, Rod, eds. *Media Economics: Theory and Practice.* New York: Erlbaum, 1993.

America's Watching: Public Attitudes Toward Television. New York: Roper Starch, 1994.

Andrews, Robert. *The Concise Columbia Dictionary of Quotations.* New York: Columbia University Press, 1993.

Aufderheide, P. "Public Television and the Public Sphere," *Critical Studies in Mass Communication* 8 (1991): 176.

Auletta, Ken. *Three Blind Mice: How the TV Networks Lost Their Way.* New York: Random House, 1991.

Avery, Robert K. and Pepper, Robert. *The Politics of Interconnection: A History of Public Television at the National Level.* Washington, DC: NAEB, 1979.

_____, Robert K., and Pepper, Robert. "An Institutional History of Public Broadcasting," *Journal of Communication* 30 (1980): 134.

Baker, Robert and Ball, Sandra, eds., *Violence and the Media.* Washington, DC: Government Printing Office, 1969.

Baldwin, Thomas F., McVoy, D. Stephens and Steinfield, Charles. *Convergence: Integrating Media, Information & Communication.* Thousand Oaks, CA: Sage, 1996.

Bandura, Albert. "Social Cognitive Theory of Mass Communication," in Jennings Bryant and Dolf Zillmann, eds. *Media Effects: Advances in Theory and Research.* Hillsdale, NJ: Erlbaum, 1994.

_____, Ross, D., and Ross, S. A. "Imitation of Film-Mediated Aggressive Models," *Journal of Abnormal and Social Psychology,* 66(1) (1963): 3–11.

Bannon, Lisa. "Kirch of Germany Gets Pay-TV Rights to Disney Movies," *Wall Street Journal,* August 30, 1996, Sec A, p. 5D.

Barnouw, Erik. *The Golden Web, A History of Broadcasting in the United States, Volume II, 1933–1953.* New York: Oxford University Press, 1968.

_____. *The Image Empire, A History of Broadcasting in the United States, Volume III, from 1953.* New York: Oxford University Press, 1970.

_____. *The Sponsor: Notes on a Modern Potentate.* New York: Oxford University Press, 1978, p. 46.

_____. *A Tower in Babel: A History of Broadcasting in the United States, Volume I, to 1933.* New York: Oxford University Press, 1966.

_____. *Tube of Plenty: The Evolution of American Television,* 2nd ed. New York: Oxford University Press, 1990.

Becker, Samuel L. "Visual Stimuli and the Construction of Meaning," in Bikkar, S. Randhawa and William E. Coffman, eds., *Visual Learning, Thinking and Communication.* New York: Academic Press, 1978.

Bellamy, Robert, V., Jr., and Walker, James R. *Television and the Remote Control: Grazing on a Vast Wasteland.* New York: Guilford, 1996.

Biddle, Fredric. "Two Giants Enter Network Fray," *Boston Globe,* January 9, 1995, p. 2.

Blumenthal, Howard J., and Goodenough, Oliver R. *This Business of Television.* New York: Billboard Books, 1991.

Boddy, William. *Fifties Television: The Industry and Its Critics.* Urbana, IL: University of Illinois Press, 1990.

Boller, Paul F., Jr. *Presidential Anecdotes.* New York: Penguin Books, 1982.

Bower, Robert T. *The Changing Television Audience in America.* New York: Columbia University Press, 1985.

_____. *Television and the Public.* New York: Holt, Rinehart, and Winston, 1973.

Bradley, William. "Behind the Megamedia Mergers," *San Francisco Chronicle,* August 6, 1996, Sec. A, p. 19.

Broach, V. Carter, Jr., Page, Thomas J., Jr., and Wilson, R. Dale. "Television Programming and Its Influence on Viewers' Perceptions of Commercials: The Role of Program Arousal and Pleasantness," *Journal of Advertising,* 24(4), 1995, pp. 45–54.

Broadcasting & Cable Yearbook 1995. Providence, RI: R. R. Bowker.

Broadcasting & Cable Yearbook 1996, Vol. 1. New Providence, NJ: R. R. Bowker.

Brooks, Tim, and Marsh, Earle. *The Complete Directory to Prime Time Network TV Shows 1946–Present,* 5th ed. New York: Ballantine Books, 1992.

Brosius, Hans-Bernd, and Kepplinger, Hans Mathias. "Linear and Non-linear Models of Agenda-setting in Television," *Journal of Broadcasting and Electronic Media,* 36, 1992, pp. 5–24.

Carman, John. "TV in Black and White," *San Francisco Chronicle,* August 26, 1996, Sec. E, p. 1.

Carnegie Commission on Educational Television. New York: Bantam Books, 1967.

Carroll, Raymond L., and Davis, Donald M. *Electronic Media Programming: Strategies and Decision Making.* New York: McGraw-Hill, 1993.

Carter, Bill. "Two Upstart Networks Courting Black Viewers," *New York Times,* October 7, 1996, Sec. C, p. 11.

———. "The Networks See Potential for Growth," *New York Times,* February 2, 1996, Sec. D, p. 6.

"CBS Reports: Don't Touch That Dial." New York: CBS News, 1982.

Charlton, W. "Perceptions of Commercial Activities in Public Broadcasting." [http://www.cpb.org/library/

Clark, Kenneth R. "NBC Wins Olympics for $456 Million," *Chicago Tribune*, July 28, 1993, Sec. 4, p. 3.

Collins, Richard, Garnham, Nicholas and Locksley, Gareth. *The Economics of Television: The UK Case*. Newbury Park, CA: Sage, 1988.

"Commercial Sister Network Would Subsidize Public TV," *Current*, October 9, 1995, p. 6.

Comstock, George, Chaffee, Steven, Katzman Natan, McCombs, Maxwell, and Roberts, Donald. *Television and Human Behavior*. New York: Columbia University Press, 1978.

"Conferences Okay Smaller Cuts for '96–'97," *Current*, May 15, 1995, p. 7.

Cronin, John J. and Menelly, Nancy E. "Discrimination vs. Avoidance: 'Zipping' of Television Commercials," *Journal of Advertising*, 21(2), 1992, 1–7.

Culliton, John. General Manager, WCCO-TV, Personal interview, Minneapolis, MN, Feb. 16, 1996.

Cutler, Blayne. "Where Does the Free Time Go?" *American Demographics*, November 1990, pp. 36–39.

Davenport, Walter. "Face to Face by Radio," *Collier's*, July 23, 1927.

DeFleur, Melvin L. and Ball–Rockeach, Sandra. *Theories of Mass Communication*, 5th ed. New York: Longman, 1989.

Dominick, Joseph R., Sherman, Barry L., and Copeland, Gary A. *Broadcasting/Cable and Beyond*, 3rd ed. New York: McGraw-Hill, 1996.

"Effects of CPB Recission to Public Television Stations," *America's Public Television Stations*, March 1995.

"FCC Commissioner to Step Down," *Chicago Tribune*, January 1, 1997, Sec. 3, p. 1.

"FCC Votes to Kill Fin–Syn Rules Immediately," *Electronic Media*, September 11, 1995.

Ferguson, Douglas A. "A Framework for Programming Strategies," in Susan T. Eastman and Douglas A. Ferguson, eds. *Broadcast/Cable Programming*, Belmont, CA: Wadsworth, 1997.

_____, Meyer, Timothy P. and Eastman, Susan T. "Program and Audience Research," in Susan T. Eastman and Douglas A. Ferguson, eds. *Broadcast/Cable Programming: Strategies and Practices*, 5th ed. Belmont, CA: Wadsworth, 1997.

"First CPB Cuts of Newt Era Pass House," *Current*, March 20, 1995, p. 7.

Foisie, Geoffrey. "Higher Network Revenue Gain Projected," *Broadcasting & Cable*, July 25, 1994, p. 79.

Fouhy, Ed. "The Dawn of Public Journalism," *National Civic Review, 83*, 1995, p. 259.

Francese, Peter. "America at Mid-Decade," *American Demographics*, February, 1995, pp. 23–31.

Frank, Betsy. "And Now a Word From Our. . . ZAP," *Marketing and Media Decisions*, July, 1984, pp. 162–166.

Friedland, L. "Public Television as Public Sphere: The Case of the Wisconsin Collaborative Project," *Journal of Broadcasting and Electronic Media* 39 (1995): 158.

Fritz, Sara and Morris, Dwight. *Handbook of Campaign Spending*. Washington, DC: Congressional Quarterly, 1992.

"Funding Scramble is 'Nature' of Public TV," *Broadcasting and Cable*, January 31, 1994, p. 22.

Garramone, Gina M. "Effects of Negative Political Advertising: The Roles of Sponsor and Rebuttal," *Journal of Broadcasting & Electronic Media, 29* (1985): 147–159.

Gerbner, George. "Women and Minorities on Television" (a report to the Screen Actors

Guild and the American Federation of Radio and Television Artists, Annenberg School, University of Pennsylvania, Philadelphia, June, 1993).

_____ and Gross, Larry. "Living with Television: The Violence Profile," *Journal of Communication,* 26(2) (1976): 173–199.

_____, Gross, Larry, Morgan, Michael, and Signorielli, Nancy. "Growing Up with Television: The Cultivation Perspective," in Jennings Bryant and Dolf Zillmann, eds. *Media Effects: Advances in Theory and Research.* Hillsdale, NJ: Erlbaum, 1994, pp. 27–28.

Gibson, George H. *Public Broadcasting, The Role of the Federal Government, 1912–76.* New York: Praeger, 1977.

Gomery, Douglas. "Mass Media Merger Mania," *American Journalism Review,* December, 1995, p. 46.

"Gore Assails 'All Out Attack' on Enrichment for Kids," *Current,* March 6, 1995, p. 14.

Graham, Jefferson. "UPN: Funny Has No Color," *USA Today,* July 3, 1996, Sec. B, p. 9.

Greenberg, Bradley S. *Life on Television: Content Analyses of U.S. Television Drama.* Norwood, NJ: Ablex, 1980.

_____ and Brand, Jeffrey E. "Minorities and the Mass Media: 1970s to 1990s," in Jennings Bryant and Dolf Zillmann, eds. *Media Effects: Advances in Theory and Research.* Hillsdale, NJ: Erlbaum, 1994.

Gunter, Barrie. "The Question of Media Violence," in Jennings Bryant and Dolf Zillmann, eds. *Media Effects: Advances in Theory and Research.* Hillsdale, NJ: Erlbaum, 1994, pp. 192.

Hall, Lee. "Price War Giving DBS a Big Push," *Electronic Media,* September 2, 1996, pp. 1 & 2.

Halonen, Doug. "Historic Rewrite Finally Passes," *Electronic Media,* February 5, 1996, pp. 1 & 54.

_____. "It's a Deal," *Electronic Media,* March 4, 1996, pp. 1 & 26.

Haring, Bruce. "PCs as TVs: Dramas Kick Off Cyberspace Networks," *USA Today,* April 16, 1996, Sec. D, p. 3.

Harris, Irvin. "Scanning Devices: What They Do and How to Make Them?" *Popular Radio and Television,* May 1928, pp. 389–90, 431.

Hawver, Walt. *Capital Cities/ABC The Early Years: 1954–1986.* Radnor, PA: Chilton, 1994.

Head, Sydney W., Sterling, Christopher H., and Schofield, Lemuel B. *Broadcasting in America: A Survey of Electronic Media,* 7th ed. Boston: Houghton Mifflin, 1994.

Hirsch, Paul. "On Not Learning from One's Own Mistakes: A Reanalysis of Gerbner et al.'s Findings on Cultivation Analysis: Part II," *Communication Research,* 8 (1981): 3–37.

Horowitz, David. *The Problem with Public TV.* Center for the Study of Popular Culture, 1991.

Hoynes, William. *Public Television for Sale: Media, Market, and the Public Sphere.* Boulder: Westview, Inc., 1994.

Inglis, Andrew F. *Behind the Tube: A History of Broadcasting Technology and Business.* Boston: Focal Press, 1990.

Jamieson, Kathleen Hall, and Campbell, Karlyn Kohrs. *The Interplay of Influence,* 3rd ed. Belmont, CA: Wadsworth, 1992.

Jankowski, Gene F. and Fuchs, David. *Television Today and Tomorrow.* New York: Oxford, 1995.

Jones, Tim. "Hot Media Properties? Plain Old TV," *Chicago Tribune,* July 28, 1996, Sec. W, pp. 1 & 6.

_____. "An Old Glow, and Dynamic Prospects," *Chicago Tribune,* December 16, 1996, Sec. 4, p. 1.

_____. "The Visible Hand of Wall Street Rewrites Newspaper Giants' Script," *Chicago Tribune,* September 29, 1996, Sec. 5, p. 1.

Kelly, Keith J. "Bright Prospects Seen for Cable TV, New Media," *Advertising Age,* August 19, 1996, p. 8.

Kerbel, M. R. *Edited For Television: CNN, ABC, and the 1992 Presidential Campaign.* Boulder, CO: Westview, 1994.

Kief, Susan. Sales Department, KARE Channel 11, Personal Interview, St. Paul, March 22, 1996.

Klapper, Joseph T. *The Effects of Mass Communication.* New York: Free Press, 1960.

Klopfenstein, Bruce C. "From Gadget to Necessity: The Diffusion of Remote Control Technology," in James R. Walker and Robert V. Bellamy, Jr., eds. *The Remote Control in the New Age of Television.* Westport, CT: Praeger, 1993.

Klopfenstein, Bruce C. and Sedman, David. "Technical Standards and the Marketplace: The Case of AM Stereo," *Journal of Broadcasting & Electronic Media,* 34, 1990, pp. 171–194.

Kogan, Rick. "WFLD Rolls Dice on Cosby Magic," *Chicago Tribune,* September 30, 1988, Sec. 5, p. 4.

Krugman, Dean M., Cameron, Glen T., and White, Candace McKearney. "Visual Attention to Programming and Commercials: The Use of In-Home Observations," *Journal of Advertising,* 24(1), 1995, 1–12.

Lachenbruch, David. "Commercial-Killing VCR," *Electronics Now,* April 1995, p. 89.

Lashley, Marilyn. *Public Television: Panacea, Pork Barrel, or Public Trust?* New York: Greenwood Press, 1992.

Lawrence, Ron. "The Battle for Attention," *Marketing & Media Decisions,* 24(2), 1989, 80–84.

Lazarsfeld, Paul F. and Stanton, Frank N. *Radio Research 1942–43.* New York: Essential Books, 1944.

Lin, Carolyn A. "Network Prime-Time Programming Strategies in the 1980s," *Journal of Broadcasting & Electronic Media,* 39(4), 1995, pp. 482–495.

Lord, Kenneth R. and Burnkrant, Robert E. "Attention Versus Distraction: The Interactive Effect of Program Involvement and Attentional Devices on Commercial Processing," *Journal of Advertising,* 22(1), 1993, 47–60.

Lowry, Brian. "Debates Offer Opportunity for UPN, WB," *Los Angeles Times,* October 4, 1996, Sec. F, p. 26.

MacFarland, David T. "Television: The Whirling Beginning," in Lawrence W. Lichty and Malachi C. Topping, eds. *American Broadcasting: A Source Book on the History of Radio and Television.* New York: Hastings House, 1976.

Macy, John, Jr. *To Irrigate a Wasteland: The Struggle to Shape a Public Television System in the United States.* Berkeley: University of California Press, 1974.

Maddox, Kate. "The Big Picture: Visions of a New TV Begin to Merge," *Electronic Media,* November 8, 1993, p. 23.

Maisel, L. Sandy and Bassett, Charles. *Political Parties and Elections in the United States: An Encyclopedia.* New York: Garland, 1991.

Mandese, Joe. "How Much? Try a Million a Minute," *Electronic Media,* September 16, 1996, p. 3.

_____. "Media World on Brink of M & A Frenzy," *Advertising Age,* July 25, 1994, pp. 1–2.

Marcus, Ruth. "Loophole Lets Dems Stretch Scarce Cash for TV Ads," *Chicago Sun-Times,* July 1, 1996, p. 16.

Marton, Andrew. "Ad Makers Zap Back," *Channels,* September 1989, pp. 30–31.

Mast, Gerald. *A Short History of the Movies,* 2nd ed. Indianapolis, IN: Bobbs-Merrill, 1976.

Matzer, Marla. "Contented Kingdoms," *MediaWeek* (Superbrands Supplement), October 7, 1996, pp. 28–35.

McClellan, Steve. "NBC Posts $1 Billion in Earnings," *Broadcasting & Cable,* December 16, 1996, p. 64.

_____. "TVB Sees Ad Growth in '96," *Broadcasting & Cable,* October 2, 1995, p. 36.

McCombs, Maxwell. "News Influence on Our Pictures of the World," in Jennings Bryant and Dolf Zillmann, eds. *Media Effects: Advances in Theory and Research.* Hillsdale, NJ: Erlbaum, 1994.

McCombs, Maxwell and Shaw, Donald L. "The Agenda-Setting Function of the Mass Media," *Public Opinion Quarterly,* 36 (1972): 176–187.

McConnell, Chris. "FCC Enumerates TV's Future," *Broadcasting & Cable,* August 19, 1996, pp. 17–22.

McConville, Jim. "Everybody Wants to Get into the Game," *Broadcasting & Cable,* April 8, 1996, pp. 50–51.

"Meet the New Media Monsters," *The Economist,* March 11, 1989, pp. 65–66.

Melder, Keith. *Hail to the Candidate: Presidential Campaigns from Banners to Broadcasts.* Washington, DC: Smithsonian Institution, 1992.

Mermigas, Diane. "Colossal Combos," *Electronic Media,* August 7, 1995, pp. 1 & 30.

Mickelson, Sig. *From Whistle Stop to Sound Bite: Four Decades of Politics and Television.* New York: Praeger, 1989.

Mogelonsky, Marcia. "Coping With Channel Surfers," *American Demographics,* December 1995, pp. 13–15.

Monush, Barry, ed. *International Television & Video Almanac.* New York: Quigley, 1996.

Moriarty, Sandra E. and Everett, Shu-Ling. "Commercial Breaks: A Viewing Behavior Study," *Journalism Quarterly,* 71(2), 1989, 346–355.

"Networks Freed from Prime-Time Rule," *Chicago Tribune,* July 29, 1995, Sec. 2, pp. 1 & 3.

Nielsen 1992–93 Report on Television. New York: Nielsen Media Research.

"Night-by-Night Nielsen Prime-Time Household Ratings," *Electronic Media,* February 19, 1996, p. 30.

"Now, a Flurry of Options for the Future," *Current,* March 6, 1995, p. 1.

O'Conner, Donald. General Manager, KTMA Channel 23, Personal Interview, St. Paul, Minnesota, November 10, 1995.

Owen, Bruce M., Beebe, Jack H., and Manning, William G., Jr. *Television Economics.* Lexington, Mass.: Lexington Books, 1974.

_____. and Wildman, Steven S. *Video Economics.* Cambridge, MA: Harvard University Press, 1992.

Pahwa, Ashok. "Boom Generation More Receptive to Quality TV Ads," *Marketing News,* September, 1990, pp. 8, 17.

Palmgreen, Philip, Wenner, Lawrence A., Rosengren, Karl Erik. "Uses and Gratifications Research: The Past Ten Years," in Karl Erik Rosengren, et al., *Media Gratifications Research: Current Perspectives.* Beverly Hills, CA: Sage, 1985.

Pavlik, John V. "Competition: Key to the Communications Future?" *Television Quarterly,* 1996, 28:2, pp. 35–43.

Pfau, Michael, Moy, Patricia, Radler, Barry, and Bridgeman, Michael K. *Influence of Individual Communication Media on Public Confidence in Democratic Institutions,* a paper presented at the International Communication Association Conference, May 1996.

Picard, Robert G. *Media Economics: Concepts and Issues.* Newbury Park, CA: Sage, 1989.

Pohlmann, Ken C. "Channel Envy," *Video,* September, 1996, pp. 23–25.

Potter, W. James. "Cultivation Theory and Research: A Conceptual Critique," *Human Communication Research,* 19 (1993): 564–601.

_____. "Does Television Viewing Hinder Academic Achievement among Adolescents?" *Human Communication Research,* 14 (1987): p. 27.

Powers, Angela. "Competition, Conduct and Ratings in Local Television News: Applying the Industrial Organizational Model," *Journal of Media Economics,* 6, 1993, pp. 37–51.

Pridmore, Jay. "From 1860 to 1968, Chicago Was the Political Convention Capital," *Chicago Tribune* online archive, July 26, 1996.

"Pubcasters Pull Together a Plan for Congress," *Current,* May 1, 1995, p. 13.

Quinlan, Sterling. *Inside ABC: American Broadcasting Company's Rise to Power.* New York: Hastings House.

Rice, Lynette. "Round Three: UPN vs. The WB," *Broadcasting & Cable,* August 26, 1996, pp. 5, 10.

Robinson, John P. "I Love My TV," *American Demographics,* September 1990, pp. 24–27.

_____. "Quitting Time," *American Demographics,* May 1991, pp. 34–36.

Robinson, Michael J. "Public Affairs Television and the Growth of Political Malaise: The Case of 'The Selling of the Pentagon,'" *American Political Science Review,* 70 (1976): 409–432.

Rosenthal, Ed. "Latest Sony News Gear Aims for Flexibility," *Electronic Media,* March 18, 1996, p. 24.

Ross, Chuck. "Blacks Drawn to Indy TV, Cable," *Advertising Age,* March 4, 1996, p. 8.

Rowland, Williard D., Jr. "Continuing Crisis in Public Broadcasting: A History of Disenfranchisement," *Journal of Broadcasting and Electronic Media* 30 (1986): 265.

_____. *The Politics of TV Violence.* Beverly Hills, CA: Sage, 1983.

Saettler, Paul. *A History of Instructional Technology.* New York: McGraw-Hill, 1968.

Sandomir, Richard. "Dumb like a Fox? 4th Network Wins Rights to NFC Games," *Chicago Tribune,* December 18, 1993, Sec. 3, pp. 1 & 4.

Schramm, Wilbur. "Procedures and Effects of Mass Communication," in N. B. Henry, ed. *Mass Media and Education II: 53rd Yearbook of the National Society for the Study of Education.* Chicago: University of Chicago Press, 1954.

_____, Lyle, Jack, and Parker, Edwin B. *Television in the Lives of Our Children.* Stanford, CA: Stanford University Press, 1961.

Schultz, Don E. "Is Television Advertising Obsolete?" A presentation made to the NAB Management Development Seminar for Television Executives, Northwestern University, July 1992.

"Season-To-Date," *Electronic Media,* July 14, 1997, p. 43.

Shapiro, Eben. "Chris-Craft's 4th-Period Net Fell 67% on Start-Up Losses at UPN," *Wall Street Journal,* February 15, 1996, p. B–7.

Shister, Gail. "Philly Stations Overhaul Local News," *Electronic Media,* February 26, 1996, p. 44.

Siegal, Ed. "TV Wars: Has Local TV Gone Tabloid," *The Boston Globe Magazine,* February 12, 1995, pp. 18–26, 29–31.

Slide, Anthony. *The Television Industry: A Historical Dictionary.* Westport, CT: Greenwood Press, 1991.

Smith, F. Leslie, Meeske, Milan and Wright, John W. *Electronic Media and Government.* White Plains, NY: Longman, 1995.

Smith, Steven Cole. "Infomercials Flourish Everywhere Since Deregulation," *Minneapolis Star Tribune,* August 1995, p. 8E.

Smythe, Dallas W. *Three Years of New York Television.* Urbana IL: National Association of Educational Broadcasters, 1956.

Spring, Jim. "Exercising the Brain," *American Demographics,* October 1993, pp. 56–59.

Spring, Jim. "Seven Days of Play," *American Demographics,* March 1993, pp. 50–53.

Statistical Abstract of the United States, 115th ed. Washington, DC: Government Printing Office, 1995.

Steiner, Gary A. *The People Look at Television: The Study of Audience Attitudes.* New York: Knopf, 1963.

Sterling, Christopher H. and Kittross, John M. *Stay Tuned: A Concise History of American Broadcasting,* 2nd ed. Belmont, CA: Wadsworth, 1990.

Stone, David M. *Nixon and the Politics of Public Television.* New York: Garland, 1985.

Stone, Vernon. "News Operations at U.S. TV Stations," jourvs@showme. missouri.edu, 1995.

_____. "Paychecks and Market Baskets: Broadcast News Salaries and Inflation in the 1990s," jourvs@showme.missouri.edu, 1995.

Stout, Patricia A. and Burda, Benedicta L. "Zipped Commercials: Are They Effective?" *Journal of Advertising,* 18(4), 1989, 23–32.

Sturcken, Frank. *Live Television: The Golden Age of 1946-1958 in New York.* Jefferson, NC: McFarland, 1990.

"Super Bowl Ads Again Go for Record Price," *Chicago Tribune,* January 8, 1997, Sec. 4, p. 2.

Television and Behavior: Ten Years of Scientific Progress and Implications for the Eighties. Washington, DC: Government Printing Office, 1982.

Television and Growing Up: The Impact of Televised Violence. Washington, DC: Government Printing Office, 1971.

"Television Trends in Ownership," *Time Almanac of the 20th Century,* CD–ROM. Time, 1995.

Television's First Year. A pamphlet published by National Broadcasting Company, 1940.

"The 10 Biggest Campaign Bankrolls," *Time,* November 18, 1996, p. 41.

Thomas, Laurie, and Litman, Barry. "Fox Broadcasting Company, Why Now? An Economic Study of the Rise of the Fourth Broadcast Network," *Journal of Broadcasting and Electronic Media,* 35, 1991, pp. 139–156.

Thomas, Vicki, and Wolfe, David B. "Why Won't Television Grow Up?" *American Demographics,* May 1995, pp. 24–29.

Tiegel, Eliot. "'Hawaii Stars' Singin' Along," *Electronic Media,* January 8, 1996, p. 52.

Tiltman, Ronald F. "Television in Natural Colors Demonstrated," *Radio News,* October, 1928, pp. 320, 374.

U.S. Congress, *House Subcommittee on Telecommunication and Finance on H.R. 4118,* 100th Cong., 2d. sess., 1988, pp. 525–527.

U.S. Congress, Senate, *Subcommittee Hearings on Communications on S.2120,* 103rd Cong., 2nd. sess., 1994, p. 21.

Udelson, Joseph H. *The Great Television Race: A History of the American Television Industry 1925–41.* University, AL: University of Alabama Press, 1982.

USA Today, April 1, 1996.

Van, Jon. "Digital TV Promises an Unclear Revolution," *Chicago Tribune,* April 7, 1996, Sec. 5.

Vedehra, Dave. "Viewers Report Fewer Negative Responses to Commercials," *Advertising Age,* March 4, 1994, p. 20.

"Voter Turnout," *Time,* November 18, 1996, p. 41.

Walker, James R. "How Media Reliance Affects Political Efficacy in the South," *Journalism Quarterly,* 65 (1988): 746–750.

_____. "Old Media on New Media: National Popular Press Reaction to Mechanical Television," *Journal of Popular Culture, 25,* 1990, 21–29.

_____ and Bellamy, Robert V., Jr. "Gratifications of Grazing: An Exploratory Study of Remote Control Use," *Journalism Quarterly, 63,* 1991, 422–431.

Walker, Paul A. "The Time to Act Is Now," in Carrol V. Newsom, ed., *A Television Policy for Education.* Washington, DC: American Council on Education, 1952.

Wall Street Journal, October 21, 1996, Sec. B, p. 11.

Weaver, Pat with Coffey, Thomas M. *The Best Seat in the House: The Golden Years of Radio and Television.* New York: Knopf, 1994.

Webster, James and Lichty, Lawrence W. *Ratings Analysis: Theory and Practice.* Hillsdale, NJ: Erlbaum, 1991.

"What If Congress Tips toward the GOP?" *Current,* October 31, 1994, p. 15.

"What to Kill First? CPB Is Nominated to Save Tax Money and 'Privatize the Left,'" *Current,* December 12, 1994, p. 1.

"Will 'Glide Path' Reach Beyond 1997?" *Current,* April 17, 1995, p. 1.

Wimmer, Roger D. and Dominick, Joseph R. *Mass Media Research: An Introduction,* 4th ed., Belmont, CA: Wadsworth, 1994.

Wood, Donald N. and Wylie, Donald G. *Educational Telecommunications.* Belmont: Wadsworth, 1977.

The Works of Aristotle, Vol. II. Chicago: Encyclopedia Britannica, 1952.

World Almanac and Book of Facts, The. New York: Newspaper Enterprise Association, 1995.

Wright, Keith. "Robots in the News: Camera Robot Navigation in Television Studios," *Industrial Robot, 21,* 1994, p. 17–19.

Zillman, Dolf, Gibson, Rhonda, Ordman, Virginia, and Aust, Charles. "Effects of Upbeat Stories in Broadcast News," *Journal of Broadcasting and Electronic Media, 38,* 1994, pp. 65–78.

Zufryden, Fred S., Pedrick, James H., and Sankaralingam, Avu. "Zapping and Its Impact on Brand Purchase Behavior," *Journal of Advertising Research, 33*(1), 1993, 58–66.

Index

The Allyn & Bacon
Series in Mass Communication

Available Now

New Media Technology: Cultural and Commercial Perspectives, 2/e by John V. Pavlik (Professor and Executive Director of the Center for New Media at Columbia University) is a timely and comprehensive guide to the new media landscape. It includes a new chapter on the Internet and coverage of such topics as laboratory experimental technologies, marketing issues, and legal ramifications affecting the industry.

The Recording Industry, by Geoffrey Hull (Middle Tennessee State University), is a comprehensive examination of the industry that drives the music business. It is about how and why the industry is now centralized in six international entertainment conglomerates.

The Cable and Satellite Television Industries, by Patrick R. Parsons and Robert M. Frieden, both of Pennsylvania State University, captures the scope and detail of the impact of new technologies in the world of television and examines the convergence and competition of emerging television industries.

The Motion Picture Mega-Industry is an in-depth exploration of the movie industry, from early developments to its current multibillion dollar influence on today's society. Barry Litman (Michigan State University) has produced a truly unique text drawing on contributions from some top scholars.

The Broadcast Television Industry, by James R. Walker (Saint Xavier University) and Douglas A. Ferguson (Bowling Green State University), is a current, comprehensive review of the dominant distributor of television programming in the United States. The book reviews the history and current practices of both commercial and public television.

The Magazine Publishing Industry, by Charles P. Daly, Patrick Henry, and Ellen Ryder, provides a current and thorough examination of the fascinating field of magazine publishing. It explores advertising, circulation principles, production, and editorial techniques in detail and examines the current state of the industry and the inner workings of magazines.

The Newspaper Publishing Industry presents a timely, all-inclusive approach to the alluring newspaper business. Robert Picard and Jeff Brody, both of California State University at Fullerton, offer insight into the economics of a newspaper as a product that delivers both advertising and information.

The Book Publishing Industry offers a thoughtful study on book publishing's great traditions and its unyielding quest for perfection. This text covers everything from contracts to censorship, mergers to marketing, sales to shipping, and much more. Series editor and author, Albert N. Greco (Fordham University Graduate School of Business Administration) delves into all aspects of the industry — social, technological, and economic.